THIS IS OUR FAITH

Series Authors: **Janaan Manternach**
Carl J. Pfeifer

Authors: **Jacqueline Jambor**
Joan R. DeMerchant
Maureen Gallagher

Consulting Editor: Jean Marie Weber

Contributing Authors: Robert Hamma
Kate Sweeney Ristow

SILVER BURDETT GINN
PARSIPPANY, NJ

THIS IS OUR FAITH
SCHOOL PROGRAM

Contributing Authors: James Bitney, Sister Cecilia Maureen Cromwell, I.H.M., Patricia Frevert, Robert M. Hamma, Mary Lou Ihrig, Paula A. Lenz, Judene Leon, Yvette Nelson, Sister Arlene Pomije, C.S.J., Sister Carolyn Puccio, C.S.J., Anna Ready, Kate Sweeney Ristow, Sister Mary Agnes Ryan, I.H.M., Sister Maureen Shaughnessy, S.C., Brother Michael Sheerin, F.M.S., Barbara Carol Vasiloff

Opening Doors: A Take-Home Magazine: Peter H.M. Demkovitz, Janie Gustafson, Margaret Savitskas

Day to Day: Skills for Christian Living: Susan G. Keys

Advisory Board:
Rev. Louis J. Cameli
Philip J. Cunningham
Sister Clare E. Fitzgerald
William J. Freburger
Greer G. Gordon
Sister Veronica R. Grover, S.H.C.J.
Rev. Thomas Guarino
Rev. Robert E. Harahan
Kathleen Hendricks
Rev. Eugene LaVerdieré, S.S.S.
Rev. Frank J. McNulty
Rev. Msgr. John J. Strynkowski

Consultants: Linda Blanchette, Anita Bridge, Fred Brown, Rod Brownfield, Sister Mary Michael Burns, S.C., Patricia Burns, Bernadine Carroll, Mary Ellen Cocks, Sister Peggy Conlon, R.S.M., Mary Ann Crowley, Pamela Danni, Sister Jamesetta DeFelice, O.S.U., Sister Mary Elizabeth Duke, S.N.D., Mary M. Gibbons, Yolando Gremillion, Sister Angela Hallahan, C.H.F., Alice T. Heard, Sister Michele O'Connoll, P.B.V.M., Sister Angela O'Mahoney, P.B.V.M., Sister Ruthann O'Mara, S.S.J., Sandra Okulicz-Hulme, Judy Papandria, Rachel Pasano, Sallie Ann Phelan, Sister Geraldine M. Rogers, S.S.J., Mary Lou Schlosser, Patricia Ann Sibilia, Margaret E. Skelly, Lisa Ann Sorlie, Sister Victorine Stoltz, O.S.B., Sister Nancy Jean Turner, S.H.C.J., Christine Ward, Judith Reidel Weber, Kay White, Elizabeth M. Williams, Catherine R. Wolf, Florence Bambrick Yarney, Kathryn K. Zapcic

Nihil Obstat

Kathleen Flanagan, S.C., Ph.D.
Censor Librorum

Ellen Joyce, S.C., Ph.D.
Censor Librorum

Imprimatur

✠ Most Reverend Frank J. Rodimer
Bishop of Paterson
November 8, 1996

The *nihil obstat* and *imprimatur* are official declarations that a book or pamphlet is free of doctrinal and moral error. No implication is contained therein that those who have granted the *nihil obstat* and *imprimatur* agree with the contents, opinions, or statements expressed.

ACKNOWLEDGMENTS

Scripture selections are taken from *The New American Bible* With Revised New Testament Copyright © 1991, 1986 by the Confraternity of Christian Doctrine, Washington, D.C. 20017 are used with permission. All rights reserved.

"Blessings of a Pet" reprinted with permission from the *New St. Joseph's People's Prayer Book* (page 1037), Copyright © 1980 by Catholic Book Publishing Co., New York, NY. All rights reserved.

Excerpts from the English translation of *Rite of Marriage* © 1969, International Committee on English in the Liturgy, Inc. (ICEL); excerpts from the English translation of *Rite of Baptism for Children* © 1969, ICEL; excerpts from the English translation of *Rite of Holy Week* © 1972, ICEL; excerpts from the English translation of *The Roman Missal* © 1973, ICEL; excerpts from the English translation of *Rite of Penance* © 1974, ICEL; excerpts from the English translation of *Rite of Confirmation*, Second Edition © 1975, ICEL; excerpts from the English translation of *Pastoral Care of the Sick: Rites of Anointing and Viaticum* © 1982, ICEL. All rights reserved.

Excerpts from the English translation of *The Liturgy of the Hours* © 1974, International Committee on English in the Liturgy, Inc. All rights reserved.

Excerpts from *The Long Loneliness* by Dorothy Day. Copyright © 1980, 1952. Harper & Row, Publishers, Inc., NY

CREDITS

Cover: Pamela Johnson

Gatefold art: Robert LoGrippo

Scripture art: Barbara Epstein Eagle, Roberta Morales, Arvis Stewart

Day to Day art: Diana Thewlis

Map: Karen Minot

All other art: George Baquero, Denny Bond, Ralph Brillhart, Jenny Campbell, Julie Carpenter, Gwen Connelly, Eulala Conner, Carolyn Croll, Renee Daily, Ric Del Rossi, Kathleen Dunne, John Dyess, Barbara Epstein Eagle, Len Ebert, Sarah Jane English, Jack Freas, Patrick Gnan, Ethel Gold, Riva Greenberg, Meryl Henderson, MeeWha Lee, Richard Loehle, Bob Marstall, Claude Martinot, Katie Monaghan, Roberta Morales, Patricia Philbin, Julie Peterson, Steven James Petruccio, Tom Powers, Don Robinson, Ed Saulk, Sally Schaedler, Den Schofield, Karen Strattner, Susan Swan, Deb Troyer, Susan Hunt Yule

Contents

Let Us Pray

Sign of the Cross

In the name of the Father,
  and of the Son,
  and of the Holy Spirit.
Amen.

Señal de la Cruz

En el nombre del Padre,
  y del Hijo,
  y del Espíritu Santo.
Amén.

The Lord's Prayer

Our Father, who art in heaven,
  hallowed be thy name;
thy kingdom come;
thy will be done on earth
  as it is in heaven.
Give us this day our daily bread;
and forgive us our trespasses
  as we forgive those
  who trespass against us;
and lead us not into temptation,
  but deliver us from evil.
Amen.

Padre Nuestro

Padre nuestro, que estás en el cielo
  santificado sea tu nombre;
venga a nosotros tu reino;
hágase tu voluntad en la tierra
  como en el cielo.
Danos hoy nuestro pan de cada día;
perdona nuestras ofensas,
  como también nosotros perdonamos
  a los que nos ofenden;
no nos dejes caer en la tentación,
  y líbranos del mal.
Amén.

Hail Mary

Hail Mary, full of grace,
  the Lord is with you.
Blessed are you among women,
  and blessed is the fruit
  of your womb, Jesus.
Holy Mary, Mother of God,
  pray for us sinners, now,
  and at the hour of our death.
Amen.

Ave María

Dios te salve, María llena eres de gracia,
  el Señor es contigo.
Bendita tú eres entre todas las mujeres,
  y bendito es el fruto
  de tu vientre, Jesús.
Santa María, Madre de Dios,
  ruega por nosotros, pecadores, ahora
  y en la hora de nuestra muerte.
Amén.

Glory Be to the Father

Glory be to the Father,
  and to the Son,
  and to the Holy Spirit.
As it was in the beginning,
  is now, and ever shall be,
  world without end.
Amen.

Gloria al Padre

Gloria al Padre,
  y al Hijo,
  y al Espíritu Santo.
Como era en el principio,
  ahora y siempre,
  por los siglos de los siglos.
Amén.

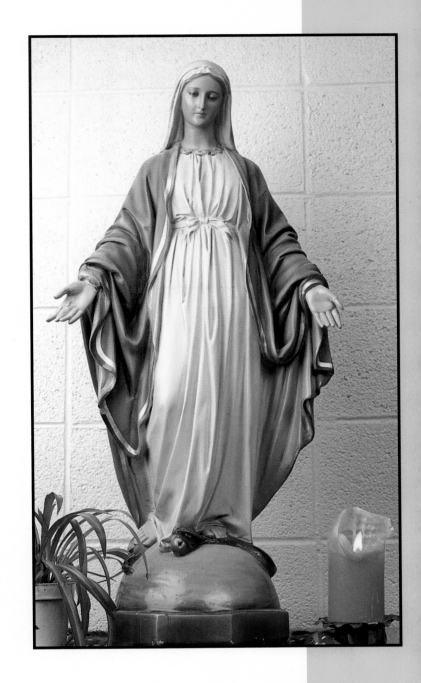

Let Us Pray

Grace Before Meals

Bless us, O Lord, and
    these your gifts,
    which we are about to receive
    from your goodness,
    through Christ our Lord.
Amen.

Grace After Meals

We give you thanks
    for all your gifts,
    almighty God,
    living and reigning now
    and forever.
Amen.

A Morning Prayer

Loving God, bless the work we do.
Watch over us and guide us
    in school and at home.
Help us realize that everything we do
    gives praise to you.
We make this prayer in Jesus' name.
Amen.

Evening Prayer

O Lord, support us all the day long, until the shadows
    lengthen and the evening comes, and the busy world is
    hushed, and the fever of life is over, and our work is done.
Then, Lord, in thy mercy grant us a safe lodging, and a
    holy rest, and peace at last, through Jesus Christ our Lord.
Amen.

Nicene Creed

We believe in one God
    the Father, the Almighty,
    maker of heaven and earth,
    of all that is seen and unseen.

We believe in one Lord, Jesus Christ,
    the only Son of God,
    eternally begotten of the Father,
    God from God, Light from Light,
    true God from true God,
    begotten, not made, one in Being with the Father.
    Through him all things were made.
    For us men and for our salvation
        he came down from heaven:

By the power of the Holy Spirit
    he was born of the Virgin Mary, and became man.

For our sake he was crucified under Pontius Pilate;
    he suffered, died, and was buried.
    On the third day he rose again
        in fulfillment of the Scriptures;
    he ascended into heaven
        and is seated at the right hand of the Father.

He will come again in glory to judge the living and the dead,
    and his kingdom will have no end.

We believe in the Holy Spirit, the Lord, the giver of life,
    who proceeds from the Father and the Son.
    With the Father and the Son he is worshiped and glorified.
    He has spoken through the Prophets.
    We believe in one holy catholic and apostolic Church.
    We acknowledge one baptism for the forgiveness of sins.
    We look for the resurrection of the dead,
        and the life of the world to come.
  Amen.

Let Us Pray

Act of Contrition

My God,
I am sorry for my sins with all my heart.
In choosing to do wrong and failing to do good,
  I have sinned against you
  whom I should love above all things.
I firmly intend, with your help,
  to do penance,
  to sin no more,
  and to avoid whatever leads me to sin.
Our Savior Jesus Christ suffered and died for us.
In his name, my God, have mercy.

Revised Rite of Penance

Prayer to the Holy Spirit

Come, Holy Spirit, fill the hearts of your faithful
  and kindle in them the fire of your love.
Send forth your Spirit, and they shall be re-created;
  and you will renew the face of the earth.

Beginning the Journey

Whenever we go on a journey, we rely on signs to show us the way. Life is a journey, too. There are signs of life and love all around us, showing us the way. As Catholics, these signs can help us discover Jesus, who is present in every moment of our lives.

You are beginning a year-long journey to learn about some of the signs of Christ's presence and actions in your life and in the world around you. Begin this journey by thinking about your own experience of Jesus' presence.

Draw your own sign—something that tells others about you—who you are, what you are like, or what your talents are. *Example:* Someone who likes music might draw a musical instrument or musical notes.

Who or what is a sign to you that Jesus is with you?

_____

_____

_____

Name one current event that seems to be a sign that Jesus is present in the world today.

_____

_____

_____

Prayer for the Journey

Leader: This is the Bible, the book of God's word. Through the words of the Bible, God reveals to us signs of Christ's presence with us.

All: Your word, O Lord, is a lamp that guides me and a light on my path.

Based on Psalm 119:105

Leader: The Gospels reveal to us signs that tell us who Jesus is and why he came among us. Listen carefully.

When he was in prison, John heard of the works of the messiah. He sent his disciples to Jesus with this question. "Are you the one who is to come, or should we look for another?" Jesus said to them in reply, "Go and tell John what you hear and see: the blind can see again, the lame walk, lepers are cleansed, the deaf can hear, the dead are raised, and the poor have the good news proclaimed to them."

Based on Matthew 11:2–61

All: Praise to you, Lord Jesus Christ!

Leader: Jesus is with us and the whole world at large through many different signs.

All: Lord, open our minds and hearts to the signs of your presence and love.

Leader: May God bless each of us as we begin our journey together. May we learn to recognize signs of Christ's presence in our lives. And may God bless these books that will guide our journey.

All: Amen!

THIS IS OUR FAITH

✣ A Preview of Grade 5

SILVER BURDETT GINN • SCHOOL PROGRAM 5

THIS IS OUR FAITH ✣

OPENING DOORS
A Take-Home Magazine ™

You are cordially invited…

A Profile of the Fifth-Grade Child

No one knows your child better than you! It may be helpful and interesting to you as a parent or guardian, however, to explore some of the characteristics of the fifth grader.

Fifth graders

- are very curious.
- enjoy reading.
- need warm and supportive reinforcement from parents and other adults.
- need guidelines and rules to follow.
- respect rules and expect others to follow them as they do.
- are sensitive to criticism but beginning to realize that criticism is necessary and helpful.
- have a strong interest in helping others.
- are much more influenced by the peer group than in earlier years.
- have an increased interest in sexuality.
- dislike being criticized in front of their friends.
- like doing things together and being together with their friends.

Time Out You may want to make a special effort this week to discuss with your child a special interest of his or hers. Also, take the time to share with him or her a special interest of yours.

4

to continue on the journey of faith you first began on the day you presented your child for Baptism. Throughout the years you have been—and continue to be—the most important person of faith for your child. As your fifth-grader commits to this year's faith journey, you are invited as the primary educator in faith to journey along with your child, in whatever way is most comfortable for you. This Is Our Faith is privileged to assist you in this important task.

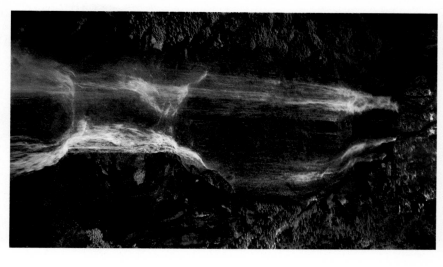

This Year in Grade 5

This year your fifth grader will study the sacramental life of the Catholic Church. Your child will also learn that the Church is the sacrament or sign of Christ in the world. They will come to appreciate the difference Jesus makes in our lives.

In Unit 1 your child will learn that there are many signs of Christ's loving presence in our daily lives. People, especially, but also special, or sacred things, places, and times reveal the presence of God.

OPENING DOORS
A Take-Home Magazine™

As your child completes each unit of This Is Our Faith, you will receive *Opening Doors: A Take-Home Magazine*. Each magazine will include the following features to help you and your family share your faith.

A Closer Look

includes discussion starters, points for reflection and an article relating the unit theme to a particular aspect of the Mass.

Being Catholic

explains a particular aspect of our Catholic heritage.

Growing Closer

suggests activities to help you and your family integrate your faith into everyday life.

And also . . . .

Looking Ahead

A preview of the next unit of This Is Our Faith

UNIT 1

SACRAMENTS: CELEBRATIONS OF LIFE

What are some things in your life you want to celebrate?

THINGS ARE SIGNS OF GOD'S LOVE

SOMETHING MEMORABLE

What is one object you have that reminds you of a special person whenever you look at it or hold it?

Neeraj and Greg had been friends since first grade. They were on the same soccer team and learned karate at the same karate studio. Even though they didn't look like each other and were from different countries, they seemed closer than brothers. Neeraj and Greg were always together. Until last July . . .

One evening Neeraj called Greg. "My dad just told me we're moving!"

Greg was shocked. "I can't believe it. When will you leave? Where are you going?"

"Akron, Ohio. It's over a thousand miles away. And we have to leave in two weeks."

Greg ran downstairs to find his mom and tell her the news. She listened and seemed to understand why Greg was so upset. Finally, she shared her own experience.

"The same thing happened to me when I was about your age," she confided. "My best friend also moved away. Before she left, Linda gave me a necklace with half a heart on it. She kept the other half of the heart around her neck. Every time I saw or touched my half of the heart, I thought of Linda. We are still close friends even though she now lives in Europe."

(to be continued)

Discuss

1. Greg's best friend is moving away. How might Greg feel about Neeraj's move?

2. Linda gave Greg's mom a sign of her presence when she moved. What do you think Greg might do when Neeraj moves away?

SIGNS OF GOD'S PRESENCE

Jesus loved the world of things that God creates for people. He enjoyed the birds and the flowers. He liked to walk along the seashore. He enjoyed eating and drinking with his family and friends.

Jesus knew that God gives us all the good things of creation. He learned to enjoy them, to use them, to care for them, to share them. He knew that everything God creates is good. Jesus also learned to recognize God's presence and care for us in all creation. Everything spoke to him of God.

Activity

We are called to appreciate created things as God's gifts and signs of his presence and care. Imagine each of the things pictured below. Each is a gift from God and a sign of what God is like. Decide what each sign tells you about God and write it on the line below each picture. The first one is done for you.

God is healing.

SOMETHING MEMORABLE *(continued from page 12)*

Greg decided right away to do something like what his mother's friend did. He waited until the day before Neeraj was moving. On that day he gave Neeraj his favorite photo of himself, the one in which he was making the winning goal in last year's soccer tournament. To Greg's surprise, Neeraj gave him a picture of himself receiving his brown belt in karate.

Greg put Neeraj's photo on his desk. A week later he received a card from his friend. It ended with "Your picture is on top of my dresser. I see it all the time. Your friend, Neeraj."

Discuss

1. Why did Neeraj and Greg give something special to each other when Neeraj moved away?

2. What effect did the two pictures have on them?

3. What similar experiences have you had?

Activity

Look at the objects pictured below. Each is a real thing that is also a sign of something else. On the lines provided, write what each sign means to you. Then draw one of your own signs and tell what it means to you.

 _____    _____

 _____   _____

 _____   _____

SACRAMENTALS

Just as Greg's photo of himself reminded Neeraj of their friendship, other objects such as hearts and flags can remind us of someone's presence. Some things are special to Catholics because they speak more clearly about Jesus. These are called **sacramentals**. Sacramentals are blessings, objects, or actions that the Church uses to help us remember that the risen Christ is with us and is active in our lives.

Here are some sacramentals Catholics use to become more aware of God's presence.

 **Crucifixes** remind us that Jesus suffered and died for us and that he rose again.

 **Medals** are worn to remind us of God's continuing presence and care.

 Holy water is water that has been blessed. It reminds us of our Baptism.

 The **rosary** is a reminder of Mary, a very special sign of God's presence.

 The **Bible** is the book that tells us the story of God's continuing presence. It is the inspired word of God. God guided the writers of the Bible to think and write about God's presence in their lives.

 **Statues** remind us of particular people who have been signs of God's presence in the world, such as Jesus, Mary, and the saints.

 **Palms** remind us of Jesus' entry into Jerusalem just before his crucifixion.

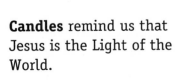 **Candles** remind us that Jesus is the Light of the World.

Vocabulary

sacramental: a blessing, an action, or an object that reminds us of Jesus' presence with us and God's care for us

JESUS POINTS OUT SIGNS OF GOD'S CARE

One day, Jesus was teaching a large crowd of people on a mountainside. He knew that the people had problems with the good things of the world. Some of the people liked things so much that they neglected God. They often forgot to care about other people. Others worried because they did not have enough of the good things of the world.

"Look at the birds in the sky," Jesus told them. "They do not sow or reap, yet your heavenly Father feeds them. Which of you by worrying can add a moment to your lives?

"As for clothes, why be concerned? Learn a lesson from the way the wildflowers grow. They do not work; they do not spin. Yet look how beautiful they are! If God can clothe wildflowers with such beauty, will he not provide much more for you?

"Your heavenly Father knows all that you need. Seek first God's rule over you, his way of holiness, and all these things will be given to you besides. Do not worry about tomorrow. Let tomorrow take care of itself."

Based on Matthew 6:26–34

Discuss

1. What things in today's world cause people to neglect God and to forget to care about others?

2. What did Jesus mean when he said, "Your heavenly Father knows all that you need. Seek first God's rule over you and all these things will be given to you besides"?

Based on Matthew 6:32–33

ALL CREATION SPEAKS OF GOD

God gives us the whole world of created things. God asks us to enjoy them, to respect and care for them, and to use them for our good and the good of others. God asks us to share things and to work so that everyone has a rightful share of the good things of creation.

Jesus teaches us that all of creation speaks to us of God's presence and care for us. He shows us how every created thing can help us become aware of God's presence and care for us. We can learn to let creation speak to us of God's care for us. Everything can be a sign of God's loving presence.

We Believe

God creates everything for us to enjoy, use, respect, and care for. All created things are signs of God's presence and care. We can learn to discover through all the things around us that God is with us and is acting for our good.

BLESSINGS

Just as things are signs of God's presence and care, people are images of God's love. We know that God is with us and cares for us through the things or gifts that he has given us and through people who love us. As a way of thanking and praising God for people and things, the Church has given us prayers called **blessings**. We can ask God's blessings on people as well as on things.

When we use words that ask God to bless something, we are asking God to make it holy. "Bless this food, O Lord, which we are about to share."

When we thank God for his presence and care, we praise him. "Blessed be God, blessed be his holy name."

When we pray, "Bless us, O God, in our work and in our play. Keep us in your loving care in all we do," we ask God's blessing on one another and on ourselves.

Activity

Blessings can be found in the Bible and in many other books. Look up each of the following blessings found in the Bible. Then tell on whom or on what it is asking a blessing.

Psalm 3:8 _____

Mark 8:6–7 _____

Mark 10:13–16 _____

Mark 14:22–24 _____

Activity

The Church has daily blessings, seasonal blessings, blessings for special occasions, as well as many other blessings for things and for people. Read "Blessing of a Pet" below. Then write a blessing for your own pet or other favorite thing. Remember to bless your pet or favorite thing when you go home.

BLESSING OF A PET

Lord God,
you have made all living things and
you are even more wonderful than the
things you have made.
We thank you for giving us our pets
who are our friends and who give us
so much joy in life.
Bless this pet. May it give us joy
and remind us of your power.
May we realize that as our pets
trust us to take care of them,
so we should trust you to take care of us.
Grant us this through Christ our Lord.
Amen.

MY BLESSING

_____

_____

_____

_____

_____

Vocabulary

blessing: a prayer praising or thanking God for someone or something and asking God to be present

PRAYING A BLESSING

Leader: Let us remember that we are in the presence of God as we gather now in prayer.

All: In the name of the Father, and of the Son, and of the Holy Spirit. Amen.

Leader: Loving God, you have created all things to remind us of your continuing presence and care for us. Look upon these young people in your love and bless them. Let them know of the care you have for them, and the care that we have for one another. We call upon you now to bless each of us.

Reader 1: Bless our foreheads: May our minds hold just and loving thoughts, and may our minds learn more about God and about God's Son, Jesus, this year.

Reader 2: Bless our eyes: May our eyes see God's presence in all creation and in one another.

Reader 3: Bless our ears: May our ears be open to the message of God's love and the Gospel of Jesus.

Reader 4: Bless our lips: May our lips speak only the truth, and may we speak to one another in kindness and gentleness.

Reader 5: Bless our hands: May our hands reach out to one another in support, and may we always be willing to lend a helping hand.

Leader: God of all creation, we ask that through this prayer we will become a blessing for one another and for our families. Be with us each day and remind us to use our senses to see your presence all around us.

All: Amen.

Chapter Review

God gives us nature as a special sign of his presence. We are called to care for and respect all of nature. Name one part of nature that is sometimes misused by people.
Then name something you can do to respect that part of nature.

_____

_____

_____

_____

Tell what each sacramental reminds us of.

_____

_____

_____

_____

_____

_____

Fill in the answers to the first two questions.

1. What is meant by a *blessing*?

_____

_____

2. What does Jesus want us to learn from the good things of creation?

_____

_____

3. Discuss how we can develop a habit of being aware of God's presence and care in created things.

From the greatness and beauty of created things, we can see their Creator.
Based on Wisdom 13:5

PLACES ARE SIGNS OF GOD'S PRESENCE

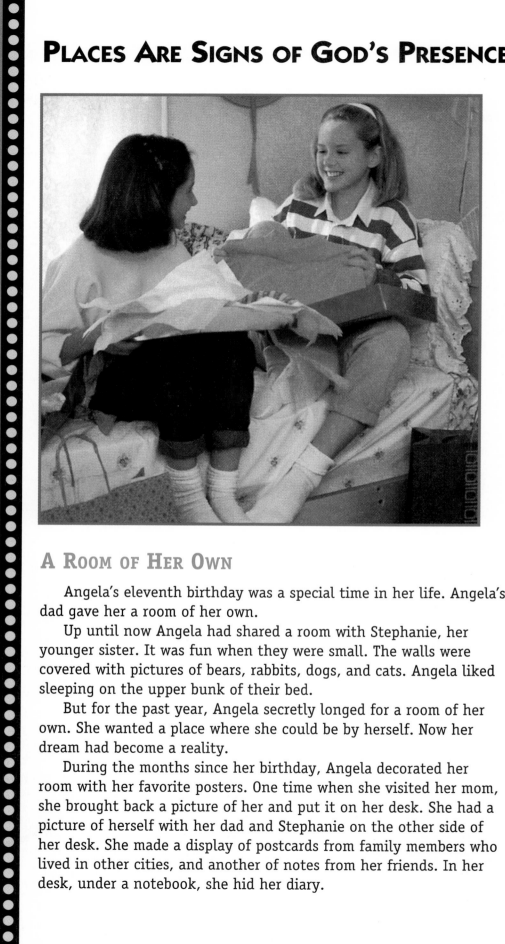

What is your favorite place? What makes it special?

A ROOM OF HER OWN

Angela's eleventh birthday was a special time in her life. Angela's dad gave her a room of her own.

Up until now Angela had shared a room with Stephanie, her younger sister. It was fun when they were small. The walls were covered with pictures of bears, rabbits, dogs, and cats. Angela liked sleeping on the upper bunk of their bed.

But for the past year, Angela secretly longed for a room of her own. She wanted a place where she could be by herself. Now her dream had become a reality.

During the months since her birthday, Angela decorated her room with her favorite posters. One time when she visited her mom, she brought back a picture of her and put it on her desk. She had a picture of herself with her dad and Stephanie on the other side of her desk. She made a display of postcards from family members who lived in other cities, and another of notes from her friends. In her desk, under a notebook, she hid her diary.

It felt so good to Angela to have her very own place. Sometimes she read or wrote stories, or did her homework there. Other times she listened to music or just stretched out on her bed and let her mind wander.

In her room Angela really felt at home. Alone there, Angela somehow felt close to those whose pictures and notes surrounded her. At times she felt that her mom, whom she missed very much, was right there in the room with her.

Angela's room was now her favorite place in all the world, even if her dad didn't think it was as neat as it should be.

Discuss

1. What made Angela's room special to her?
2. How did she feel when she was in it? Why?
3. If you could make a room your very own, what would you put in it? What would you do in it?

Activity

Jesus had special places where he liked to be. The gospels reveal some of them, such as quiet places in the hills, the desert, and along the seashore. Discover some other favorite places of Jesus. Look up the following Scripture passages. Next to each, write the name of the place referred to in the Scripture passage.

Matthew 4:12–14 _____

Mark 10:46–52 _____

John 12:1–8 _____

Matthew 21:1–2 _____

JESUS ENTERS JERUSALEM

One day, Jesus went into Jerusalem riding on a donkey. Crowds of people lined the road. They cheered Jesus as their king. They covered the ground with palm branches.

When Jesus caught sight of the city, he began to weep. He knew that Jerusalem, the city he loved, was in danger from its enemies outside it.

"If only you knew today the path to peace!" Jesus said sadly, talking to Jerusalem itself. "The time will come when your enemies will surround you. They will destroy you and your people within your walls. They will not leave a stone upon a stone."

Then Jesus went into the Temple. The traders and merchants were noisily selling animals for sacrifice and exchanging money. Jesus became angry. He said to them, "God's Temple is to be a house of prayer. But you have made it a place for thieves." He began to drive out the noisy traders and merchants.

Based on Luke 19:28–47

JESUS LOVED JERUSALEM

Jesus, like all Jews of the first century, had a special love for Jerusalem and its holy Temple. Both places were filled with memories and meaning. Mary and Joseph had brought him to the Temple when he was a baby to dedicate him to God (Luke 2:22–35). He had probably gone there with his family each year as he was growing up. Jesus called the Temple, "my Father's house" (Luke 2:41–52). In the city of Jerusalem and especially in its Temple, Jesus celebrated God's holy presence with other devout Jews.

Sacred Places Around the World

Jerusalem remains a very special place for Jews, and also for Muslims and Christians. The Temple of Herod was destroyed about forty years after Jesus died. Only part of one of the walls, the Western Wall, remains. Devout Jews go to Jerusalem to pray at the Western Wall.

Jews, Christians, and Muslims from all over the world make **pilgrimages** to Jerusalem and Israel, which Christians often call the Holy Land. The **Holy Land** is sacred to Christians because it is the place where Jesus lived.

The city of Jerusalem in the Holy Land

The Western Wall in Jerusalem

Vocabulary

pilgrimage: a religious journey to a sacred place

Holy Land: Israel, the land where Jesus lived

Nuestra Señora y Juan Diego (Our Lady and Juan Diego)

We can experience and celebrate God's loving presence in sacred places and ordinary places. Juan Diego experienced God's presence in a special way on a hill called Tepeyac.

Juan Diego was a poor Aztec Indian. He lived in Mexico. Every Saturday he walked to the village of Santiago to celebrate the weekly Mass in honor of Mary, the mother of Jesus.

Early one Saturday morning, Juan Diego was on his way to the church. He was walking by the hill of Tepeyac when he heard beautiful music.

He looked up and saw a bright white cloud at the top of the hill. Juan Diego was curious. He climbed up the hill.

As he came near the cloud, he heard a woman calling him. The cloud opened up and within it was a beautiful lady.

"Listen carefully," the beautiful lady said, very kindly. "I want you to go to the bishop of Mexico. Tell him that I, the Mother of God, want him to build a church right here."

A reproduction of the original painting of Our Lady of Guadalupe located at the Church of Our Lady of Guadalupe, Mexico

Juan Diego was amazed. He told the bishop what Mary had said. The bishop told Juan Diego to go back to the hill. "Ask the lady for some kind of sign that she is the mother of Jesus and really wants me to build a church."

The next morning Juan Diego met Mary at the foot of the hill. "Climb back up the hill to where we met," she told him. "Cut the roses you find there. Put them in your cloak. Then come back here to me."

Juan ran up the hill. "No roses grow on this hill," he thought to himself. "Besides, it's winter." But there, at the top of the hill, were hundreds of roses. He cut as many as he could carry in his cloak.

"Take them to the bishop," Mary told him. "Do not show them to anyone along the way."

Juan Diego carried the roses carefully to the bishop. When Juan opened his cloak, the roses fell to the floor. The bishop knelt down. Juan noticed that the bishop was staring at the empty cloak. On Juan's cloak was a beautiful painting of the lady he had seen on the hill.

The bishop quickly had a small church built on the hill of Tepeyac. He placed Juan Diego's cloak with the painting of Mary in the new church. The church is called the Church of Our Lady of Guadalupe. Many people come every year to pray to Mary and to see her picture on Juan Diego's cloak.

SPECIAL SACRED PLACES

Catholics also believe that certain other places are sacred because people experience God's presence there in special ways. Two of these are the city of Rome and the **Basilica** of St. Peter in that city. Some others are the **shrines** of Our Lady of Guadalupe (Mexico), Our Lady of Lourdes (France), Our Lady of Fatima (Portugal), and Sainte Anne de Beaupré (Canada). In some countries there are small shrines along the roadsides. Many Hispanic Catholic families have small shrines in their homes called *altarcitos*.

The Church of Our Lady of Guadalupe, Mexico

Activity

We know that God is present everywhere. However, like Juan Diego, we often find it easier to experience God's presence in a special place.

Where do you find it easiest to think of God and feel his presence?

_____
_____
_____

What is it about this place that helps you feel God's presence?

_____
_____
_____

Vocabulary

basilica: a Catholic church that the pope honors for a special reason

shrine: a sacred place where God is worshiped

LOCAL SACRED PLACES

Saint Patrick's Cathedral, New York

The Church community experiences God's presence in sacred places everywhere, both around the world and locally. These are special places where we recognize God's presence in a special way. In these sacred places we can pray with the community that is gathered, or we can pray alone.

Most Catholics belong to a **parish**. A parish usually has a church, where the Catholic community can gather for worship. Each parish belongs to a **diocese.** A diocese usually has a **cathedral**, the official church of the bishop. Within a diocese there will be many parish churches. There also might be convents, rectories, Catholic elementary schools and high schools, monasteries, Catholic hospitals, and many other Catholic institutions.

Activity

Complete the following sentences.

The diocese in which I live is the

_____ diocese.

Our bishop's name is

_____ .

The name of our cathedral is

_____ .

Our cathedral is located in

_____ .

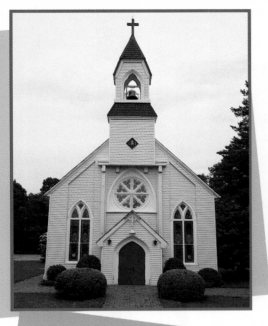

PLACES FOR MEETING GOD

The sacred places pictured above are special places for meeting God. They can make us more aware that God is with us in every place. We can learn to recognize God's presence with us everywhere.

Activity

The name of my parish is _____.

A church I have visited is _____.

My favorite sacred place is _____

because _____

_____.

Vocabulary

parish: a local church where the Catholic community gathers

diocese: a Catholic community made up of many parishes

cathedral: the official church of the bishop or head of a diocese

We Believe

God is with us everywhere and we can meet him in every place. Some places are sacred because we may experience God's presence there in special ways, or they help us to know God's presence everywhere.

PRAYING FOR OURSELVES AS SACRED DWELLING PLACES

Leader: Holy are you Lord, God, Creator of all. You give us times and seasons and reasons for glad celebration. We come into your presence this day in prayer. Make us ready now to hear your word and to offer our prayers to you.

All: Amen.

Reader: We are the temple of the living God; as God said:
"I will live with them and move among them,
and I will be their God
and they shall be my people."

2 Corinthians 6:16

The Word of the Lord.

All: Thanks be to God.

Leader: God, you have chosen to make each of us your dwelling place. We are holy because you live in us. May we always live in ways that show to others that we believe that your presence makes our bodies, our minds, our entire selves sacred places. And may we always respect each other and find you dwelling there. Amen.

Teacher: (*Name*), remember that you are a sacred place and that God dwells in you.

Student: Amen.

Leader: Blessed are you, Lord our God, who blesses us with life and with one another. It is with happy hearts that we thank and praise you for making each of us a sacred place where we can find you near. We offer this prayer in Jesus' name.

All: Amen.

Chapter Review

Help "build" this church by completing the sentences below and writing the correct answers in the spaces provided.

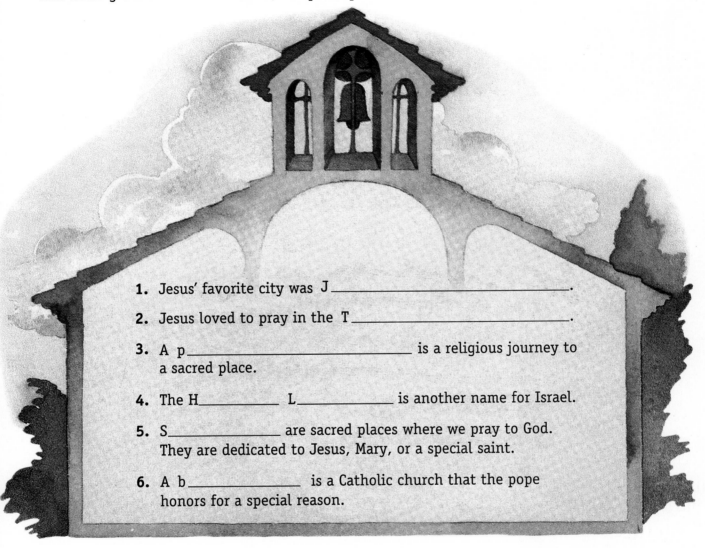

1. Jesus' favorite city was J_____.

2. Jesus loved to pray in the T_____.

3. A p_____ is a religious journey to a sacred place.

4. The H_____ L_____ is another name for Israel.

5. S_____ are sacred places where we pray to God. They are dedicated to Jesus, Mary, or a special saint.

6. A b_____ is a Catholic church that the pope honors for a special reason.

Fill in the answers to the first two questions.

1. What is a *parish?*

   _____

2. If God is everywhere, why do we need special, sacred places?

   _____

   _____

3. Discuss how we can become more aware of God's presence with us in sacred places and ordinary places.

O Lord, I love the house in which you dwell.
Psalm 26:8

TIME IS A CONSTANT SIGN OF GOD'S PRESENCE

Activity

List some of your favorite times. Be ready to explain why they are so special for you.

My favorite hour is

My favorite day is

My favorite week is

My favorite month is

My favorite season is

My favorite year is

My favorite time to be with my family is

My favorite time to be with my friends is

My favorite time to be aware of God's presence is

Activity

Some people may feel that time is endless—it goes on and on. Others may feel that time is very short— there is never enough of it. Think of what time feels like to you. Then finish the sentence below.

Time is

What are some of the best times you've ever had? What made them so special for you?

Jesus teaches us that time is precious because God enters our lives at every moment.

THE TIME OF THE LORD'S COMING

One day, Jesus was talking with his disciples. He told them a story about time.

"Be dressed and ready to go. Have your lamps burning. Be like servants waiting for their master to come home from a wedding. As soon as he arrives and knocks, they open the door right away.

"Happy are those servants who are awake and ready when the master returns, even if it is very late. Their master will put on an apron. He will seat them at his table and he will wait on them."

Jesus stopped for a moment. His disciples thought about what he had said. Then he said the same thing with a slight twist.

"You know as well as I that if the head of the house knew when the thief was coming, he would not let him break into his house. Be ready then. The Lord will come when you least expect him."

Based on Luke 12:35–40

GOD IN EVERY MOMENT

Every moment of time is precious. Every moment is a sign of God's presence. We can become more aware of God's presence by taking time regularly to pray. God is always with us.

Activity

Think about how often you take advantage of the following times to turn to God in prayer. Then put a ✔ in the appropriate column for each prayer time listed.

	NEVER	ALMOST NEVER	OCCASIONALLY	FAIRLY OFTEN	VERY OFTEN	ALL OF THE TIME
When I get up in the morning						
When I eat						
When I'm going to bed						
When I'm taking a test						
When I'm playing an important game						
When I want something badly						
When I'm afraid						
When I'm thankful for something good						
When I'm tempted						

CELEBRATING SPECIAL TIMES

Jesus urged his followers to be open to God at every moment of life. He and his first disciples had special times to become aware of God and to remind themselves that God was always with them. Like faithful Jews then and now, Jesus and his disciples prayed in the morning, at midday, and in the evening. They celebrated the weekly Sabbath and yearly feasts, such as Passover.

Later, Christians chose Sunday as their Sabbath. For them, Sunday became the first day of the week, and it was on this day that the early Christians celebrated their greatest feast day, the resurrection of Jesus. The first Christians continued the practice of Jesus and the disciples by praying in the morning, at midday, and in the evening.

TIMES AND SEASONS

Time is a most precious gift. Without time, nothing is possible. Time never stops. We must be careful of how we use time, because we never get back a past moment.

Activity

Think about the four seasons of the year: winter, spring, summer, and fall. How do you usually spend your time during each of these seasons? How could you use time to become aware of God's presence during each season?

Seasons	I usually spend my time	I could use my time to become aware of God's presence by

A parish community lights the Advent wreath.

OBSERVING SPECIAL TIMES

Catholics and many other Christians observe special times each day, each week, and each year. We prepare for Easter by fasting, praying, and doing penance for forty days. This time of preparation is called **Lent**. We celebrate the birthday of Jesus at Christmas, after four weeks of preparation called **Advent**. We also celebrate other moments in Jesus' life, as well as moments in the lives of Mary and the saints. We continue the tradition of the first Christians by praying in the morning, at midday, and in the evening. We continue each week to celebrate the Sabbath Day on Sunday.

The liturgical calendar on page 37 shows many of the feasts, seasons, holy days, and Sundays that make up the **liturgical year**. These special times can help us remember that the risen Christ is with us at every moment of every day, week, and year. Time is a constant sign of the loving presence of God. Celebrating these feasts and seasons makes us more aware of God's presence. The liturgical year reminds us of the great moments of our Catholic heritage and faith.

THE LITURGICAL YEAR

Study the liturgical year calendar on page 37. Notice that the liturgical year is divided into seasons: Advent, Christmas, Lent, Easter, and Ordinary Time. A new liturgical year begins on the first Sunday of Advent. Easter, Christmas, and Ordinary Time provide a special focus for our prayer and our awareness of God's presence. Like the early Christians, we prepare during the liturgical season of Advent for Christmas and during the season of Lent for Easter. During Ordinary Time, we celebrate events in the life of Jesus as recorded in the gospels.

Activity

Write in the outer circle, near each of the seasons and feasts, the dates they are celebrated this year. Add other special dates you will celebrate this year.

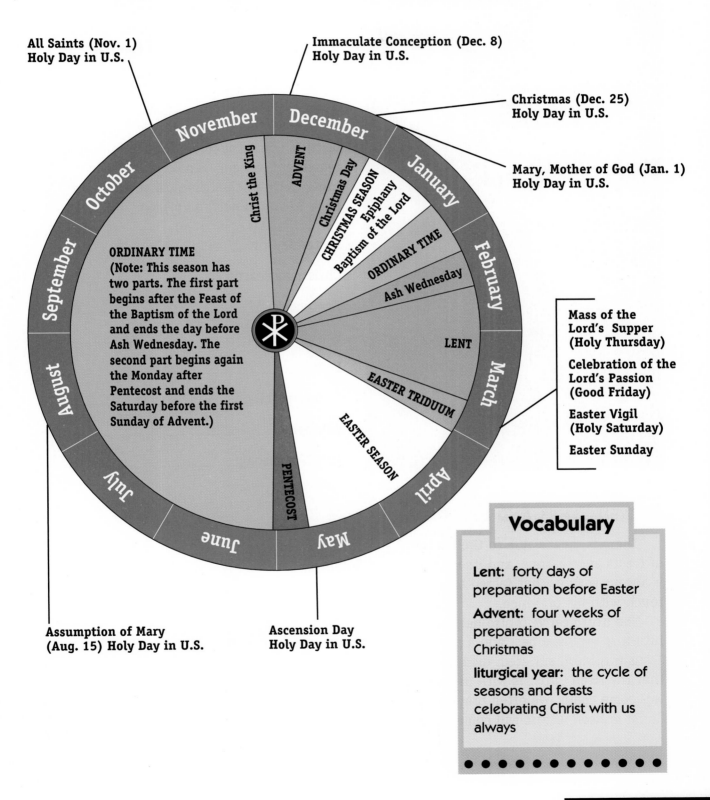

All Saints (Nov. 1)
Holy Day in U.S.

Immaculate Conception (Dec. 8)
Holy Day in U.S.

Christmas (Dec. 25)
Holy Day in U.S.

Mary, Mother of God (Jan. 1)
Holy Day in U.S.

November

December

October

January

September

February

August

March

July

April

June

May

Christ the King

ADVENT

Christmas Day

CHRISTMAS SEASON

Epiphany

Baptism of the Lord

ORDINARY TIME

Ash Wednesday

LENT

EASTER TRIDUUM

EASTER SEASON

PENTECOST

ORDINARY TIME
(Note: This season has two parts. The first part begins after the Feast of the Baptism of the Lord and ends the day before Ash Wednesday. The second part begins again the Monday after Pentecost and ends the Saturday before the first Sunday of Advent.)

Mass of the Lord's Supper (Holy Thursday)

Celebration of the Lord's Passion (Good Friday)

Easter Vigil (Holy Saturday)

Easter Sunday

Assumption of Mary
(Aug. 15) Holy Day in U.S.

Ascension Day
Holy Day in U.S.

Vocabulary

Lent: forty days of preparation before Easter

Advent: four weeks of preparation before Christmas

liturgical year: the cycle of seasons and feasts celebrating Christ with us always

LITURGICAL COLORS

During the liturgical year the Catholic Church uses color to call our attention to the various feasts and seasons. We see liturgical colors used in banners, in altar linens, and in the vestments that the priest wears.

Activity

List the liturgical colors for the following feasts and seasons. (Look back at the inner circle of the liturgical calendar on page 37 if you need help.)

Easter Season _____

Christmas Season _____

Pentecost _____

Advent _____

Lent _____

Ordinary Time _____

Epiphany _____

Ash Wednesday _____

SACRED TIMES AND SEASONS

There is great value to the liturgical year with its cycle of feasts and seasons, and its holy days and Sundays. God is always with us, but sacred times help us to be more in touch with his presence.

The liturgical year also helps us to see that there is a future as well as a past and a present. We remember that Jesus was born, suffered, died, and rose again. We know that the risen Christ is with us now. We believe that Jesus will come again. We often pray at Mass, "Christ has died, Christ is risen, Christ will come again."

Activity

One way to find out more about the events in the life of Jesus is by reading the Bible. Look up each Scripture passage below. On the lines provided write the liturgical season that celebrates the event mentioned in each Scripture reading.

Luke 2:1–7 _____

Luke 24:50–51 _____

Matthew 2:1–12 _____

Mark 16:2–8 _____

Mark 14:22–26 _____

John 19:25–30 _____

Did you know that . . .

. . . Lent is the forty days of preparation for Easter?

. . . The Easter Triduum runs from Holy Thursday evening to Easter Sunday evening?

. . . Easter Sunday is followed by fifty days of the Easter season? This is one of the oldest liturgical seasons in the Church's year.

. . . Advent is a period of preparation for Christmas?

. . . Christmastime lasts from Christmas day to the Feast of the Baptism of Jesus? It includes the Feast of the Epiphany.

We Believe

We celebrate special times during the liturgical year to help ourselves be more open to the risen Christ who brings us God's love and grace at every moment of our lives.

PRAYING WITH THANKS AND GRATITUDE

Dear God,

I thank you for the gift of time, most especially for the time that I use to

_____ .

I thank you for the sacred feasts and seasons, most especially the feast or season of

_____

which reminds me of _____ .

I thank you for the time when I knew you were with me. It was _____

_____ .

I am going to make better use of your gift of time to me by

1. _____

2. _____

3. _____

Please help me do this.

Love,

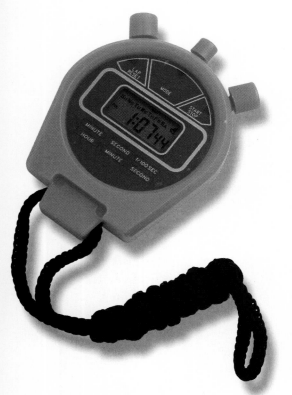

A TIME FOR EVERYTHING

For everything there is a season,
and a time for everything under heaven.
A time to be born, and a time to die;
A time to plant, and a time to uproot.
A time to tear down, and a time to build.
A time to weep, and a time to laugh;
A time to mourn, and a time to dance.
A time to embrace, and a time not to embrace.
A time to seek, and a time to lose;
A time to keep, and a time to throw away.
A time to tear, and a time to sew;
A time to be silent, and a time to speak.

Based on Ecclesiastes 3:1–7

Chapter Review

Write your daily, weekly, and seasonal activities in the appropriate spokes of the wheel. Then circle those activities that are sacred times or that remind you of God's presence.

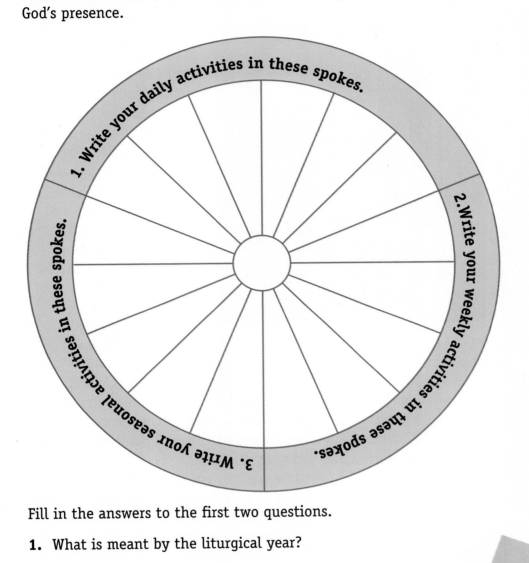

Fill in the answers to the first two questions.

1. What is meant by the liturgical year?

_____

_____

2. Why do we celebrate special, sacred times?

_____

_____

_____

3. Discuss how we can make better use of the gift of time.

> **Now is the acceptable time! Now is the day of salvation!**
> 2 Corinthians 6:2

PEOPLE ARE IMAGES OF GOD'S LOVE

LIKE PARENT, LIKE CHILD

Justin and his younger sister Megan were talking at the kitchen table with their dad and their grandparents last weekend.

"Know what?" eleven-year-old Justin asked. "Look at my hands and dad's hands." He took his father's right hand and placed his own right hand on top of it. "They're exactly the same shape," Justin announced proudly.

"What about me?" asked Megan, feeling a bit left out. "I look like Mom *and* Dad," she boasted.

"When I look at each of you, I see your mother and father," their grandmother commented, trying to head off an argument.

"You're the images of your dad and mom in more ways than just your looks," their grandfather observed. "I think you each have some of your mom's and dad's best qualities."

They all spent the next few minutes naming more important ways Justin and Megan resembled their parents. They talked about things like neatness, patience, thoughtfulness, and generosity.

"We'll be late for the soccer game if we don't hurry," their dad broke in. Justin and Megan hurriedly gathered their jackets and kissed their grandparents goodbye.

As they raced each other to the car, Justin stopped long enough to look at himself in the hall mirror. He smiled. He was the image of his mom and dad, yet somehow Justin was more than that—he was also himself!

Discuss

1. Whom do people say they see in you? Whom are you most like?

2. How are you like that person in how you think, feel, and act?

What do people mean when they say they can see one of your parents or relatives in you?

Activity

The psalms tell us what God is like. What do these psalms tell you about God?

Psalm 103:17 _____

Psalm 135:7 _____

Psalm 136:1 _____

Psalm 149:4 _____

THE IMAGE OF GOD

In the first book of the Bible called the Book of Genesis, we read that human beings are created in God's own image. "God created humankind in God's image; in the divine image God created them; male and female God created them."

Based on Genesis 1:27

Activity

What are some other qualities that you think God has? On the lines below, write words that you would use to describe God.

_____

_____

_____

_____

_____

When God looks at you, which qualities listed above does God see?

_____

_____

_____

_____

Now read a gospel story about Jesus, who saw something of God's goodness in everyone, especially in people others despised or looked down upon.

JESUS SAW GOD IN EVERYONE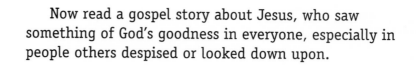

One day Jesus was in Bethany. He was a dinner guest in the home of Simon.

During the meal a woman, who was thought to be a sinner, came into the room in which they were dining. She carried a container of expensive perfume. Everyone was surprised to see her.

She walked over to Jesus. She took the top off the container, and began anointing Jesus' head with perfume.

Some of the guests were angry with the woman. The guests felt she was wasting the perfume. They said, "That perfume could have been sold for a lot of money. The money could have been given to the poor."

Jesus defended the woman. "Leave her alone," he said. "Why are you criticizing her? She has done a great kindness for me. The poor will always be with you, and you can be generous to them whenever you wish. You will not always have me. She has done what she could."

The other guests were still angry with her. But they were afraid to say anything more against the woman.

"I tell you," Jesus said, "wherever the gospel is proclaimed throughout the world, what she has done for me will be told in her memory."

Based on Mark 14:3–9

WHAT JESUS SAW

Jesus saw God's image in the sensitive, courageous woman who anointed his head with perfume. He also saw something of God in Simon, who was so hospitable and generous. Jesus could even see God's image and likeness in the angry guests whom he knew yearned to be good, caring persons. Jesus believed each human being is created in God's image and likeness, deserving of respect and care.

Activity

Think about the image of God you see in each group of people listed. Place a ✔ in the appropriate column to indicate if it is easy or difficult for you to see God's image in each group.

Look at your completed chart. For each group that you checked "Easy", describe the image of God you see. Write your descriptions on the lines below.

Group	Easy	Difficult
the elderly		
young children		
family members		
neighbors		
teachers		
coaches		
friends		
classmates		
teammates		
other _____		

Activity

1. What does it mean to be holy? _____

_____

_____

2. Do you know someone who is holy? _____

3. Do you see yourself as holy? Why or why not? _____

_____

_____

Thomas More was canonized a saint in 1935.

SAINTS ARE IMAGES OF GOD'S LOVE

Because of Jesus' openness and compassion toward all, his disciples came to see God's image reflected in him. The disciples admired Jesus and began to live more and more as Jesus lived. Gradually, people began to see Jesus' traits in his disciples. To those who never knew Jesus, the disciples became the image of Jesus because they reflected Jesus' presence.

Many Christians reflect Christ's presence and way of life in both ordinary and extraordinary ways. Those who do can be models for us. You may find some of these Christians in your family, neighborhood, or school.

The Church **canonizes** some exceptional followers of Jesus and calls them **saints**. All who belong to the community of Jesus' followers, both living and dead, are part of the **Communion of Saints**. The greatest of all saints is Mary, the mother of Jesus.

RELATING TO THE SAINTS

The Church honors the saints throughout the year and especially on All Saints Day. Here is how we can relate to the saints who can help us to become better Christians.

1. **We can learn about the saints.** As we learn more about our faith, we also learn more about the people who have lived before us and those who have been faithful followers of Jesus. By reading about their lives, we are inspired to live as friends of Jesus.

2. **We can honor the saints.** We honor these Christian men and women by taking their names at Baptism, naming churches and other places after them, placing their statues or pictures in our churches and homes, and celebrating their feasts. At every Mass we remember and honor them.

3. **We can pray to the saints.** We can ask the saints to pray for us because we believe that we are united with them in the Communion of Saints.

4. **We can imitate the saints.** The saints are models or examples of how we can live in the Spirit of Jesus. We, too, can respect and love all people, especially those who are poor and in need. We can learn to see an image of God in everyone.

Activity

If I could recommend people for canonization, I would recommend

1. _____ because
   _____.

2. _____ because
   _____.

3. _____ because
   _____.

Vocabulary

canonize: the way in which the Church names someone a saint

saint: someone the Church singles out as an outstanding model of what it means to be like Jesus

Communion of Saints: the entire community of Jesus' followers, both living and dead

We Believe

All people are made in the image and likeness of God and deserve respect and care. All who are united with Christ are members of the Communion of Saints. The Church honors some exceptionally Christlike persons as saints, the greatest of whom is Mary.

How Jesus Lived

The Beatitudes summarize how Jesus lived. They teach us how to find everlasting happiness. Jesus promises that if we live the Beatitudes, we can begin to bring about God's kingdom, which will be fulfilled when Christ comes again.

When Jesus saw the crowds, he went up on the side of a mountain and sat down. Jesus' disciples gathered around him, and he taught them:

"Happy are the poor in spirit. The kingdom of God is theirs.
Happy are the sorrowing. They will be comforted.
Happy are the gentle. They will receive all that God has promised.
Happy are those who hunger and thirst for justice. They will be satisfied.
Happy are those who show mercy to others. They will receive mercy.
Happy are the single-hearted. They will see God.
Happy are the peacemakers. They will be called children of God.
Happy are those who are treated unfairly for doing what is right.
The kingdom of God is theirs."

Based on Matthew 5:1–12

How We Live the Beatitudes

We are the poor in spirit when we listen to God and trust in God's goodness.
We are the sorrowing when the sin and suffering in the world makes us sad.
We are the gentle when we use the gifts that God has given us to help others.
We are those who hunger and thirst for justice when we long for God's peace, love, and justice for all people.
We show mercy to others when we forgive those who hurt us and are patient with everyone.
We are single-hearted when we do what God wants us to do and when we show our love for God by loving our neighbor.
We are peacemakers when we choose to reconcile with others and to make peace.
We are doing what is right when we carry on Jesus' work in the world, speak out against injustice, and stand up for what is right, even when it is not always easy.

Activity

Choose a beatitude you would like to try to live. Name two ways you could live it.

_____

_____

REFLECTING THE IMAGE OF JESUS

Like the earliest followers of Jesus, and all those saints and other Christians who have gone before us, we are called to live in such a way that others can see and hear Jesus in us. We are the community of Jesus' followers, and we are part of the Communion of Saints.

Jesus calls each of us to live in a way that is caring and respectful. Everyone is a son or daughter of God and is deserving of respect and love. We reflect God's love by the way we try to be like Jesus.

Activity

How well do you reflect God's image to others? For each statement below, check the box that is most true for you.

I Reflect God's Image When	Always	Often	Seldom	Never
I share with others.				
I help others.				
I treat others with respect.				
I thank others.				
I admit my mistakes.				
I forgive others.				
I treat others fairly.				
I treat things with respect.				
I ask forgiveness.				
I am honest.				

PRAYING THE LITANY OF THE SAINTS

Leader: We have learned that all followers of Jesus, both living and dead, belong to the Communion of Saints. The Church calls on the saints to pray for us through a traditional prayer called a litany. A person leads a litany by calling on the saints' names. The other members of the community respond by answering "pray for us" or a similar short prayer.

Leader:	**Students:**
Lord, have mercy.	Lord, have mercy.
Christ, have mercy.	Christ, have mercy.
Lord, have mercy.	Lord, have mercy.
Holy Mary, Mother of God,	pray for us.
Holy angels of God	pray for us.
Saint Joseph	pray for us.
Saint Peter and Saint Paul	pray for us.
Saint Mary Magdalene	pray for us.
Saint Benedict and Saint Scholastica	pray for us.
Saint Augustine and Saint Dominic	pray for us.
Saint Francis and Saint Clare	pray for us.
Saint Catherine of Siena	pray for us.
Saint Thérèse of Lisieux	pray for us.
(Other saints' names may be added.)	pray for us.
All holy men and women	pray for us.
Lord, be merciful.	Lord, save your people.
From all evil,	Lord, save your people.
By your death and rising to new life,	Lord, save your people.

Leader: Let us pray.
God of our ancestors, we are grateful for all those holy people whose lives showed us Jesus, your Son, and who now live forever with you. Keep us united with all the saints in heaven and with all who love you here on earth. We join our prayer with the prayer of the entire Communion of Saints through Jesus, our Lord.

All: Amen.

Chapter Review

Name five ways people can be images of God.

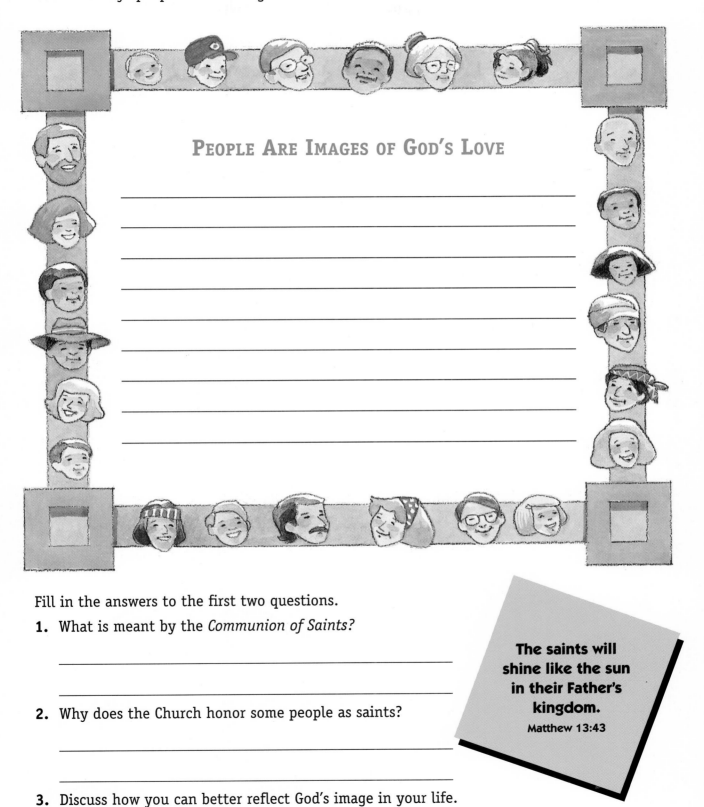

PEOPLE ARE IMAGES OF GOD'S LOVE

Fill in the answers to the first two questions.

1. What is meant by the *Communion of Saints?*

_____

_____

2. Why does the Church honor some people as saints?

_____

_____

3. Discuss how you can better reflect God's image in your life.

The saints will shine like the sun in their Father's kingdom.
Matthew 13:43

UNIT **1** ORGANIZER

Each picture below stands for a chapter in this unit. Write two important words or ideas about that chapter on the lines provided.

Time

Things

SIGNS AND IMAGES OF GOD'S LOVE AND PRESENCE

People

Places

UNIT 1 REVIEW

Match the phrases in Column A with the phrases in Column B to complete the sentences.

Column A

1. God gives us all the

2. All created things are

3. God's gifts are

4. A most precious gift is

5. A sacramental is a blessing, an action, or an object

6. The Bible is the book

7. The crucifix reminds us

8. A blessing is a prayer praising God

Column B

_____ life.

_____ that Jesus suffered, died, and rose for us.

_____ that reminds us of Christ's presence with us.

_____ everywhere.

_____ or thanking him for someone or something and asking God to be present.

_____ good things of creation.

_____ signs of God's presence and care.

_____ that tells the story of God's continuing presence.

Write the correct word or words in the blanks to complete the sentences.

1. The land where Jesus lived is now called Israel. Christians often refer to it as

   _____.

   | Egypt | Asia | the Holy Land |

2. A religious journey to a sacred place is a _____.

   | basilica | vacation | pilgrimage |

3. When Jesus traveled to Jerusalem he visited the _____.

   | Temple | church | cathedral |

4. The bishop's church in a diocese is a _____.

   | shrine | basilica | cathedral |

5. On Juan Diego's cloak was a beautiful painting of _____.

   | Jesus | roses | Mary |

UNIT **1** REVIEW

Match the phrases in Column A with the phrases in Column B to complete the sentences.

Column A

1. Advent is four weeks

2. Time is

3. The symbolic color for Easter and Christmas

4. The greatest feast day for the followers of Christ

5. The liturgical year is the cycle of seasons and feasts

6. Lent is the forty days

Column B

_____ is white.

_____ celebrating the presence of Jesus Christ with us at all times.

_____ of preparation for Easter.

_____ of preparation for Christmas.

_____ a most precious gift.

_____ is Easter Sunday.

Unscramble the letters in parentheses and write the correct word on the lines.

1. All people are made in the image and likeness of God and deserve

   (tpseecr) _____ and (vole)_____ .

2. The presence of (hCrsit) _____ can be discovered in every human being.

3. The (crhhuC) _____ sees each person as a brother or sister of Jesus Christ.

4. The saints learned to see everyone as made in God's (megia) _____.

5. To (zonaince) _____ means to officially name someone a saint.

6. The saints are (eldmso)_____ of how people can live according to the Spirit of Jesus.

7. (ryMa) _____ is the greatest saint.

WHAT DOES BEING a PEACEMAKER MEAN?

Peacemakers are people who recognize that they and others are loved by God. A peacemaker spreads God's love by acting in ways that show compassion, forgiveness, kindness, and gentleness.

Activity

In the ovals below, write words or phrases that describe the people in your life. The small oval in the middle represents you. The outer oval represents the people with whom you feel closest.

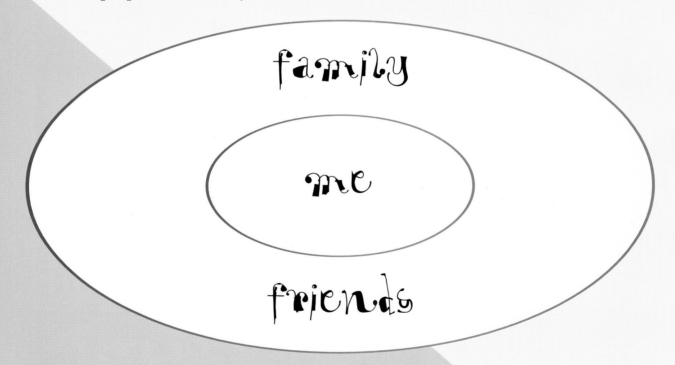

family

me

friends

Our Actions Affect Others

When a stone is skipped across a pond, the water breaks into ripples. Like the action of a skipping stone, your actions have an effect on those around you. You are also affected by the "ripple" from the actions of others. When you treat others with love, kindness, compassion, and gentleness, there is a greater chance that they in turn will treat you and others in the same way.

Activity

On the lines below, write about a time when you were a peacemaker. Perhaps you were a peacemaker with one of the people named in your ovals.

How did you spread God's love by acting in ways that showed compassion, forgiveness, kindness, or gentleness?

_____

_____

How did it feel to be a peacemaker?

_____

Was this easy or difficult to do?

_____

Now tell about a time when someone was a peacemaker for you.

How did this person show God's love to you?

_____

_____

How did you feel and respond?

_____

_____

Following Jesus

Jesus calls us to love one another. When we treat others with kindness, compassion, and gentleness, and when we forgive someone who has hurt us, we are being peacemakers. We are teaching others about Jesus.

PRAYER

Jesus, I know you love me and I feel your love in my heart. Help me to be a sign of your love for others through my actions. Amen.

OPENING DOORS
A Take-Home Magazine™

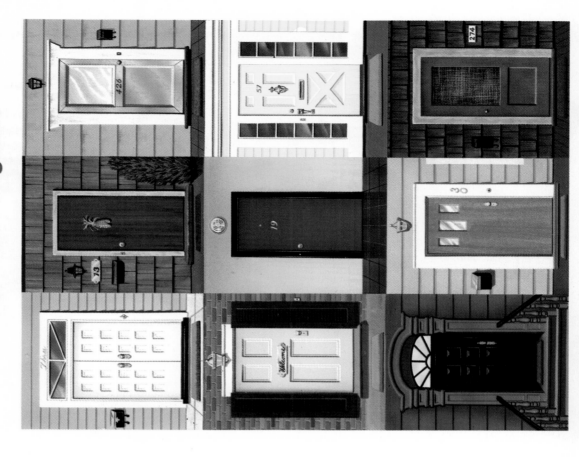

THIS IS OUR FAITH

Growing Closer

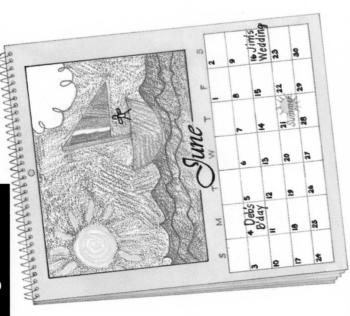

MAKE A FAMILY CALENDAR to post in your kitchen. Use photographs or family drawings to illustrate each month. On the calendar, fill in family birthdays, holidays, and anniversaries. Also fill in the feasts and seasons of the Church that are important to you. As you do so, talk about seasonal family traditions. Share with your child your own memories and experiences concerning the feasts and seasons of the Church.

Looking Ahead

In the coming weeks your fifth-grader will learn that Jesus is true God and true man. Jesus speaks God's word. He brings us God's healing power. Jesus brings us to God in prayer.

A Closer Look

Time Passages

An acrostic is a puzzle in which the beginning letters of each line you add to the puzzle form a word. Look at the example of the acrostic for TIME. Make your own family acrostic for PRESENT, PAST, or FUTURE.

Time is very precious.

In our family we should

Make every day

Extra special.

Crucifixion. *Scrimshaw, U.S.A., 19th century.* (page 181). *(whalebone art)*

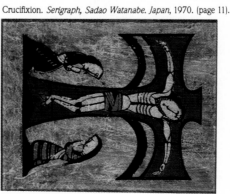

The Face of Jesus. *Plaster plate. Norman LaLiberté. U.S.A., contemporary.* (page 227).

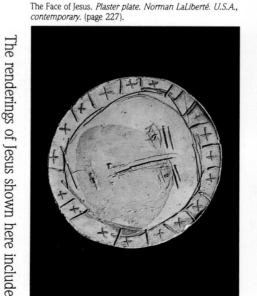

The renderings of Jesus shown here include the work of artists in different parts of the world. In each case the Jesus shown reflects the artist's own time, world, and culture.

Crucifixion. *Serigraph, Sadao Watanabe. Japan, 1970.* (page 11).

Photographs from *The Faces of Jesus,* Riverwood/Simon and Schuster, New York, 1974.

The Gift of Time

Use the following questions for self reflection and/or family discussion.

- Do I think of time as a precious gift of God?
- What is my favorite time of the day? Why?
- What is my favorite day of the year? Why?
- Do I really have time for everything I try to do?
- How do I organize my priorities and time?
- Am I so busy and preoccupied with work that I live superficially?
- Do I try to fill up all my time with activity?
- Do I plan quiet time during each day in which to meet God?
- Do I have time for each member of my family—every day, each week?

The Many Faces of Jesus

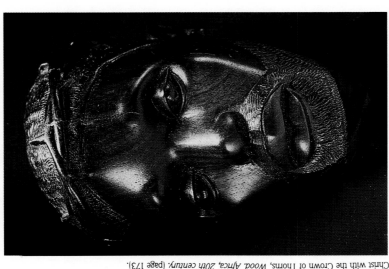

Christ with the Crown of Thorns, Wood, Africa, 20th century (page 173).

None of the authors of the gospels gave us a description of Jesus. Their only interest was to hand down his message, to spread the good news of his great love for us. But down through the ages, artists in many different cultures have tried to show us Jesus. In wood, oils, ceramic, metal, and stone, they have told us what Jesus meant to them and what he might mean to us.

The Church Calendar

The Church celebrates Eucharist day in and out, year after year after year. And in essence the Mass never changes. But the externals change. The mood and tone of the celebration changes from season to season, according to the major feasts of the Church year. One of the more noticeable changes is the color of vestments worn by the priest. Most parishes also rearrange and/or redecorate according to the season: flowers and foliage, banners, Christmas trees, Advent wreaths, Lenten crosses, palms and Easter lilies.

The readings from Scripture and the responsorial psalm clearly reflect the season. The opening prayer states the theme; songs set the tone.

The liturgical calendar takes us through the life of Christ on Sundays. On weekdays we celebrate and commemorate holy days, feasts of Mary and other saints of the Church. The rhythmic cycle of feasts, seasons, holy days, and Sundays forms a pattern in our lives that colors everything else. It's not that God is more present or active at these special times; these special times help us get more in touch with God.

Advent

Christmas

Lent

Easter

Ordinary Time

Pentecost

UNIT 2

JESUS: SACRAMENT OF GOD'S PRESENCE

When you think of Jesus, what's the first thing that comes to your mind?

JESUS TEACHES GOD'S WORD

JOSÉ AND MR. SANTOS

José didn't say much during class. He didn't say much on the playground. At lunch time he often sat alone.

When José's classmates called him stupid, he was hurt. Mr. Santos could feel José's hurt. Some children made fun of José because he didn't speak English very well.

Mr. Santos gave José a big notebook and some colored pens. He told José to draw and write whatever he wished. José spent a lot of time alone, writing and drawing with his notebook. He would not let anyone except Mr. Santos see his work.

One day Mr. Santos asked José to help him after school. "I know you are hurting," Mr. Santos said. "What is making you so sad?"

José could not explain the hurt he felt inside. He just looked at Mr. Santos with tears in his eyes. His teacher seemed to sense how José felt and why he felt that way.

"When I came here," Mr. Santos said to José, "people laughed at me and called me dumb because I didn't speak English well. I felt bad. But I knew I was not dumb. I decided that what others said or thought wasn't what really mattered. I just did my best."

José looked up at his teacher with wide eyes. He could not imagine people ever laughing at Mr. Santos.

"Your pictures and writings are good," Mr. Santos continued. "Show the class your drawings and writings. Then they will see that you are not stupid."

Who is the best teacher you have ever had? What is so special about that teacher?

Mr. Santos and José made a display of José's work. The next morning José's classmates were surprised. From the pictures they could see what it was like in José's homeland, Honduras.

One picture showed beautiful green hills. Another showed how a banana farm looks. A third showed a big city with busy streets. A fourth showed a poor family standing in front of a little house made of boxes. A fifth showed soldiers.

The words he had written under the pictures showed some of José's thoughts and feelings. Under the picture of the hills, he had written: "The green hills are like God, strong and peaceful."

Under the picture of the poor family, he had written: "Why are some people so poor?" Beside the picture of the soldiers, José had written: "Why do people fight and kill each other?"

Mr. Santos smiled as José's classmates looked with amazement at the pictures and what José had written. No one laughed at José or made fun of him after that. Instead they began to understand José better.

Discuss

1. What do you think about Mr. Santos as a teacher?

2. What did he teach José?

3. What are some of the ways in which he taught José?

4. What did the other children learn?

JESUS, TEACHER OF GOD'S WORD

People called Jesus **rabbi**, which means "teacher." Like other rabbis of his time, Jesus taught in the local **synagogues,** which are Jewish houses of worship, and in the Temple. He also taught in homes, in the streets and marketplaces, in fields, on hillsides, and even along the seashore.

People came from all over to listen to Jesus. He taught them much about life and about God, mostly through stories and by the way he lived.

People wondered how Jesus had learned all that he taught. For when Jesus taught, the people recognized God's word. They felt God's presence when he spoke to them. Because of this they also called him a **prophet**, someone called by God to speak in his name.

Vocabulary

rabbi: Hebrew word that means "teacher"

synagogue: house of worship and a community center of the Jewish people

prophet: someone called by God to speak in his name

We Believe

Jesus was a teacher and a prophet. The Church believes that Jesus Christ speaks God's word to us.

JESUS, THE GREAT TEACHER

The crowds sat quietly on the hillside. They had been listening to Jesus for hours.

Now it was getting late. The bright red sun was sinking low in the sky. Shadows of the hills stretched darkly over the calm sea. Jesus ended his teachings for the day with two short stories.

"Anyone who hears my words and puts them into practice is like the wise man who built his house on rock. When the rainy season came, heavy rains poured down. Rivers flooded and winds blew hard against the house. But the house did not fall down, because it was built solidly on rock."

Jesus paused a moment to let the crowds think about the story. Then he went on.

"Anyone who hears my words but does not put them into practice is like a foolish man who built his house on sand. Heavy rains fell. The rivers flooded. Strong winds beat against the house. And the house fell down and was washed away."

Jesus stopped talking. He stood up and began to walk down the hill with his disciples.

The crowd sat for a moment in silence. They were amazed at what Jesus said and how he taught them. They sensed that Jesus taught with more authority than other teachers they had heard.

Based on Matthew 7:24–29

Activity

List three characteristics of sand.

1. _____

2. _____

3. _____

List three characteristics of rock.

1. _____

2. _____

3. _____

Why do you think Jesus told the story about the house built on rock and the house built on sand?

_____

_____

_____

_____

Name three decisions you can make to build your life on solid Christian "rock."

1. _____

_____

2. _____

_____

3. _____

_____

JESUS SPEAKS AND WE RESPOND

As followers of Jesus, we are called to learn from Jesus' teachings and to share those teachings with others. Jesus continues to teach us through the gospels.

Activity

Read the following gospel passages and complete the chart.

Gospel Reference	Based on Mark 9:35	Based on Matthew 7:12	Based on Luke 12:20
Gospel Passage	At Capernaum, Jesus overheard his disciples arguing about which of them was the greatest. Jesus responded, "If anyone wishes to be first, he must be the last of all and the servant of all."	Jesus once told a group of people, "Do unto others whatever you would have them do to you."	Jesus told a story about a man who lived only to build bigger barns so he could make more money. In the story, God says to the man, "Fool, this night your life will be taken from you; and the things you have prepared, whose will they be?"
In this Gospel passage, I think Jesus is talking about…			
Jesus seems to be telling me…			

ANGELA'S RESPONSE

As a follower of Jesus, Angela Kimlinger, a high school student from White Bear Lake, Minnesota, learned from Jesus' teachings. She learned about God and about how we are to care for others. Angela and fifty other young people from her parish youth group volunteered to spend part of their summer vacation in Missouri. They rebuilt and repaired the homes of families in need. Angela's youth group was joined by four hundred other young people from all over the United States. The young people slept in the town's high school, ate their meals together, and prayed together. Each person in their work crew of six was from a different part of the country. For six hours a day, in 90 degree heat and humidity, the young people responded as followers of Jesus. Here are some of her thoughts about her experience.

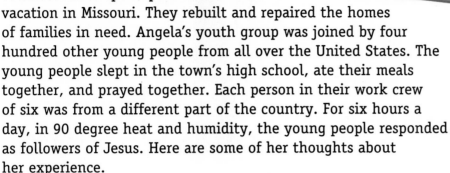

Day 2: "Wow! Missouri has sure been an amazing experience. My faith and relationship with God have been renewed. It seems our lives are a never-ending search to meet God and understand God. I met God in the members of my work crew and in the people whose homes we worked on."

Day 15: "Daily prayer is also very important to me. Being close to God in prayer more than once a day is so comforting and reassuring. God is like a good friend. We like to see or talk with our good friends each day, so why not talk to God each day?"

Day 26: "When you come right down to it, the only thing we have control of is our actions. So, we must follow God's ways, as Jesus taught us. We must love and do unto others as we would want done to us."

Day 33: "Every one of us, you and me, are truly special people. We are gifts of God."

Activity

What if, like Angela, you volunteered to help rebuild and repair the homes of people who are in need? How do you think you could help them? How do you think helping them would change your relationship with God? Write about it on the lines below.

_____

_____

_____

Activity

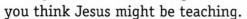

The risen Christ continues to speak God's word to us. One way he does so is through our daily experiences. Each picture below shows a situation in which Jesus could be teaching an important lesson through another person. On the lines near each picture, write what you think Jesus might be teaching.

_____

_____

_____

_____

_____

_____

_____

_____

_____

JESUS TEACHES BY EXAMPLE AND WORD

In the Bible, we read that Jesus taught people about God. He taught them how to live and how to pray. The people learned from Jesus not only by what he said, but also by what he did. They learned how they should treat people by watching how Jesus treated people throughout his life. He taught others by his example as well as by his words.

Sometimes you will be asked to teach others about God with your words. More often, you will teach about God and share the teachings of Jesus by your example.

Activity

Jesus taught by his teachings and actions. List examples of how Jesus lived out each of his teachings. Then list specific ways you can respond to his teachings.

Teachings of Jesus	Actions of Jesus	How I Can Respond
"Love one another." *John 15:17*		
"Do not put your light under a bushel basket." *Based on Mark 4:21*		
"Come. You have my Father's blessing!... For I was hungry and you fed me." *Based on Matthew 25:34-35*		
"I am the good shepherd. A good shepherd lays down his life for his sheep." *John 10:11*		

PRAYING AND LISTENING TO GOD

How does God's word come to us? Often God's word comes to us through the Scriptures we read or hear proclaimed. But God's word can also come to us when we listen to what he might be telling us or asking of us in prayer. Use the outline below to complete a letter to yourself from God. Then reread God's letter and listen to what he has to say to you.

Dear _____ ,

I hope you know how much I love you. You are such a good person, _____ . especially the way you _____

I know that sometimes school might seem difficult, but I hope that you _____ .

I know, too, that at times you are very busy, and that is good. But, _____ . I hope you always will be sure to take time to _____

I also know how much fun you have. When you are having fun I _____ hope you _____ .

Try also to be honest, in particular, be sure to _____ _____ .

Remember always how much your family loves you. I hope that in _____ . your family you are _____

Please remember also to pray often about _____ _____ and to listen carefully to what I may want to say to you. You can always come to talk to me in prayer. I'll be waiting for you.

Blessings!

Your friend,
God

Chapter Review

Write the answers to the following questions on the lines provided.

1. What is a prophet?

   _____

   _____

2. Whom did people call teacher and prophet?

   _____

3. What are three ways in which Jesus continues to speak God's word to us?

   _____

   _____

   _____

4. What are four things you can do to teach others about God and share Jesus' teachings by your example?

   _____

   _____

   _____

   _____

◆ ◆

Fill in the answers to the first two questions.

1. What does the word *rabbi* mean? _____

   _____

2. Why did people who heard Jesus teaching come to praise, thank, and love God as well as wonder at Jesus' words?

   _____

   _____

3. Discuss how the risen Christ continues to teach us today.

> Lord, to whom shall we go? You have the words of eternal life.
>
> **Based on John 6:68**

JESUS HEALS WITH GOD'S POWER

Activity

Look carefully at the photographs on the page. Tell a story about what might have happened in each. Describe how you think each person feels and what he or she needs most.

What is one thing you can do to help someone who is hurting or feeling sad?

JESUS RESPONDS TO PEOPLE IN NEED

The gospels show Jesus as a very **compassionate** man. Jesus helped the sick, the blind, and the lame. He healed and comforted them. Jesus gave them words that were full of hope. He forgave and healed many of them.

We do not know how many people Jesus actually healed. But there is no question that he healed people in a way that amazed those who watched. It is also certain that he forgave sinners in a way that shocked many of the religious leaders.

When Jesus helped or forgave someone, people felt the presence and power of God, their merciful and compassionate Healer.

Activity

Read each Scripture passage below. On the lines provided, describe the ways that Jesus responded to people's needs.

Mark 1:40–45 _____

Luke 7:11–17 _____

Matthew 9:27–31 _____

Luke 13:10–17 _____

John 11:1–44 _____

Vocabulary

compassionate: caring for and about other people

///////////////////

We Believe

Jesus healed and forgave people by his words and actions. The Church believes that Jesus continues to bring us God's healing power.

JESUS HEALED PEOPLE'S PAIN

One day, when Jesus was teaching in a house where he was staying, some men came to the house carrying a paralyzed man on a mat. They wanted to bring him to Jesus. They hoped that Jesus would cure him. But the house was so crowded that they could not get inside.

So they climbed up on the flat roof. They made a hole in the roof. They carefully let the mat down into the room where Jesus was. The man came to rest at Jesus' feet in the middle of the crowd.

Jesus was impressed with their faith in him. He bent over the man and said, "My friend, your sins are forgiven."

Some of the people gathered there were upset. They thought that Jesus was claiming to be God. They said to one another, "Who is this man who speaks **blasphemy**? Who can forgive sins but God alone?"

Jesus overheard their discussion. "Why do you have such thoughts?" Jesus asked them. "Which is easier: to say, 'Your sins are forgiven you,' or to say, 'Get up and walk'?"

As they thought about his question, Jesus spoke to the paralyzed man, "I say to you, get up! Take your mat with you and go back home."

The man stood up before everyone. He picked up the mat he had been lying on. He went home, praising God. Everyone was amazed. They all praised God, saying, "We have seen wonderful things today!"

Based on Luke 5:17–26

Activity

Pretend that you are a guest at the house where Jesus is staying in the gospel story. On the lines provided, answer the following questions.

What impressed you most about the healing you just witnessed?

_____

_____

What do you think about Jesus now?

_____

_____

_____

_____

Vocabulary

blasphemy: an insult to God or to his holy leaders

////////////////////

One way the risen Christ continues to bring God's healing and forgiveness is through people, including ourselves. We can learn from people who care enough to make a difference in the lives of others.

A Compassionate Healer

Peter Claver was born in Catalonia (today, Spain) about 400 years ago to a family of wealthy farmers. When Peter was twenty, he joined the Society of Jesus, or the Jesuits. Peter was eventually ordained a priest and sent as a missionary to South America.

Father Peter did not like what he saw in Cartagena, a port city in the country known today as Colombia. Ships would dock with men and women from Africa who were to be sold as slaves. They were all very sick from their journey, which had lasted five or six weeks. No one else seemed to care for them.

Father Peter decided to help the slaves all he could. He would hurry to the ships with medicine, food, clothing, and water. Peter then nursed them back to health and taught them how much God loved them. He baptized many of the slaves.

Above all, Father Peter treated the slaves with great kindness and respect. He cared for them because Peter knew that Jesus wanted to heal these broken people through him.

In 1650, Father Peter became ill during an epidemic that had fallen on Cartagena. He lived four more years in poor health, all the while continuing to care for the slaves as best he could.

Pope Leo XIII canonized Peter Claver in 1888 and declared him the patron saint of missionaries who work with Africans.

Activity

Look again at the three photographs on page 72. Select one of them. Then on the lines provided, write how you might help with your heart, eyes, ears, and hands. You will discover ways you can bring Jesus' healing and forgiveness to others as the people shown on this page are doing.

With my heart I can _____

_____

_____

_____ .

With my eyes I can _____

_____

_____

_____ .

With my ears I can _____

_____

_____

_____ .

With my hands I can _____

_____

_____

_____ .

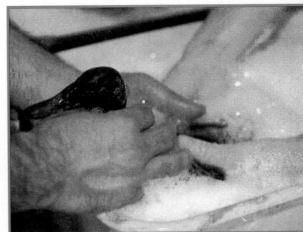

By words and actions, Jesus taught us about compassion. In the following parable, we learn more about bringing God's healing power and compassion to others.

THE GOOD SAMARITAN

One day a young man saw Jesus and asked him this question: "Who is my neighbor?" Jesus told the young man the following story.

One day a man fell victim to robbers as he went down from Jerusalem to Jericho. The robbers attacked him and stole his money, leaving him almost dead.

Later, a priest was going down that road, but when he saw the victim, he passed by on the opposite side.

Soon a Levite walked by. He saw the man lying on the side of the road, but he kept on walking.

Then a Samaritan traveler who came upon him was moved with compassion at the sight. He went up to the victim, poured oil and wine over his wounds, and bandaged them. Then he lifted the man onto his donkey, took him to a nearby inn, and cared for him. The next day the Samaritan gave money to the innkeeper with the instruction, "Look after this man until I come back. If you need to spend more money, I'll pay you when I return."

When the story was finished, Jesus looked at the young man and asked him, "Which of these three people acted like a neighbor to the injured man?"

"The one who was kind to the injured man," the young man answered.

Jesus said to him, "Then go and do the same."

Based on Luke 10:29–37

EXAMINING THE STORY WITH A STORY MAP

Fill in the story map below to retell the parable on page 78.

Beginning

Who are the people in the Scripture story? _____

_____

Where does the story take place? _____

_____

Middle

What is the problem? _____

_____

_____

_____

Ending

How was the problem solved? _____

_____

_____

_____

Reflection

What does the Scripture story say to you? _____

_____

_____

_____

PRAYING TO BE HEALERS

Leader: Lord Jesus, we ask you to look lovingly on us as we gather here to pray. We ask that you will help us bring healing into our hurting world.

All: Amen.

Reader: This is a reading from Acts of the Apostles. *(Read Acts of the Apostles 5:12, 15–16.)* The Word of the Lord.

All: Thanks be to God.

Leader: Lord, let our eyes watch for opportunities to help those who are in need, we pray to the Lord.

All: Lord, hear our prayer.

Leader: Lord, let our lips speak only words of comfort and kindness, we pray to the Lord.

All: Lord, hear our prayer.

Leader: Lord, may our ears hear the words of Jesus and his teachings of care and healing, we pray to the Lord.

All: Lord, hear our prayer.

Leader: Lord, may our feet always hasten to help others, we pray to the Lord.

All: Lord, hear our prayer.

Leader: *(Name)*, may your hands never bring harm, only healing and help.

Student: Amen.

Leader: We pray this prayer as we pray all prayers, through your Son, Jesus.

All: Amen.

Chapter Review

Circle **T** if a sentence is true. Circle **F** if a sentence is false.
Correct any false sentences by rewriting them on the lines below.

1. Catholics believe the risen Christ continues
    to reach out, heal, and comfort suffering people.   T   F

2. Jesus healed people and forgave sinners in a way that   T   F
    drew no attention from the religious leaders.

3. Blasphemy is an insult to God or to his holy leaders.   T   F

4. When Jesus forgave someone, people felt the presence and   T   F
    power of God.

5. In the parable about the Good Samaritan, Jesus tells a story   T   F
    about God's forgiveness.

_____

_____

_____

_____

_____

_____

_____

Fill in the answers to the first two questions.

1. What does it mean to be *compassionate*?_____

    _____

2. How did Jesus heal and forgive people? _____

    _____

3. Discuss what we can do to allow Jesus to heal and
    forgive through us.

**I, the Lord, am
your healer.**
Exodus 15:26

7 Jesus Brings Us to God in Prayer

Do you know anyone who prays often? Have you ever prayed with this person?

A Special Moment of Prayer

It was Julie's birthday. Her parents allowed Julie to invite her best friend, Molly, to stay for dinner after Julie's birthday party.

It seemed as if everyone was feeling something different that day. Julie's mother was feeling relieved because the party had gone so well. Julie's dad had just lost a sale that afternoon and was having a hard time warming up to Julie's birthday celebration. Molly was so glad to be the one friend invited to the dinner. And Grandma was happy to be feeling well enough to share in her granddaughter's birthday celebration.

When dinner was ready and all were seated at the table, Julie's dad took the family "blessing cup" in his hands. He prayed a brief silent prayer and drank a sip from the cup. He passed it to his wife, who prayed, drank, and passed it on. Each person at the table held the blessing cup, prayed silently, sipped, drank from the cup, and passed it to the next person.

Activity

Look carefully at the picture on page 82. Identify each person in the story. Write in the balloon above each person's head what you think that person may have prayed when it was his or her turn to hold the blessing cup.

PRAYER

Prayer is conversation with God. Whether we are alone or with others, when we pray we recognize that God is with us.

When Jesus wanted to be close to God, he knew that he could be with God in prayer. Jesus prayed often and everywhere. He prayed at home, in the synagogue, and in the Temple. He also prayed in the streets, in busy marketplaces, and in the midst of crowds. We read in the gospels that Jesus went to the mountains as well as to the desert to pray. He prayed on the hillsides and at the seashore. We also read that he always prayed when he was faced with a difficult decision.

Activity

Look up the following Scripture passages. On the lines provided, write the names of the places where Jesus prayed. Then describe the places where you pray.

Scripture	Places Where Jesus Prayed
Mark 1:35	_____
Luke 6:12-13	_____

Places Where I Pray

The places that I like to pray are

_____

_____

_____

Vocabulary

prayer: conversation with God

/////////////////////

JESUS PRAYS TO HIS FATHER

Jesus was praying in a certain place. When he finished, one of his disciples said to him, "Lord, teach us to pray, just as John taught his followers." So Jesus said to them, "When you pray, say:

Father, blessed be your name.
May your kingdom come.
Give us each day our daily bread.
Forgive us for our sins
as we ourselves forgive everyone
who has done us wrong,
and do not allow us to be tempted."

Based on Luke 11:1-4

JESUS AND PRAYER

Jesus' entire life was filled with prayer. No matter how busy or tired he was, Jesus took time out of his day to pray. He prayed everywhere and at all times.

Jesus seemed to pray in a very personal way. Jesus' disciples heard him call God by the names *Holy One, Almighty One*, and even *Abba*, which means "Daddy" in Aramaic, the spoken language of Jesus. Many young children in Israel even today call their own fathers by the affectionate name of *Abba*.

The Jewish people of Jesus' time knew that God was loving. However, there is no evidence that they addressed God in prayer by such a tender, loving title as *Abba*. This loving name tells us today that God loves us like a loving father, whom we can feel free to speak with about anything.

The Lord's Prayer

His disciples were so impressed with Jesus' life of prayer that they asked him how to pray. Jesus responded by teaching them The Lord's Prayer, a special prayer that begins with the words, "Our Father."

The Lord's Prayer is still the prayer shared today by all Christians because it is a prayer given to us directly by Jesus. It includes praise to God, blessing his holy name. The Lord's Prayer asks favors of God—daily bread and safety from harm and temptation. The prayer demands that we forgive one another so that our sins will be forgiven. It is also a prayer of hope that asks for God's kingdom to come and that God's will be done on earth as it is in heaven. And this prayer of Jesus allows us to call God *Father* or *Abba*.

Activity

Describe how Jesus' way of praying was different from how most people in Jesus' time prayed.

_____

_____

_____

We Believe

Jesus prayed often and everywhere. His prayer showed that he had a special relationship with God. He called God his Father.

THE SEVEN PETITIONS

The Lord's Prayer contains seven petitions or requests. The first three petitions give glory to God. The last four petitions ask God for help with our own needs and wants.

	Petition	Explanation
First Petition	Our Father, who art in heaven, hallowed be thy name	May your name be held holy.
Second Petition	thy kingdom come	May your kingdom begin with us on earth.
Third Petition	thy will be done on earth as it is in heaven.	May we do what you ask now.
Fourth Petition	Give us this day our daily bread	Give us everything we need as your children.
Fifth Petition	and forgive us our trespasses, as we forgive those who trespass against us.	Forgive us our sins as we forgive those who sin against us.
Sixth Petition	And lead us not into temptation,	Keep us away from situations which may lead us to sin.
Seventh Petition	but deliver us from evil.	Protect us from all evil.

Activity

Here is an opportunity to put The Lord's Prayer into your own words. For each line of The Lord's Prayer, circle one of the alternative phrases. Then, write your new version of The Lord's Prayer on the lines provided.

Our Father, who art in heaven,	**a.** Loving God, **b.** Abba, **c.** Creator God,
hallowed be thy name;	**a.** you are holy; **b.** your name is holy; **c.** blessed be your name;
thy kingdom come, thy will be done on earth as it is in heaven.	**a.** help us to bring your word into the world. **b.** let the world be full of your goodness.
Give us this day our daily bread;	**a.** Give us all that we need; **b.** Remember us every day;
and forgive us our trespasses as we forgive those who trespass against us	**a.** pardon our sins; help us to pardon others **b.** and forgive us as we forgive others
and lead us not into temptation,	**a.** keep us from sin, **b.** help us to know what is right,
but deliver us from evil.	**a.** keep us safe. **b.** keep us close to you.
Amen.	**a.** So be it. **b.** May this be so.

The Lord's Prayer According to _____

_____

_____

_____

_____

_____

The Psalms

Jesus calls us to pray often and everywhere as he did. The prayer he taught his disciples, The Lord's Prayer, grew out of Jesus' own prayer to his Father. He also prayed the **psalms**, as did all Jews of Jesus' time. The psalms are an ancient collection of 150 prayer songs.

Activity

There are psalms for many feelings and expressions, such as faith, hope, thanks, and sorrow. Look up the psalms listed below. Find one verse or line in each psalm that you could pray easily and often. Write it on the lines provided.

Prayer of Faith, Psalm 25 _____

_____

Prayer of Hope, Psalm 71 _____

_____

Prayer of Love, Psalm 18 _____

_____

Prayer of Praise, Psalm 104 _____

_____

Prayer of Thanks, Psalm 9 _____

_____

Prayer of Sorrow, Psalm 51 _____

_____

Prayer of Petition, Psalm 30 _____

PRAYER SONGS

The most common types of psalms plead with God for help. There are also many psalms of thanksgiving and praise. Sometimes a psalm speaks of a problem or teaches a lesson.

Though the psalms were originally meant to be sung, over the centuries they have become spoken prayers as well. Thousands of years later, Jews and Christians continue to pray and sing the psalms.

Jesus was always aware of God's presence. Read this beautiful psalm that sings of God's presence.

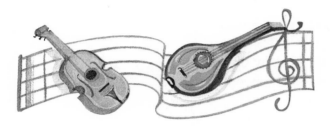

Psalm 139

O Lord, you know me well.
You know when I sit and when I stand. . .
You understand my thoughts. . .
You are familiar with all my ways.
You are with me on every side.
You rest your hand on me.

Where can I go from your spirit?
From your presence, where can I flee?
If I go up to the heavens, you are there.
If I sink deep below the earth, you are
    present there.

If I fly farther East than the sunrise,
Or live beyond the sunset in the West,
Even there your hand shall guide me.
There your right hand will hold me fast.

Based on Psalm 139:1-10

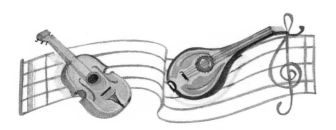

Vocabulary

psalms: prayer songs from the Old Testament

PRAYING THE PSALMS

Leader: Let us put ourselves into God's presence by silently recalling his love for each one of us.

(*pause*)

We have learned that the psalms are ancient prayers that are still prayed today by Jews and Christians. Let us now pray together Psalm 103.

All:

O LORD, I praise you; I praise your holy name.
My entire being praises you and does not forget your kindnesses.
You forgive all my sins and heal all my illnesses.
You save me and give me love and mercy.
You give me all good things and you give me life.

O LORD, you are fair to those who are hurt by others.
You showed your ways to Moses and to the people of Israel.
You are merciful and kind.
You do not get angry quickly and you have great love.
You do not always blame us and you always forgive us.

Based on Psalm 103:1-9

Leader: Thank God for someone in your life.
Praise God for something in creation.
Tell God you are sorry for something you have done.
Pray for someone else.
Ask God for help with something you need.
Praise the Lord, and God's presence within you.

Make up your own psalm by completing the outline below.

Remember all God's _____.

God forgives _____

    and God heals _____.

The Lord saves us from _____

    and surrounds us with _____.

God fills our lives with _____
and we are made new.

Based on Psalm 103

Chapter Review

Write about your own experience of prayer by answering the question and completing the sentences.

a. What events, times, or places remind you to pray?_____

_____

_____

b. My favorite times to pray are _____

_____

_____

c. My favorite prayers are _____

_____

_____

d. To me, prayer is _____

_____

_____

Fill in the answers to the first two questions.

1. What is *prayer*?_____

2. Where are some of the places that Jesus prayed? What did Jesus' prayer show?

_____

_____

_____

_____

> **At every opportunity pray in the Spirit.**
> Ephesians 6:18

3. Discuss how we can pray as Jesus did.

JESUS IS THE SACRAMENT OF GOD

MAKING KNOWN WHAT IS INVISIBLE

Signs and gestures send different kinds of messages. Look at the pictures below. Each one shows a sign or gesture that tells us something. What does each gesture or sign say to you?

Some people are so filled with the spirit of a group or an ideal that their lives make that spirit known to others. The spirit within them becomes so strong that to know them is to know something about the spirit of the group.

What is the first thing you remember hearing about Jesus?

Activity

Write the name of one person you know who is filled with the spirit of a group or an ideal. Then explain how his or her life makes that spirit known to others.

_____

_____

_____

_____

JESUS MAKES GOD VISIBLE

The crowds who listened to Jesus and watched him asked themselves what sort of man Jesus was. Something about Jesus led them to marvel and question.

According to the gospels, Jesus spoke and acted like God, whom he called his Father. He spoke God's word as teacher and prophet. He brought God's mercy, forgiveness, and freedom as **Savior**. He encouraged people to let their light shine for all to see and to do great things for God.

Jesus' words and actions, all that he was, showed people that God was really, truly with them. In the Gospel of Matthew, Jesus is called **Emmanuel**, a Hebrew name that means "God is with us." If we want to know who God is, we look to Jesus.

The Church came to believe and understand that Jesus is both God and man. Slowly, the Church found the right words to say what it believed about Jesus. We call him the *sacrament of God* because he makes known in himself the loving presence of God with us now. Catholics speak of Jesus as "God become man," God incarnate. We wonder at the **Incarnation**—God's Son becoming human.

Activity

Write three things you know about God because you know Jesus. Then complete each sentence by explaining how you know each thing.

1. I know that God must be_____

   because Jesus is _____

   _____.

2. I know that God must be_____

   because Jesus is _____

   _____.

3. I know that God must be_____

   because Jesus is _____

   _____.

Vocabulary

Savior: Jesus Christ, who brought us God's mercy and forgiveness and freed us from sin

Emmanuel: a title for Jesus that means "God is with us"

Incarnation: God's Son becoming human while remaining God. Jesus Christ is both God and man.

We Believe

The Church believes that Jesus' life and teachings make known the loving presence of God with us now. The life, death, and resurrection of Jesus reveal him as both God and man.

WHO IS JESUS OF NAZARETH?

One day Jesus and his disciples stopped near a town called Caesarea Philippi.

Jesus asked his friends a question: "Who do people say that I am?"

The disciples knew what the crowds had been saying about Jesus. They told Jesus they had heard people saying different things about him.

"Some say you are John the Baptizer," they told Jesus. "Others say you are Elijah. Still others say you are Jeremiah or one of the other prophets."

People believed that Jesus might be one of those great prophets come back to life. They thought that because his words and teachings were like those of prophets—full of love and power.

Jesus made the question more personal. "And you," he asked them, "who do you say that I am?"

The disciples thought for a moment. They were impressed, even more than the crowds had been, with the power and the love of Jesus' words. They were also amazed at how Jesus healed the sick and forgave sinners. They were becoming aware that Jesus spoke and acted in ways the Bible often showed God speaking and acting.

They were impressed with how close to God Jesus always seemed to be.

Simon Peter spoke up. "You are the Son of the living God."

For a moment Jesus was silent. Peter called Jesus God's Son because he knew that Jesus had a very special relationship with his Father.

The others looked at Jesus and at Simon Peter. Would Jesus agree with what Peter said, or deny it? Jesus smiled and praised Peter. He told Peter that God in heaven had helped Peter understand.

Based on Matthew 16:13-20

Discuss

1. What were some of the answers the friends of Jesus gave when he asked, "Who do people say that I am?"

2. What did Simon Peter answer when Jesus asked, "Who do you say that I am?"

Activity

Read Luke 5:1-11. Then answer the following questions.

1. After Jesus said, "Move the boat into deep water and lower the fishing nets" (based on Luke 5:4), what did Simon do? Why?

_____

_____

_____

2. When Jesus said: "Don't be afraid, you will be catching people" (based on Luke 5:10), how did Simon and the others respond? Why?

_____

_____

_____

3. When you hear Jesus say to you, "Who do you say that I am" what is your response?

_____

_____

_____

_____

A Visual Creed
Here is how some early Christians summed up their beliefs about Jesus and hid them from their enemies. Each letter of the Greek word for "fish," $IXOY\Sigma$, stands for a new word. Together the words say: "Jesus Christ, Son of God, Savior."

Madonna, Sapieha/Art Resource, Haiti

Miracle of the Loaves and Fishes (lithograph), Jean Heiberg, 20th century, Contemporary, USA

IMAGES OF JESUS

People in different times and places have tried to know more and more about Jesus. What did he look like? What foods did he eat? What places did he visit?

Look at the three different images of Jesus. What kinds of things can you learn about Jesus just by looking at them?

The Holy Face (oil on cardboard), Georges Roualt, 20th century, France

We can learn much about Jesus by reading the gospels. The gospels tell us interesting facts, such as, that Jesus traveled long distances on foot and often slept outdoors. We learn that prayer, forgiveness, and compassion were important to Jesus: "At that time, Jesus went to a mountain to pray. He spent the entire night praying to God" (based on Luke 6:12). It might even surprise us to learn that Jesus cried when he experienced great sadness: "When Jesus saw Mary weeping because her brother Lazarus had died, he was deeply moved, and he began to cry" (based on John 11:33, 35). It probably wouldn't surprise us to know that Jesus loved children: Jesus said, "Let the children come to me. Do not stop them. God's kingdom belongs to children like these" (based on Luke 18:15-16).

All of these known facts about Jesus give us a hint as to who Jesus was. Jesus continues to reveal himself to us so that we can know him as our friend and our savior. Each person who knows Jesus could tell us who Jesus is. Who is Jesus for you?

Activity

Interview an adult member of your family to find out who Jesus is for that person. Write your findings below. Be sure to mention the name of the person you interviewed.

_____

_____

_____

_____

_____

_____

_____

_____

Activity

List two ideals of your family that would show others the values by which your family lives.

1. _____ 2. _____

Who in your family best reflects your family's spirit and ideals? _____

REVEALING GOD'S LOVING PRESENCE

Just as we reflect who our families are by the way we speak and act, Jesus reflected who God the Father is by the words he spoke and by the way he treated others. Jesus is the sacrament of God, the visible sign of God's presence. Each time Jesus spoke words of peace and forgiveness, God's peace and forgiveness was experienced. Each time Jesus reached out to others to heal them, to comfort them, or simply to be present to them, it was God who healed, comforted, or was present. To experience Jesus is to experience God the Father.

As followers of Jesus, we are called to become more and more like Jesus. We are called to continue his work of making God's presence visible by who we are and by the things we say and do.

Activity

Think of a specific time when Jesus taught others, showed care for someone, forgave someone, and prayed. Describe Jesus' actions. Then tell what things you can do to reflect Jesus' spirit.

Jesus taught others when he _____

_____ .

I can teach others when I _____

_____ .

Jesus showed care for someone when he _____

_____ .

I can show care for someone when I _____

_____ .

Jesus forgave someone when he _____

_____ .

I can forgive someone when I _____

_____ .

Jesus prayed when he _____

_____ .

I can pray when I _____

_____ .

PRAYING WITH FAITH

Whenever we pray, we pray with faith—faith in God. As Catholics, we believe many things about God, Jesus, the saints, the Church, and about life itself. When we list these beliefs together in a prayer, we call it a creed. A creed is a statement of beliefs. The word *creed* comes from the Latin word *credo*, which means "I believe."

At the Sunday liturgy, we often pray together the Nicene Creed or the Apostles' Creed. These prayers list the most important beliefs of our faith.

MY BELIEFS

Think about what it is that you believe about God, Jesus, the saints, the Church, and life. Create your own creed by completing the prayer below. Then pray your creed alone or with one of your classmates.

MY CREED

I believe in _____ , who _____

_____ .

I believe in _____ , who _____

_____ and _____ .

I believe that _____

and that _____ .

I believe in _____

and in _____

and in _____ .

Most of all, I believe _____

_____ .

Amen.

Chapter Review

Read the statements below. Then tell what you can do to be more aware of Jesus, the sacrament of God, in your life.

Jesus teaches us God's word. Jesus is God's word. What can you do to hear God's word or to share his word with others whom you meet each day?

_____

_____

_____

Jesus brings us God's healing and forgiveness. Jesus is our Savior, Redeemer, and Liberator. What can you do to receive Jesus' healing or forgiveness, or to share Jesus' healing and forgiveness with others?

_____

_____

_____

Jesus prays to God as Father. Jesus is God's Son. How can you pray to God as Father?

_____

_____

Fill in the answers to the first two questions.

1. What is meant by the *Incarnation*?

_____

_____

2. How did Christians come to recognize Jesus as the sacrament of God?

_____

_____

3. Discuss what we can do to be more aware of Jesus in our lives.

Jesus Christ is the image of the invisible God.
Based on Colossians 1:15

The words in the circle, the arrow, and the box when read together name the title of a chapter in this unit. For example, *Jesus Teaches God's Word*. Write two important ideas about each chapter on the lines provided.

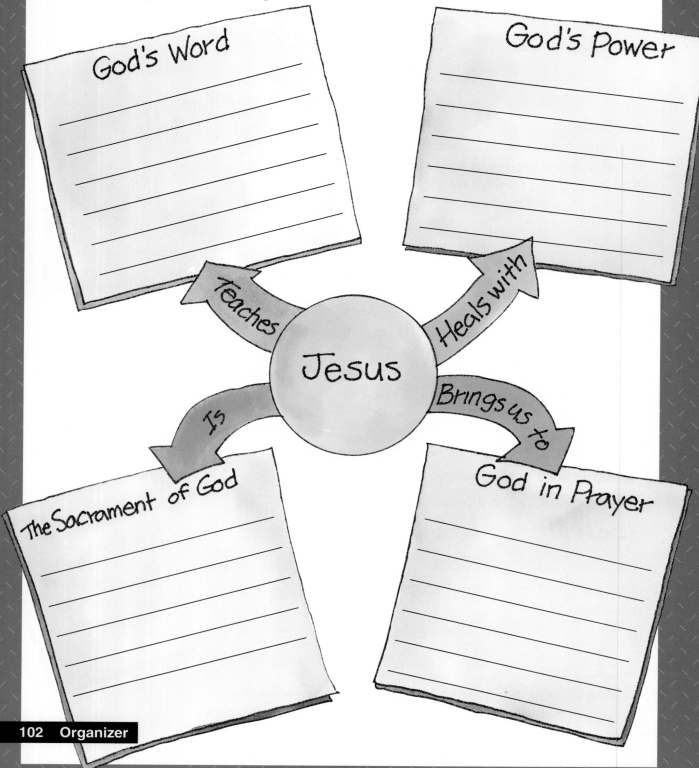

God's Word

God's Power

Teaches

Heals with

Jesus

Is

Brings us to

The Sacrament of God

God in Prayer

UNIT **2** REVIEW

Match Column A with Column B.

Column A

1. rabbi

2. synagogue

3. prophet

4. Teacher

5. Jesus' followers

6. Jesus taught others

7. The Church believes

Column B

_____ someone called by God to speak in God's name

_____ a special name for Jesus

_____ a house of worship and a community center of the Jewish people

_____ are called to learn and share Jesus' teachings

_____ Hebrew word that means "teacher"

_____ that Jesus speaks God's word to us

_____ by his example and by his words

Match Column A with Column B to complete the sentences.

Column A

1. Jesus healed and forgave people

2. The Church believes Jesus brings us

3. When Jesus healed or forgave someone,

4. In Exodus 15:26, we read

5. The risen Christ continues to bring healing and forgiveness through

Column B

_____ people felt the presence of God.

_____ "I, the LORD, am your healer."

_____ by his words and actions.

_____ people.

_____ God's healing power.

UNIT **2** REVIEW

Write the answers to the following questions.

1. What is prayer? _____

_____

2. When and where did Jesus pray? _____

3. What did Jesus call God? _____

4. What does the name that Jesus called God mean? _____

5. What is the name of the special prayer that Jesus taught his disciples when they

   asked him how to pray? _____

6. What do the first three petitions of The Lord's Prayer give to God? _____

7. What do the last four petitions of The Lord's Prayer ask of God?

_____

_____

Write **T** if a sentence is true. Write **F** if a sentence is false.

_____**1.** Jesus is not only God's Son, he is God.

_____**2.** Jesus' disciples were not surprised at his life and teachings.

_____**3.** Wherever Jesus was, people could sense God's presence.

_____**4.** "Incarnation" means that God's Son became a man while remaining God.

_____**5.** Jesus is the sacrament of God because he makes known in himself the loving
presence of God with us now.

_____**6.** Some people thought that Jesus was their Lord.

HOW CAN I BE a PEACEMAKER for MYSELF?

Coping with Difficult Thoughts and Feelings

I can feel at peace within myself when I feel unhappy or upset if I remain open to God's love. Yet, how can I be open? Sometimes it seems as if my problems will never be solved and I will never feel happy again. Sometimes I am angry with God for allowing me to feel this way. What can I do?

"TAMARA SHOULD BE MY FRIEND BECAUSE I'VE JUST INVITED HER TO MY PARTY."

When Trying to Cope with Difficult Feelings and Thoughts

1 Keep your body healthy. Get enough rest and exercise. Eat healthy foods. A healthy body can better handle stressful feelings and thoughts.

2 Stop and think before you act! Count to ten and take a deep breath to stay calm while trying to think of positive solutions to problems. If you feel angry and are about to lose control, move away from the situation. Find a place where you can be calm and regain your control.

3 Change negative thoughts to positive ones. Feelings can come from what we tell ourselves about the problem we are facing. We refer to these thoughts as "self-talk." When our thoughts are "I should," "I must," "he should," or "she must," we become upset when what we expect doesn't happen. It is healthier to change our "self-talk" from "I should" and "I must" to "I'd prefer."

4 Stay busy. Do things with people you enjoy. It is okay to cry. Tears express your feelings.

5 Share feelings and thoughts with someone you can trust who will listen. This might be a parent, an older brother or sister, an aunt or uncle, a neighbor, a teacher, or a counselor. Though friends your age can be good listeners, older and more experienced people can help you cope with strong feelings and thoughts.

6 Pray. Remember that you are loved and you can always share your thoughts and feelings with Jesus. Jesus always listens.

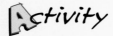 **Activity**

Draw a picture or write a story about yourself, or someone you know, trying to cope with difficult feelings and thoughts. Show how one of the suggestions on page 105 might help.

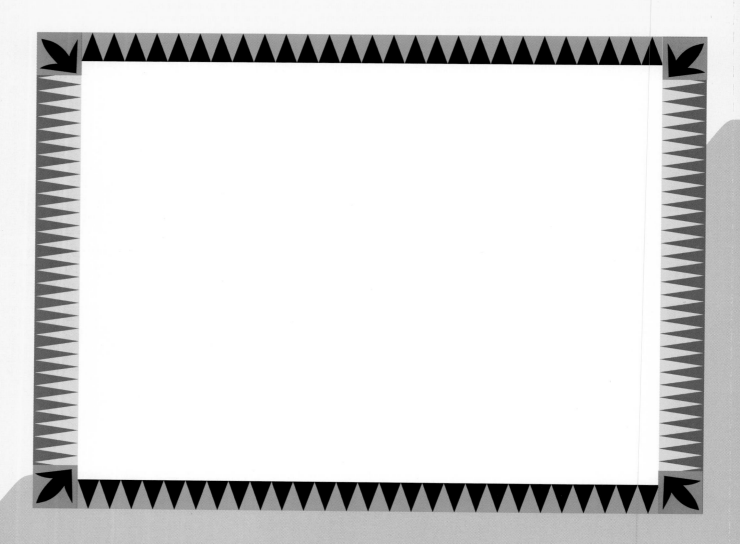

Following Jesus

Jesus realizes that the call to be a peacemaker is not an easy one. It is especially difficult when our own thoughts and feelings disturb our peace. Jesus greeted his disciples after his resurrection with the words "Peace be with you..." (John 20:19). Jesus wishes us to be at peace also.

PRAYER

While sharing a sign of peace with your classmates, pray the words, "Peace be with you."

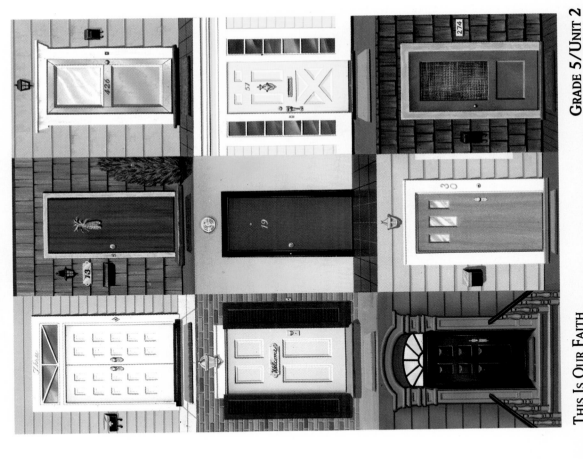

OPENING DOORS

A Take-Home Magazine™

Growing Closer

THE WORD OF GOD, Scripture, is the daily sustenance we need in living the Christian life. Help your family be nourished in both body and spirit at every family meal. Use a slice of bread to make a pattern. Cut twelve or more slices of "bread" out of construction paper or a brown grocery bag.

Enlist your fifth-grader's help in making the bread. On each slice of bread write one of the following quotes from Scripture.

Put the slices of bread on a bread plate or basket and place it on your dining table. Before or after your family meal, have one member take a slice of bread and read the Scripture. Take time to share thoughts about the passage.

Lk 8: 4–8 11–15

Mk 2: 1–12

Mt 5: 14–16

Mt 7: 24–29

Mk 4: 35–41

Lk 12: 32–34

Looking Ahead

In the coming weeks your fifth-grader will learn that the Church is the sacrament (sign) of Christ in the world. We, the Church, in the way we live and deal with people reveal the presence and activity of the risen Christ. The Church speaks to today's questions and issues as teacher and prophet. The Church reaches out to suffering people around the world as healer and reconciler. The Church works to bring God and people closer through prayer. In all these activities, we are Jesus Christ for today's world.

THIS IS OUR FAITH

Dear Luis,

Last night, I decided to put a question mark after your favorite saying, "A picture is worth a thousand words." We had a family crisis last night — no sound on the television set. Imagine our dismay when we sat down to watch our favorite family sitcom, and Tom discovered a snag in the sound system.

I really was disappointed because I needed some relaxation and humor after an extremely hectic day at work. So Susan suggested that we watch the show anyway. Each of us took one of the characters' parts and added our own words. We all were holding our sides from laughing at what we would have said in the family crisis shown on the screen. We're just sorry you weren't here to add your own humorous touch.

Your sister,
Maria

All the cycles begin each year on the First Sunday of Advent. Other major dates in the *Lectionary* depend upon the date of Easter (the first Sunday after the first full moon after the spring equinox). Lent occupies the six weeks preceding Easter. Ascension Day is forty days after Easter. Pentecost is fifty days after Easter. Ordinary Time stretches from the day after Pentecost to the First Sunday of Advent in the next cycle.

Today there is no reason for anyone to be a stranger to the Bible. After praying with and listening to the readings from Scripture at Mass for three years, you've covered almost the entire Bible! You truly can proclaim God's word throughout your life.

Math Facts About the *Lectionary*

- Year C is always a year that has digits that when added are divisible by 3. (For example, 1992: 1 + 9 + 9 + 2 = 21)
- Year I is always an odd-numbered year. (1991, 1993, 1995)
- Year II is always an even-numbered year. (1992, 1994, 1996)

A Picture Is Worth a Thousand Words???

📺 How would your family react to a night without television?

📺 Does television viewing help or hurt your family's communication?

📺 What means of communication help your family's communication?

📺 What means of communication hurt your family's communication?

What's in a Word?

Many parents would agree: "My child has probably heard all kinds of language, still there are certain words I don't want him or her to say." Why? Because words have meaning, power, a life of their own. By the same token, there are words parents love to hear their children say: "Please, Thank you, Okay, I did great, I'm finished, I'll help . . ."

Have you given your child a good word today? Words of love, humor, encouragement, forgiveness, and comfort have the power to build up family members and family relationships.

Proclaiming God's Word

The readings from Scripture for Mass are in a book titled *Lectionary for Mass.* Each Sunday we hear three scriptural readings from the *Lectionary.*

✜ The first reading is usually from the Old Testament.

✜ The second reading is from the Acts of the Apostles, the Book of Revelation, or one of the letters in the New Testament.

✜ The last reading is always from one of the gospels in the New Testament.

The *Lectionary* contains the following.

✜ Three-year cycle of readings for Sundays and solemn feasts—Year A, Year B, and Year C

✜ Two-year cycle of readings for weekdays—Year I and Year II

✜ A cycle of readings for the feasts of saints, readings for ritual Masses (marriage, Confirmation, and so on), and readings for Masses of various needs.

The themes of the readings are based on the liturgical seasons.

4

This Is the Word of the Lord

"On the sabbath, Jesus entered the synagogue and began to teach. The people were spellbound by his teaching because he taught with authority, and not like the scribes." See Mark 1:21–22. Jesus presented himself as a prophet who went far beyond the rabbinic tradition for his teaching. When Jesus taught, people recognized God's Word in Jesus' words. They felt God's presence when Jesus spoke to them. During the Liturgy of the Word at Mass, Jesus speaks to us through the Gospel just as surely as he taught the people assembled in the synagogue at Capernaum.

Just before the proclamation of the Gospel, the priest says: "The Lord be with you." We respond, "And also with you." These words express both a wish that the Lord will be with us and also a profound truth that the Lord is with us.

Jesus is the Word of God made flesh. His words, his actions, his whole being, make known God's invisible reality. He is God. Through him we know God. The Liturgy of the Word recalls the experiences of God among humankind, as recorded in the Scriptures. We celebrate the presence of God in our midst. Jesus is the good news of our salvation. The words of the Scriptures are not dead or empty. They have meaning, and power, and a life of their own.

Say the Word

Did you know that the words that we say just before Communion are based on the words of a Roman army officer to Jesus? See Luke 7:6–7. The officer, a centurion, a man of authority in his own right, recognized the authority and power of Jesus. He rested his faith and the health of his servant on the healing word of Jesus.

5

UNIT 3

THE CHURCH: SACRAMENT OF CHRIST'S PRESENCE

whom do you enjoy being with most?

CHRIST TEACHES THROUGH THE CHURCH

Activity

Pretend that you were asked to teach a fifth-grade class for an entire week. As part of your teaching responsibilities, your principal wants you to give the students information that will help them live happy, healthy, and successful lives. What kinds of things would you teach? How would you teach them? Write your responses below.

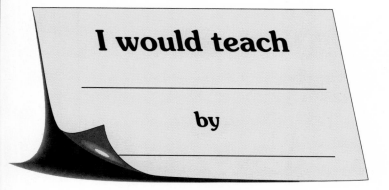

I would teach
_____
by
_____

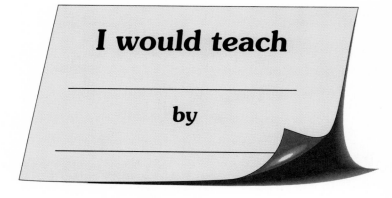

I would teach
_____
by
_____

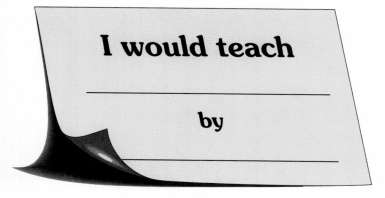

I would teach
_____
by
_____

Name someone who taught you something important about life. What did he or she teach you?

A Teaching Community

After Jesus' resurrection, his disciples taught others about him. They shared his message and spoke his words. They carried out his command: "Go, therefore, to the people of all nations and make them my disciples. Baptize them in the name of the Father, the Son, and the Holy Spirit and teach them to do everything I have told you. And know that I am with you always" (based on Matthew 28:19–20). The disciples remembered Jesus' promise to them: "Whoever listens to you, listens to me" (Luke 10:16).

Jesus' own disciples traveled all over the known world to bring Jesus' teachings to people. The Catholic Church guided by the Holy Spirit continues to teach in Jesus' name, as Jesus taught, through stories, parables, and actions. The disciples' ministry is continued today through the Church's bishops and priests and through men, women, and children who share Jesus' teachings with others by their words and examples. Through the Church and individual Christians, the risen Christ continues to teach.

Activity

Read the following Scripture passages and, on the lines provided, write what Jesus is teaching. Then write what the Church does today to continue these teachings.

In Luke 10:25–37, Jesus teaches that _____

_____

_____.

The Church continues these teachings by_____

_____.

In Luke 15:11–32, Jesus teaches that _____

_____

_____.

The Church continues these teachings by_____

_____.

JESUS' DISCIPLES
TAUGHT IN HIS NAME

After Pentecost, Peter visited the city of Caesarea. Peter, who was sent by the Spirit, was invited to the home of Cornelius, a Roman military officer. Cornelius was a good man. He prayed often and was very generous. He and his entire family believed in God and were interested in the Jewish religion.

Cornelius was eager to hear Peter's teachings. Cornelius believed that Peter had something very important to say to him and his family, so he invited all of his family and friends to come to his home and listen to Peter.

Cornelius welcomed Peter warmly. "You have been very kind to accept my invitation to come to my home. We are eager to hear the Lord's message."

Peter began to teach Cornelius, his family, and his friends. "This is the message God sends. It is the good news of peace taught by Jesus, who is Lord of all."

Everyone listened quietly as Peter told them about Jesus. "I'm sure you know what has been said about Jesus of Nazareth, starting with his baptism by John in Galilee. God anointed him with the Holy Spirit and power. Jesus went about doing good works. He healed many people of sickness and sin. God was with him. We are **witnesses** to everything Jesus did.

"Jesus was crucified by some of his enemies. But God raised him from the dead. We who ate and drank with him after he rose from the dead were chosen as witnesses. Jesus sent us to preach to the people and to bear witness that God has made Jesus judge of the living and the dead. All the prophets of old spoke about him. All who believe in him are forgiven through his name."

When Peter finished speaking, the Holy Spirit came upon all who were listening to Peter's message. Peter gave instructions that they be baptized in the name of Jesus.

Based on Acts 10:23–48

People Respond to the Teachings of Jesus

Everyone who listened with open hearts and minds, like Cornelius and his family and friends, heard Jesus speaking to them. Many became his followers. They received the Holy Spirit and were **baptized**. They were welcomed into the Christian community.

Activity

List some of the things about Jesus that Peter taught Cornelius and his family.

1. _____

2. _____

3. _____

4. _____

5. _____

List five things that you would teach others about Jesus.

1. _____

2. _____

3. _____

4. _____

5. _____

Vocabulary

witness: a person who informs others about what he or she has seen or heard

baptized: welcomed into the Christian community

Bishop ordaining priests

A Noble Task

From the early days of the Church, the title *bishop* has been used for the primary leaders of the Christian community. The word *bishop* comes from a Greek word that means "overseer." The following Scripture passage speaks about bishops.

"Whoever desires to be a bishop desires a noble task. Therefore, a bishop must be self-controlled, decent, hospitable, able to teach, gentle, and not a lover of money. He must manage his own household well, for if a man does not know how to manage his own household, how can he take care of the church of God?"

Based on 1 Timothy 3:1–5

Responsibilities of Bishops

Although the bishops have many responsibilities, their main responsibilities are to govern, to sanctify or make holy, and to teach. Bishops govern by serving the people of their dioceses—meeting their spiritual, material, social, and personal needs. Bishops sanctify by gathering the community for worship and by celebrating the sacraments.

The pope, Bishop of Rome and head of the Catholic Church throughout the world, and the bishops are the chief teachers in the Church. They are responsible for preserving Catholic doctrine and for making certain that the Church continues the teachings of Jesus. One way that bishops teach is by preaching, or explaining the Scriptures. They also teach by writing pastoral letters, which explain the Church's teachings on specific topics.

Bishop giving a homily

Bishop greeting a member of the diocese

Activity

Read the teachings of the Church below. Then write the answers to the questions on the lines provided.

1. *On Peace:* The Church teaches that nations need to stop the race to build bigger and more destructive weapons.

   What are Jesus' words on peace, according to Matthew 26:52?

   _____

   What would you teach others about peace?

   _____

2. *On Respect:* The Church teaches that everyone deserves to be treated with respect.

   What are Jesus' words on respecting others, according to Matthew 7:12?

   _____

   What would you teach people about respecting others?

   _____

3. *On Social Justice:* The Church teaches that we must help those in need and work for a more just world.

   What are Jesus' words on compassion and justice, according to Matthew 25:40?

   _____

   What would you teach others about compassion and justice?

   _____

4. *On God's Love:* The Church teaches that God loves and cares for each human being.

   What are Jesus' words on God's love, according to Matthew 6:32?

   _____

   What would you teach others about love?_____

   _____

Pastoral Letters

Some titles of pastoral letters written by the bishops are:

- *Brothers and Sisters to Us (on racism)*
- *Pastoral Statement of U.S. Catholic Bishops on Persons With Disabilities*
- *Statement of U.S. Catholic Bishops on American Indians*
- *Statement in Support of Catholic Schools*
- *The Christian Family*
- *The Hispanic Presence: Challenge and Commitment*

Activity

Think of someone in your community whom you admire. It might be a family, church, or community member, or a teacher. Write that person's name on the album cover. Then tell what you admire most about him or her.

_____

_____ :

The Person I Admire Most

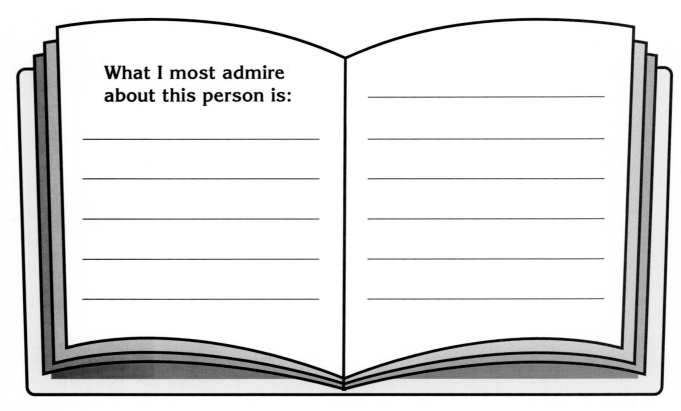

What I most admire about this person is:

THE MESSAGE OF JESUS

Although bishops are the chief teachers in the Church, they are not the only people responsible for passing on the teachings of Jesus. Jesus continues to teach us, speaking through the Church and through the words and actions of all Christians. We can hear the message of Jesus in church, at school, from our parents, our friends, and from many other people.

We can hear the message of Jesus in church when the priest or deacon explains the Scripture readings. Our families pass on the teachings of Jesus to us by their example of living as followers of Jesus and by making sure that we learn about Jesus and the Catholic faith. Our schools teach us about Jesus and his teachings through our religion teachers and by providing us with a Christian atmosphere in which to learn.

Adults aren't the only Christians called to pass on the teachings of Jesus. Our friends and classmates can teach us much about Jesus by their words and by their actions.

Activity

On the lines below, write about some experiences you have had in which individual Christians helped you to hear Jesus' message.

I heard the message of Jesus when

my teacher _____

_____

_____.

my parents _____

_____

_____.

my friend _____

_____

_____.

PRAYING A PRAYER of PETITION

In our prayer, we often ask God's help. When we ask something of God in prayer, we are praying a prayer of petition. An example of a prayer of petition is the Prayer of the Faithful or General Intercessions, which is prayed at Mass.

Pray this prayer of petition, asking God's help for the teachers of the Church.

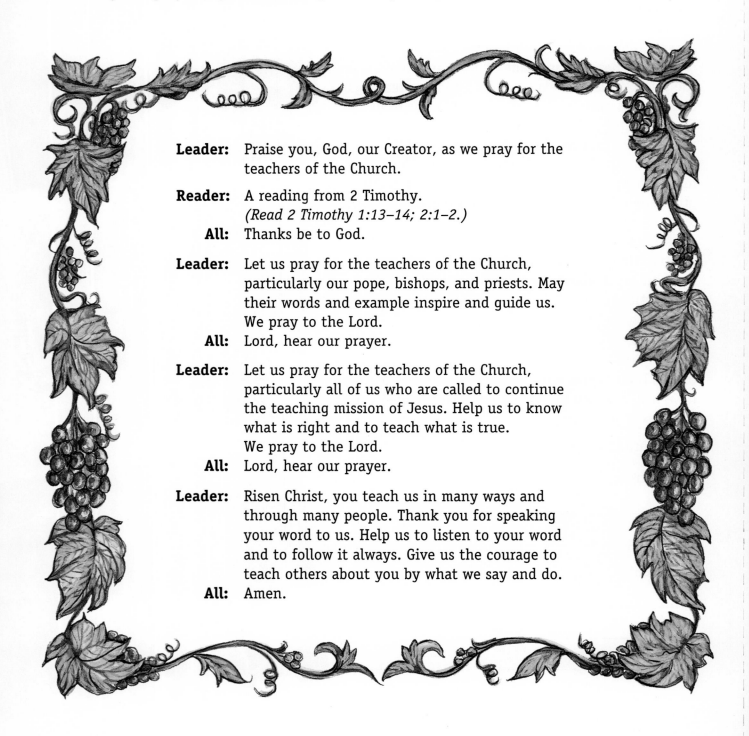

Leader: Praise you, God, our Creator, as we pray for the teachers of the Church.

Reader: A reading from 2 Timothy.
(Read 2 Timothy 1:13–14; 2:1–2.)

All: Thanks be to God.

Leader: Let us pray for the teachers of the Church, particularly our pope, bishops, and priests. May their words and example inspire and guide us. We pray to the Lord.

All: Lord, hear our prayer.

Leader: Let us pray for the teachers of the Church, particularly all of us who are called to continue the teaching mission of Jesus. Help us to know what is right and to teach what is true. We pray to the Lord.

All: Lord, hear our prayer.

Leader: Risen Christ, you teach us in many ways and through many people. Thank you for speaking your word to us. Help us to listen to your word and to follow it always. Give us the courage to teach others about you by what we say and do.

All: Amen.

Chapter Review

People witness to Jesus and his teachings by the way they live. Find a photograph of people witnessing to Jesus through their actions and paste it in the space below. Then under the picture, write the words or teachings of Jesus that the people in the photograph are living out.

Fill in the answers to the first two questions.

1. What is meant by *witness*?

_____

_____

_____

2. What are some ways in which Jesus teaches us through the Church?

_____

_____

_____

3. Discuss what you can do to better hear Jesus teaching through the Church.

**Jesus says:
"He who hears you, hears me."**
Based on Luke 10:16

CHRIST HEALS THROUGH THE CHURCH

TOUCHING A HURTING WORLD

What is one thing you and your family do, as part of your parish family, to help others who are suffering?

Dear Ruth,

You must be surprised to see that I'm writing from Nicaragua! I came here with my parish youth group about three months ago to our sister parish located in this tiny village.

I've never seen people who are so poor. Hundreds live along the railroad tracks, just a few yards from passing trains. They live in little shacks they make from cardboard, wood, tin, and plastic—anything they can find. Entire families live in one room. They have no lights. There is no running water inside. About all they ever have to eat is a little rice, beans, and tortillas.

There are no schools for most of the kids. Hardly any of the adults can find decent jobs. The kids have to do anything they can to help their parents earn money for food. Many of them have breathing problems and other kinds of illnesses. I haven't seen any doctors or medicines.

The people are really nice, especially the kids. We've all worked very hard building houses, painting, and digging irrigation trenches. Yet it doesn't seem enough, somehow. We're going back home tomorrow. I wish there was more we could do for these wonderful people.

Please write to me and let me know how you are doing at college.

Your friend,
Joan

Activity

Carefully reread the letter on page 122. Look at the photographs. Pretend you are a newspaper or magazine reporter. You have been sent to do a story on that same village in Nicaragua. Write *your* story based on interviews you've conducted with the people in the photographs. Report what the people feel they most need and what they hope others will do to help them. Give your story a title.

NICARAGUA: The People's Story

_____

_____

_____

_____

_____

_____

_____

_____

_____

_____

_____

_____

_____

_____

_____

The Church Reaches Out

In Joan's letter, she writes about the compassion she feels for the people of Nicaragua. As a follower of Jesus Christ and a member of the Church, she continues the healing ministry of Jesus.

Since the earliest days of the Church, men and women have continued to bring Christ's healing and forgiveness to suffering people. Sometimes the healings have been surprising and have caused amazement. Most of the time they have been ordinary. Yet all of the healings are signs of Jesus healing his people today. Most of the Catholic hospitals and **social services**—organized activities that help those in need—began long ago. Today Catholics continue to reach out in the name of Jesus through Catholic hospitals and social services to help those who are suffering.

Vocabulary

social services: organized activities that help people who are sick, poor, and in need

We Believe

The Church brings us Christ's healing, forgiving power. The risen Christ continues to heal us and forgive us through the Church.

JESUS' DISCIPLES HEALED MANY

When Peter and the other apostles met people who were suffering, they worked to help them. The people in Jerusalem carried friends and relatives who were sick into the streets on cots and mattresses. They hoped that when Peter passed by, at least his shadow would fall on one or more of them. Crowds from the towns around Jerusalem came too, with their sick and suffering. They all hoped to be made well. More and more people became followers of Jesus Christ.

The apostles healed people and forgave their sins in the name of Jesus. For example, on one of his many journeys, Peter visited Lydda, a town about 25 miles from Jerusalem. There Peter met a paralyzed man named Aeneas. For eight long years, Aeneas had been lying helpless in bed.

Peter said to him, "Aeneas, Jesus Christ cures you! Get up and make your bed."

The paralyzed man got up at once. All in Lydda and in nearby Sharon who saw the paralyzed man walking became followers of the Lord.

Based on Acts 5:12–16; 9:32–35

Jesus Heals Through the Apostles

Peter and the other apostles reached out to the sick and suffering in Jesus' name. The apostles knew it was the risen Christ who healed through their hands and their words. Peter told Aeneas, "Jesus Christ cures you!" (based on Acts 9:34)

The apostles saw how their healing and forgiveness were like Jesus' own compassionate cures. They and others remembered how people had carried their sick relatives into the streets so Jesus might heal them (Mark 1:32–34). They remembered how Jesus healed and forgave a paralyzed man (Luke 5:17–26), much as Peter healed Aeneas.

People who saw Peter and the other apostles heal the sick not only admired the apostles but became followers of Jesus. They believed that the risen Christ continued to heal and forgive through his disciples.

Activity

In the Acts of the Apostles, we can read of many examples of the apostles carrying on the healing ministry of Jesus. Read the following Scripture stories and, on the lines provided, describe the healing ministry.

Acts 3:1–10 _____

_____

_____

Acts 9:36–43 _____

_____

THE HEALING MINISTRY OF THE CHURCH

The Catholic Church continues the disciples' mission of healing and forgiveness through worldwide Catholic organizations such as Catholic hospitals and Catholic Relief Services. This mission is served by religious orders, by diocesan agencies, by parish groups, and by individual Christians.

Throughout the world, the missionaries of the Church serve the poor and suffering. People like Mother Teresa and those in many other religious orders provide medical help and food. Many Church organizations offer assistance by collecting clothing, volunteering their time, and helping with disaster relief.

In every local diocese, there are several social services, such as a Dorothy Day Center, which provide food and shelter to the homeless. These social services bring Christ's healing to others. The Society of St. Vincent de Paul provides food and clothing for those in need. Pro-life offices offer prenatal and newborn care, as well as adoption services for parents and their babies. And some dioceses support and send people to work in foreign missions.

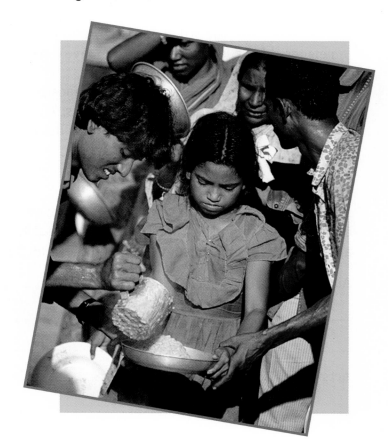

Activity

Use your diocesan newspaper to learn about Christians in your parish, neighborhood, or city who care for the suffering. Some of these people work alone. Some of them belong to groups who work together to serve the needs of others. Write about these people and tell what they do to bring Jesus' healing presence to the world. Share the information with your class.

Helping Person or Group	Who Is Being Helped?	How Are They Being Helped?

Write about the skills and abilities which you bring to healing others.

My Skills and Abilities	Who Is Being Helped?	How Are They Being Helped?

Activity

People can easily recognize the healing presence of Jesus in the world through the Church's concern for those who are suffering.

Some ways in which Jesus brings healing through the Church are shown or described below. Circle the photos and descriptions of the social projects or services that your parish is involved in.

Remember to bring infants' clothing on March 7th and 14th for our sister parish.

Volunteers are needed to collect, sort, and deliver nonperishable foods to the county food bank.

The Bereavement Committee will meet on Monday evening to discuss how we can better serve parish families during times of sorrow.

Low-cost child-care services for preschool children are available Monday–Friday at the parish center.

LOCAL PARISHES

Local parishes also do much to continue the disciples' mission of healing and forgiveness. Often parishes have parishioners who visit the sick in hospitals or at home, or who help those in need with home tasks or transportation. Also parishes may have a bereavement ministry, which helps grieving families by serving a funeral lunch, assisting at the funeral liturgy, or offering a grief support group.

Some Church communities offer their own centers, which provide food or shelter. Many times, parishes also provide holiday meals and gifts for families in their parish or community. Sometimes, parish youth groups share in the mission of healing by getting involved in serving others.

Among the most important ways that a parish cares for those who are suffering is by praying with and for them.

Activity

Your pastor has asked you to form a committee of students your age. The purpose of the committee is to come up with a plan that describes how to bring healing to your parish. Think about some ways in which additional healing can be brought to your parish and how your committee could do this. Write your ideas below.

Some ways in which healing can be brought to my parish are

_____

_____

_____.

My committee could help fill these needs by

_____

_____

_____.

PRAYING FOR HEALING

We, as Catholics, are part of a long tradition of healing prayer. Examples of healing prayer are found throughout the Scriptures, especially in the gospels. The gospels tell of the many times and ways in which Jesus healed with compassion those who were suffering. The gospels also tell us that Jesus passed on the gift of healing to his disciples. It is from them that the Church today continues to receive the gift and ministry of healing prayer.

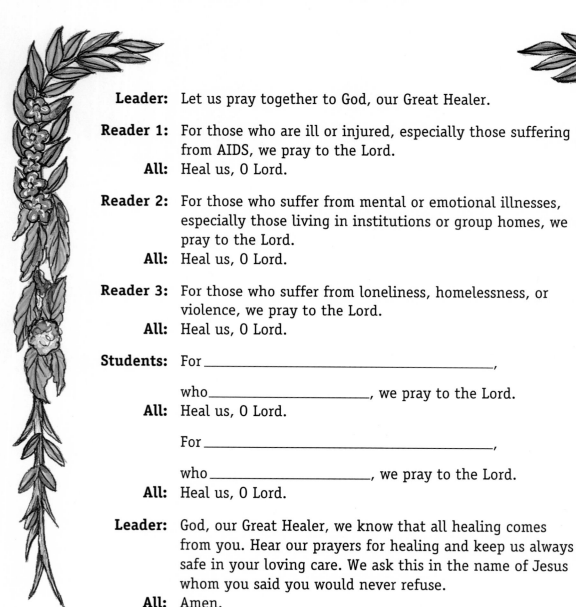

Leader: Let us pray together to God, our Great Healer.

Reader 1: For those who are ill or injured, especially those suffering from AIDS, we pray to the Lord.

All: Heal us, O Lord.

Reader 2: For those who suffer from mental or emotional illnesses, especially those living in institutions or group homes, we pray to the Lord.

All: Heal us, O Lord.

Reader 3: For those who suffer from loneliness, homelessness, or violence, we pray to the Lord.

All: Heal us, O Lord.

Students: For _____,

who_____, we pray to the Lord.

All: Heal us, O Lord.

For _____,

who_____, we pray to the Lord.

All: Heal us, O Lord.

Leader: God, our Great Healer, we know that all healing comes from you. Hear our prayers for healing and keep us always safe in your loving care. We ask this in the name of Jesus whom you said you would never refuse.

All: Amen.

Chapter Review

Jesus continues to heal others through the Church. In the spaces below, write one example of how each group brings Jesus' healing to other people.

Missionaries _____

_____

Soup kitchen volunteers _____

_____

Priests _____

_____

Hospital volunteers _____

_____

Teachers _____

_____

Parish community _____

_____

My class _____

_____

Fill in the answers to the first two questions.

1. What are *social services*?

_____

_____

_____

2. How does Jesus continue to heal and forgive people?

_____

_____

_____

Help carry one another's burdens.
Based on Galatians 6:2

3. Discuss what we can do to bring Jesus' healing power to others.

CHRIST PRAYS WITH THE CHURCH

Activity

Think about how you like to pray. Then complete the inventory below by placing a ✔ in the appropriate column.

Name one or two places where you know people are praying.

PRAYER

	ALWAYS	SOMETIMES	NEVER
I like to pray alone.	_____	_____	_____
I like to pray with others.	_____	_____	_____
I use my own words when I pray.	_____	_____	_____
I use prayers that I've learned.	_____	_____	_____
I don't use any words when I pray.	_____	_____	_____
I like to pray standing up.	_____	_____	_____
I like to kneel when I pray.	_____	_____	_____
I like to sit or lie down when I pray.	_____	_____	_____
I like to pray in church.	_____	_____	_____
I like to pray at home.	_____	_____	_____
I like to pray outdoors.	_____	_____	_____

PRAYER

Discuss

Talk with someone in your family about how he or she prays. Ask him or her to complete the prayer inventory.

PRAYERFUL PEOPLE

From the days of the early Christian communities, the Church has always stressed the importance of prayer. Jesus taught the apostles how to pray and they in turn taught the early Christians how to pray as Jesus did. Prayer was an important part of the daily life of the Christian communities. People who saw them were impressed by their praying. People were drawn to Jesus after hearing the apostles preach and seeing the first Christians pray. Somehow they sensed Jesus' presence within the prayerful communities of his followers.

The Church never forgot the words of Jesus: "For where two or three are gathered together in my name, there am I in the midst of them" (Matthew 18:20). The early Christians prayed with faith, believing that the risen Christ was with them. They believed that Jesus prayed with them when they prayed. They continued to feel his presence with them.

Activity

Think about the times you pray at home, at school, and at church.
Then complete each sentence.

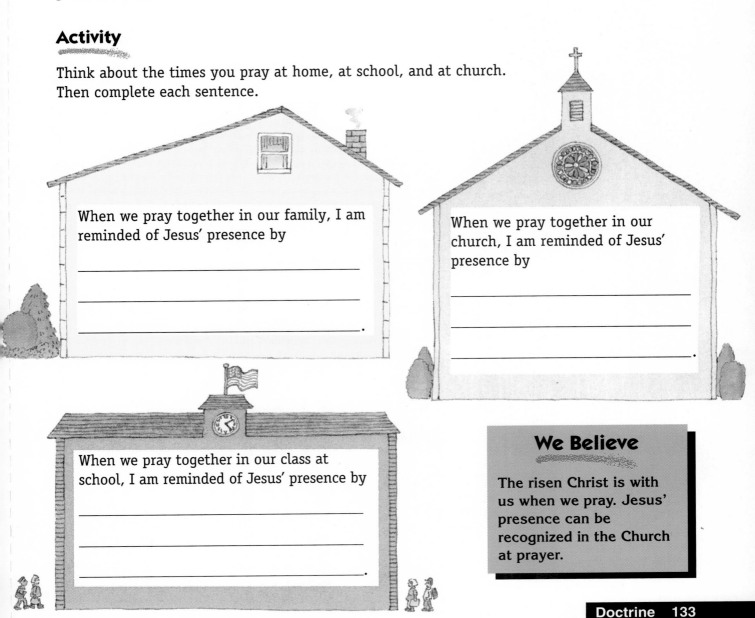

When we pray together in our family, I am reminded of Jesus' presence by

_____

_____

_____ .

When we pray together in our church, I am reminded of Jesus' presence by

_____

_____

_____ .

When we pray together in our class at school, I am reminded of Jesus' presence by

_____

_____

_____ .

We Believe

The risen Christ is with us when we pray. Jesus' presence can be recognized in the Church at prayer.

THE FIRST CHRISTIAN COMMUNITIES PRAYED

Many people in Jerusalem became followers of Jesus. They carefully learned and followed the teachings of the apostles. They lived in communities, sharing everything they had. Those who had property, or other goods, sold them. They gave what they had to those in need.

They spent much time praying. Every day they went together to the Temple to pray. In their homes they prayed and celebrated the **breaking of bread** as Jesus had commanded them to do in his memory. They ate their meals together, praising and thanking God. People who watched these followers of Jesus were drawn to them and to Jesus Christ. Their communities grew larger every day.

Based on Acts 2:42–47

A Life of Prayer

Prayer was an important part of the life of the early Christians. They celebrated the Eucharist together in their homes. Those who lived in Jerusalem went to the Temple daily to pray. One way in which they prayed was to use the psalms, prayer songs from the Old Testament. The early Christians prayed to God in the name of Jesus. They prayed at the usual Jewish prayer times: in the morning, at midday, and in the evening. In their prayer, they praised God for God's goodness. They thanked God for their many blessings. They asked God's help and forgiveness. Today, we still pray in these same ways.

Children praying in church

Activity

Read part of a letter that Paul wrote to one of the early Christian communities. Then answer the questions about Paul's letter.

> We urge you, brothers and sisters, to pray without stopping. Give thanks at all times, for this is the will of God for you in Christ Jesus.
>
> *Based on 1 Thessalonians 5:17–18*

Rabbi of an Orthodox synagogue during morning prayers

What do you think Paul is telling the early Christians?

_____

_____

_____

_____

What do you think Paul's letter means to us today?

_____

_____

_____

_____

Vocabulary

breaking of bread: the New Testament name for the Eucharist

Activity

How are the people in each photograph praying? What might each person be praying about? Write your answers on the lines provided.

_____

_____

_____

_____

_____

_____

_____

_____

_____

OFFICIAL PRAYERS OF THE CHURCH

We know that we can pray to God in our own words but it is also important to know that we can pray the Church's official prayers. Read about some of them below.

Liturgy of the Hours

The Church's daily prayer is the **Liturgy of the Hours**. The Liturgy of the Hours is prayer prayed at different times to praise God. These services include psalms, Scripture readings, songs, intercessions, and prayers. They can be prayed alone or with others.

Long ago the Liturgy of the Hours was prayed primarily by monks. Today, all kinds of people pray it—priests, businessmen and women, religious brothers and sisters, retired persons, teenagers, and many others. Like the traditional times of Jewish prayer, it is prayed in the morning, at midmorning, at midafternoon, and in the evening. It provides a way for the entire Church to be united in prayer throughout each day. You will be using some of the special parts from the Liturgy of the Hours later in this chapter.

Sacraments

The **sacraments** are also official prayers of the Church. They are special signs within the life of the Church through which Jesus truly becomes present with us and acts in our lives. The Catholic Church celebrates seven sacraments: Baptism, Confirmation, Eucharist, Reconciliation, Matrimony, Holy Orders, and Anointing of the Sick.

The most important prayer of the Church is the Eucharist. It is the central prayer around which all Catholics gather. At the Eucharist we praise and thank God. We say that we are sorry for our sins and we ask God to give us what we need. In Catholic parishes, the people gather every Sunday to celebrate the Eucharist. In most parishes, the Eucharist is also celebrated on the weekdays as well. When we celebrate the Eucharist we join in prayer with all Catholics throughout the world.

Vocabulary

Liturgy of the Hours: the Church's official prayer prayed at certain hours of the day and night

sacrament: a special sign within the life of the Catholic Church through which Christ truly becomes present with us and acts in our lives

EXPERIENCING PRAYER

The way in which we experience prayer may be different from time to time and from place to place. Sometimes we have a deeper sense of God's presence in a particular place or at a particular time because of something we see or hear. At other times the prayer may be connected to an important event such as a baptism, a wedding, or a graduation. And sometimes we have a different experience because of the community that is gathered with us for prayer. Each experience of prayer can be special if we recognize God's presence in ourselves and in one another.

Activity

Think about the prayer experiences pictured here. Then write a caption for each.

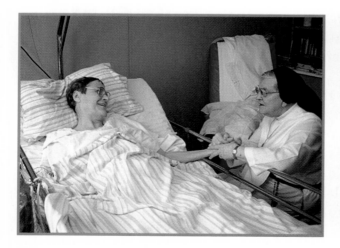

As Catholics, we continue to pray with and for the whole world through the prayers of the Church. We can sense Jesus' presence with us as we pray with the Christian community.

THOMAS MERTON—MAN OF PRAYER

We can learn from prayerful people how important prayer is. One such person was Thomas Merton.

Thomas Merton grew up with no religion. His parents died before he was sixteen. As a young man, he was full of energy and curiosity. He loved New York, where he lived. He also loved the university where he was studying. Life was exciting. He had numerous friends and went to many parties. From time to time, however, he would feel that he was missing something important.

Then one day his grandfather died. As a child, Tom had lived with his grandparents for many years. His grandfather was very special to him. On the night after his grandfather's death, Tom did something very unusual for him. He knelt down and prayed.

The next Sunday he visited a Catholic church during Mass. He did not understand what was happening, but he stayed and prayed. He went back many Sundays after that to pray. In time, Tom decided to become a Catholic. He was baptized when he was twenty-three years old.

After Thomas was baptized, he visited Gethsemani, a Trappist monastery in Kentucky. While he was there he joined the monks in prayer. Tom felt a great peace. He felt at home. He decided to stay.

Soon, Thomas became a monk. He spent his days praying and working with the other monks. He continued to write about prayer. He also wrote against war and for peace. Some of his books were bestsellers. He became very famous. Yet most of all he prayed. Thomas listened for God in everyone and in everything. He died in 1968.

Activity

Thomas Merton wrote many books on what he believed about prayer. Think about what prayer means to you. What do you believe about prayer?

_____

_____

_____

PRAYING WITH THE CHURCH EVERY DAY

The Liturgy of the Hours provides a way for the entire Church to be united in prayer throughout the day. It is an official prayer of the Church, made up of very specific parts. Pray the following prayer, using some of the Liturgy of the Hours parts—a psalm, a Scripture reading, and intercessions.

Leader: God, come to my assistance.
All: Lord, make haste to help me.

Leader: Glory to the Father, and to the Son, and to the Holy Spirit.
All: As it was in the beginning, is now, and will be for ever. Amen.

Side 1: The LORD is all I need.
Side 2: My life has been good and beautiful.
Side 1: Praise the LORD who helps me.
Even at night I feel God's calling.
Side 2: I keep the LORD before me always.
God is close to me and I will not be hurt.

Based on Psalm 16:5–8

Reader: A reading from Paul's Letter to the Ephesians. *(Read Ephesians 4:25–32)*

Leader: Blessed be God, who hears our prayers.
(pause)
Gather as brothers and sisters all people who follow Jesus.
All: Lord, bless your people.

Leader: Give our families and friends good health and peace of mind and heart.
All: Lord, bless your people.

Leader: Heal those who are sick or injured.
All: Lord, bless your people.

Leader: Welcome into your kingdom those who have died believing in you.
All: Lord, bless your people.

(All pray together The Lord's Prayer.)

Leader: May the Lord bless us, protect us from all evil and bring us to everlasting life.
All: Amen.

Chapter Review

A haiku is a poem that has three lines. Line one has five syllables. Line two has seven syllables. Line three has five syllables. Read the following example of a haiku.

My prayer says to God:
I know you care and are near
always to help me.

Now in the frame below, write a haiku that says what you believe about prayer.

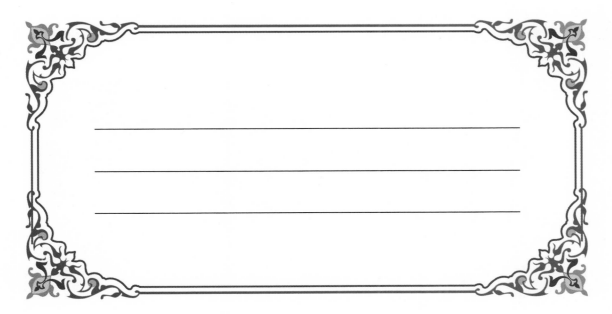

_____

_____

_____

Fill in the answers to the first two questions.

1. What does *breaking of bread* mean in the New Testament?

   _____

   _____

2. How can we recognize Jesus' presence in the Church today?

   _____

   _____

   _____

3. Discuss how you can be a more prayerful member of the Christian community.

Give thanks to God always and for everything in the name of our Lord Jesus.
Based on Ephesians 5:20

THE CHURCH IS THE SACRAMENT OF CHRIST

FAMILY SPIRIT

Everyone was excited. Kathy placed the album on the table. Her mom, dad, younger brother and sister, Jeffrey and Jessica, gathered around her so that they could see. They were eager to see pictures of Kathy's trip to California. She had gone with her best friend, Amy, and Amy's family to visit Amy's relatives in San Francisco.

There were pictures of the Golden Gate Bridge, Fisherman's Wharf, Chinatown, and trolley cars. But what Kathy's mom and dad really noticed were Amy's relatives, who were in all the photographs.

"I can hardly believe it," Kathy's mom said. "I would know they were all Amy's relatives even if you didn't tell me. They look alike."

"And they all talk the same way," Kathy added. "They talk just like Amy."

"Did you like them, Kathy?" her dad asked.

"I really did," Kathy answered. "They were all as nice as Amy, her parents, and her brother, Mike. I felt right at home with them. I felt as if I had known them for a long time. What I really liked was how they listened to me. That made me feel that what I had to say was important."

"Amy's mom has always been a good listener," Mom said.

"They were so generous, too," Kathy added. "They gave me all this film for taking pictures."

"Amy's dad is always generous," Dad recalled. "So was Amy's grandfather. He always gave me a soda when I was your age, Kathy. The rest of the family seems to have caught his spirit."

THE CHRISTIAN FAMILY AND JESUS

Saul and many other people of his time felt that it was necessary to prevent all Christians from preaching about Jesus. They went from town to town, searching out followers of Jesus in their houses of prayer.

One day Saul was on the way to Damascus. Suddenly a brilliant light from the sky flashed around him. Saul fell to the ground. He heard a voice saying, "Saul, Saul, why do you **persecute** me?"

"Who are you, sir?" Saul asked.

The voice answered, "I am Jesus, the one you are persecuting. Get up and go into the city. You will be told what to do."

Saul's friends stood there speechless. They had heard the voice but could see no one. Saul got up from the road, but he could not see. His friends led him into Damascus to the home of a follower of Jesus. For three days Saul fasted from food and drink. He still could not see. Then the Lord sent a man named Ananias to Saul. "Saul, my brother, I have been sent by the Lord Jesus, who appeared to you on the way here. He sent me so you may recover your sight and be filled with the Holy Spirit."

Immediately Saul was able to see. He was baptized. He ate a good meal and felt his strength come back.

Based on Acts 9:1–19

Vocabulary

persecute: to cause another to suffer because of his or her belief

Activity

Think of your own family. Think of all the relatives you have ever met or seen in photographs. Then complete the photo albums below with information about your family. You may use words, as well as symbols and images.

THE BODY OF CHRIST

Not long after Jesus died and rose to new life, many people began persecuting his friends. Saul was one of the leading persecutors. Yet the voice Saul heard said, "I am Jesus, the one you are persecuting."

Jesus was saying that Saul was persecuting him by persecuting his followers. Somehow, Christ and the Christians were one.

Saul lived near Damascus for almost three years after his conversion. He came to be known as Paul. He always experienced the presence of the risen Christ in the communities of Christians. These Christians tried to live as Jesus did. They tried to be caring, compassionate, courageous, and prayerful.

Many people, like Paul, who came to know the first Christians were drawn to them. They heard Jesus' word through their words. They experienced Jesus' healing and forgiveness by watching the ways in which the Christians healed and forgave one another. They experienced the presence of Jesus.

Because of Paul's experiences, he came to speak of the Church as the Body of Christ. The Church can also be called the sacrament of Jesus Christ, because we, the Church, reveal the loving presence and action of Christ by how we live, speak, and act.

In 1 Corinthians 12:12–13, Paul wrote:

"The body of Christ has many different parts, just as any other body. For in one Spirit we were all baptized into one body, whether Jews or Greeks, slaves or free persons. We each drink from that same Spirit."

Through baptism, we are members of the family of Christ, and we are called Christians. As members of the Christian family, we have special gifts or characteristics.

"My friends, there are different kinds of spiritual gifts but they come from the same Spirit. There are different ways to serve the same Lord. Yet the same God works in all of us and helps us in everything we do."

Based on 1 Corinthians 12:4–5

Activity

How do you carry the spirit of the Christian family into the world? Give three examples.

_____

_____

_____

_____

_____

We Believe

The Church is the sacrament of Jesus Christ in the world. We, the Church, reveal the presence and activity of the risen Christ in our lives.

JESUS PRESENT IN OUR LIVES

The Church is the sacrament of Jesus Christ in many different ways. We show that Jesus is with us and acting in our lives by the way in which we carry out his work and by what we say and do. Sometimes we do this as individuals. Sometimes we join with others in groups or organizations. Whether we act alone or with others, we are carrying out the mission of Jesus and revealing his presence to others.

Activity

Look up the Scripture passage below each picture. Then write how the people in the picture are showing Jesus' presence in our world.

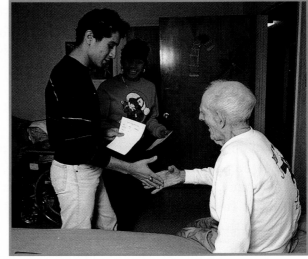

Exodus 34:6

_____

_____

_____

Mark 1:15

_____

_____

_____

Matthew 15:32–36

_____

_____

_____

REVEALING THE PRESENCE OF JESUS

All Christians are called through Baptism to reveal or show to others the living presence of Jesus in our midst. We do this by our words and our actions. Some Christians are called to do this in extraordinary ways. For instance, some in our Christian community are called to become bishops and priests so that through their leadership roles in the Church, Jesus will be known to all. Some baptized Christians are called to become missionaries, bringing the teachings of Jesus to those who have never heard of him. In our parishes, catechists, lay ministers, and members of the parish council and other communities bring the presence of Jesus to the community through the services they provide.

Activity

Create a new group that you think would help people, especially young people, discover Jesus present in their lives. Fill out this chart, describing your new church group, program, or organization.

Name of Church Group, Program, or Organization	
Purpose (Why does it exist?)	
Membership (Who can belong?)	
Responsibilities (What must members do?)	
Other Information (What makes it special or different?)	
Identifying Symbol	

Jesus' Mission—The Mission of the Church

Since the Church is the sacrament of Christ, the mission of the Church is the same as the mission of Jesus. The Church's mission has three parts.

1. **The Church must teach as Jesus taught.** This part of the Church's mission is carried out through preaching and teaching, and by proclaiming the gospel. Some examples of organizations and individuals who do this are: religious sisters and brothers who teach in Catholic schools and parishes; missionaries who bring the teachings of Jesus to distant lands; priests and deacons who preach at Mass; faith-filled men and women who teach religion. All Christians are responsible for spreading the good news of Jesus.

   Read Matthew 28:16–20 and tell what Jesus is asking his disciples to do.

   _____

   _____

   _____

   _____

   _____

2. **The Church must pray as Jesus prayed.** We carry out this part of the Church's mission when we pray at official gatherings of the Catholic community, such as during Mass and at the Liturgy of the Hours, as well as during the celebration of the sacraments. Some groups within the Church are primarily devoted to prayer. Religious orders of men and women who are examples of such groups remain separate from society.

   Read Acts of the Apostles 2:42–47 and describe what the people were devoted to.

   _____

   _____

   _____

3. The Church must serve as Jesus served.

For centuries the Church's many groups and organizations have cared for the poor and the suffering throughout the world as Jesus did. Many social services are provided by Catholic Charities, an organization which is represented in most Catholic dioceses in the United States. These services include caring for those who are homeless, hungry, sick, and dying. Basic needs of the poor are also provided by other organizations such as The Society of St. Vincent de Paul, which provides food and clothing to the poor.

Read John 13:1–15 and describe how Jesus served his disciples.

_____

_____

Activity

Since we are the Church, we are responsible for carrying on the work of Jesus in the world. Write some suggestions of how your school might do this.

We must teach as Jesus taught. I think our school can do this better by

_____

_____.

We must pray as Jesus prayed. I think our school can do this better by

_____

_____.

We must serve one another as Jesus served. I think our school can do this better by

_____

_____.

PRAYING WITH THE NEWSPAPER

Sometimes we want to pray about what's happening in our world but we may not know where to begin. Using the daily newspaper, or some other printed news source such as a magazine, can help focus our attention on world and local news events. Praying in this way can help us reach out in prayer to others while making us more aware of God's presence in our world.

Some news stories may be about someone's success or accomplishment. Other stories may be about a crime committed or a natural disaster. Whatever the story is about, remember that Jesus is present in all the situations of our lives, even when we can't easily see him there.

Use the following steps to pray with an article.

1. Choose a newspaper or magazine.

2. Find a quiet place where you can read and pray without too many interruptions or distractions.

3. After reading an article, place your hand on the article, close your eyes, and ask God's blessing or forgiveness on the people involved and on the situation described.

4. Thank God for hearing your prayer.

Repeat these steps for each newspaper or magazine you read. Your prayer doesn't have to be long. It only has to be sincere.

Chapter Review

On the lines provided, write the names of three people you know who are members of the Body of Christ, the Church. Then, after each name, write one thing that shows Christ's presence in that person's life. You may include yourself.

Member's name _____

_____

Member's name _____

_____

Member's name _____

_____

Fill in the answers to the first two questions.

1. What does *persecute* mean?

_____

_____

2. What does it mean to call the Church the "sacrament of Jesus Christ"?

_____

_____

3. Discuss what we can do to share more in the Church's task of showing Jesus to others.

You are the body of Christ. Every one of you is a member of it.
Based on
1 Corinthians 12:27

UNIT **3** ORGANIZER

THE CHURCH: SACRAMENT OF CHRIST'S PRESENCE

Each picture below stands for a chapter in this unit. Complete the
sentences about that chapter on the lines provided.

The Church gives us special teachers.
They are

_____

_____

_____ .

The Church can bring healing to a
suffering world by

_____

_____

_____ .

The Church gathers for the following
special times of prayer.

_____

_____

_____

Three parts of the Church's mission are

_____

_____

_____

_____ .

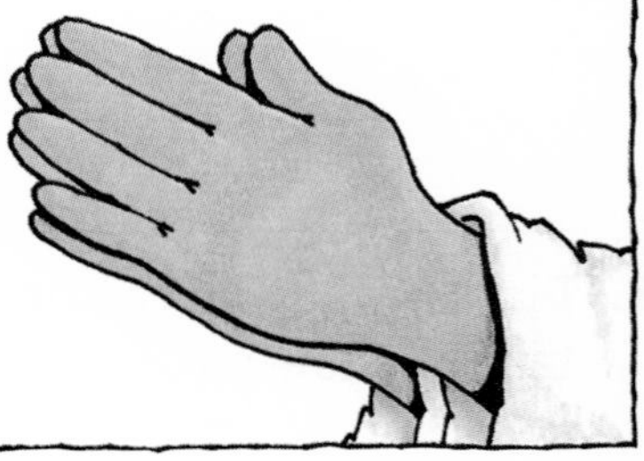

UNIT **3** REVIEW

Match the words or Bible references on the left with the
correct phrases on the right.

1. Matthew 26:51–52

2. Caesarea

3. Matthew 6:26–28

4. Matthew 7:12

5. Through the Church

_____ Christ's words are heard all over
the world.

_____ Jesus' words on peace

_____ Jesus' words at the Last Supper

_____ an important Jewish city

_____ Jesus' words on respecting others

Complete the word puzzle.

Across

1. In Jesus' name, Peter and the disciples _____.

3. It was after the _____ that the disciples began to heal
the sick and suffering.

5. Many people became _____ of Jesus after they
heard about him and saw the
healings that were done in his name.

Down

1. _____ was a great disciple of Jesus.

2. The disciples not only healed
people, they also _____ them in
Jesus' name.

4. The paralyzed man that Peter
healed was _____.

6. Each of us must help carry one
another's _____.

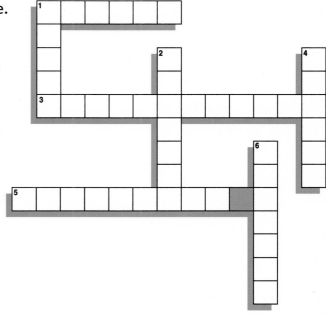

Fill in the blanks below to reveal Jesus' promise to us. Decode the message by using the letter of the alphabet that comes after the one given. (Use *A* where it occurs.)

"VGDQD   SVN   NQ   SGQDD   AQD

_____

FASGDQDC   HM   LX   MALD,   SGDQD

_____

AL   H   HM   SGDHQ   LHCRS."

_____

Write in the word that best completes each sentence.
Then read the story of Saul.

light	duty	Ananias
Christians	Holy Spirit	persecuting

Saul was against all _____. He felt it was

his _____ to stop them. To help Saul see that

what he was doing was wrong, Jesus spoke to him, "I am

Jesus, the one you are _____."

Saul had been blinded by a brilliant _____. Later, Jesus

sent _____ to heal Saul. Saul recovered his sight

and was filled with the _____.

RECOGNIZING HOW THOUGHTS and FEELINGS INFLUENCE BEHAVIOR

God created me as a person who thinks, feels, and acts. There are times when I might know the right thing to do, but I choose to behave in ways that are not good for me or others. My thoughts and feelings can influence my behavior. Some thoughts and feelings may prevent me from acting in ways I know are good.

Lee has many things going on in his life. His parents have been arguing. Lee overhears them talking about not wanting to live together. He's worried and cannot think about anything else. His school work is suffering, and he's constantly getting into fights. He doesn't even want to go outside and shoot baskets with his friends. He feels unhappy most of the time. Money is the topic of many of his parents' fights. Lee thinks that if he hadn't asked for so many things his parents wouldn't have to worry so much about money.

Jennifer and Amanda have been good friends since kindergarten. This fall a new girl has come to their school and is in their class. Amanda and the new girl have become friends. Jennifer feels left out and jealous of Amanda. She's started to talk about Amanda to her other friends. Last week Jennifer spread a rumor that hurt Amanda's feelings. Jennifer knows she hasn't been treating Amanda very nicely, but part of Jennifer feels that Amanda deserves what she's getting.

Mike's temper often gets the best of him. Sometimes he feels so angry that it seems as if he's about to explode. He gets into lots of fights and feels that he has to prove to the other person that he is tougher and stronger. Mike secretly worries about not being good enough. He knows that fighting isn't the best way to solve problems, yet he finds it hard to keep his temper in check.

Discuss

1. How are Lee, Jennifer, and Mike behaving?

2. How might their behavior affect others?

3. How do you think they are feeling?

4. What might be some of their thoughts?

5. How might their feelings and thoughts influence their behaviors?

6. How might they help themselves feel better?

Following Jesus

No matter how we feel or what we are thinking, Jesus is with us. Even if we act in ways that are not kind, forgiving, compassionate, or gentle, Jesus is with us. Jesus loves us and wants to help us when we are upset or unhappy, or when we don't think we are lovable.

PRAYER

Complete the following prayer by telling Jesus about a feeling that is troubling you or about doubts you may have about being special.

Dear Jesus,

Sometimes I wonder about _____ .

I really wish _____ .

Could you help me with _____ ?

I'm really worried about _____ .

I feel angry when _____ .

I have trouble understanding _____ .

Thank you, Jesus, for always being there to listen to me and help me.

OPENING DOORS
A Take-Home Magazine™

Growing Closer

HERE IS A GUESSING GAME to play with your fifth-grader when you're riding in the car, waiting, washing dishes, or taking a walk. Think of a person who exemplifies the Christian spirit, that is, who teaches, serves, loves, or prays as Jesus did. Begin with "I'm thinking of a person who…" Describe the person by his or her attitudes and actions, one sentence at a time, until your child correctly guesses his or her identity. Then let your child describe a person and you guess who!

Looking Ahead

In the coming weeks, your fifth-grader will be learning how we celebrate the presence and actions of Jesus in our lives through seven special signs. He or she will also study the three sacraments of initiation: Baptism (Chapter 14), Confirmation (Chapter 15), and Eucharist (Chapter 16).

A Closer Look

Family Features

Is your family famous for its short, extra-wide feet or long, narrow feet? Do you have your father's nose, your mother's chin, or your aunt's eyes? Get out your family photo album and take a peek.

What kinds of feats is your family known for? Have you inherited your grandparents' sense of adventure, your mother's musical talent, or your father's green thumb?

The Bishops as Teachers

The bishops, together with the pope, share in the responsibility of teaching. This teaching is done in the following ways.

- A council is the highest teaching authority of bishops and the pope. Vatican Council II (1962–1965) was the only council of this century.

- A synod, or meeting, of bishops from the universal Church is the second highest teaching authority. These synods, held approximately every two years, aim to provide Catholics with information on essential points of doctrine and Christian morality.

- The National Conference of Catholic Bishops meets twice each year to address issues important to the Church in the United States. They teach primarily through pastoral letters addressed to all Catholics living in the United States.

Sister Thea Bowman leads the singing at the National Conference of Catholic Bishops in Spring, 1989.

Many priests, religious, and lay people teach religion in seminaries, colleges, parishes, and religious education classrooms. However, it is important to remember that every Catholic shares in the teaching ministry of the Church. How you live your life as a follower of Jesus can be an important example to others.

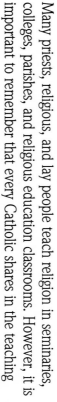

If your family were asked to participate in a family talent show, what would you do? If you were going to begin a family business, what type of business would it be? Who would have what job?

The Christian family is a community that reveals the presence and activity of God in our world. Each family member is called to teach, heal, forgive, and pray with the help of the Holy Spirit. What difference would it make in your neighborhood without your family's presence?

Go, therefore, and make disciples of all nations, baptizing them in the name of the Father, and of the Son, and of the holy Spirit, teaching them to observe all that I have commanded you.

Matthew 28:19

Teaching by Word and Example

The Pope: *The Church's Primary Teacher*

The pope teaches in the following ways.

- *Ex cathedra* statements, "from the chair" of St. Peter deal with important matters of faith and morals. These teachings are infallible—absolutely true and correct. These statements are also extremely rare.

- Encyclicals are "circular" letters sent to the universal Church. For example, in *Mater et Magistra (On Christianity and Social Progress)*, Pope John XXIII described the way we are to act together for others.

- Apostolic exhortations are documents, limited in scope and subject matter. They are often associated with an occasion. They show the Church's past and present stand on an issue but are not meant to be the final word on the subject.

A MARKED COMMUNITY

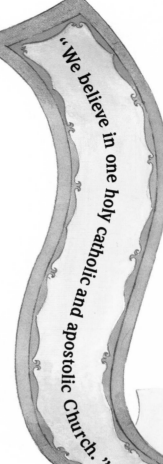

"We believe in one holy catholic and apostolic Church."

The marks of the Church—one, holy, catholic, and apostolic—are traditional ways of describing or identifying the Catholic community. These marks are gifts bestowed upon the Church by Jesus, gifts that the community of believers must strive to realize ever more fully.

Jesus is the center of our unity and community. The early Christians based their communal life on their belief in Jesus as their Lord and Savior. They met to listen to the teaching of the apostles and to pray together. They broke bread together—celebrated the Eucharist.

As the early Christians did, we believe in Jesus as Lord and celebrate our unity in the Eucharist. We seek to use our diverse talents and gifts to continue the work of Jesus. Each parish community is called to reveal the presence and activity of the risen Christ in our world today. We do this by teaching, healing, forgiving, and praying.

Support Group

In the past few years, we've heard about and experienced the successes of support groups. They have given many people the understanding and strength they needed to cope with or overcome problems or difficult situations. Do you realize that you belong to a support group, a very large and strong one, the Christian community? Your group meets every week on Saturday evening or Sunday to pray together, to be nourished by the Word and at the Table of the Lord, to be renewed and strengthened to meet the responsibilities and challenges of Christian living throughout the coming week.

Check your parish bulletin. Your parish may list the support groups (for example, groups for widowed, separated, divorced) in the local community.

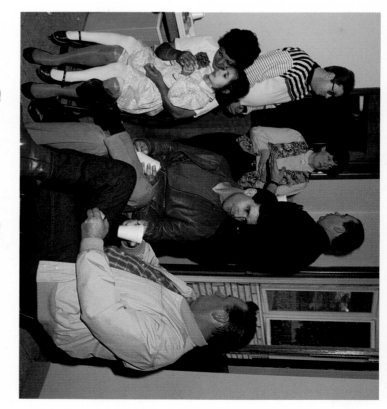

UNIT 4

SACRAMENTS OF INITIATION

What most helps you feel welcome in a new group?

13

THE CHURCH CELEBRATES SEVEN SACRAMENTS

Special Signs

We use objects, gestures, and actions as signs. These types of signs are often used to express what we are thinking or feeling or to give importance to what we say. Sometimes they are used to call attention to something that's not obvious.

Look at the picture on the right. Tell a brief story about what is happening in the picture now, what happened before the picture was taken, and what will happen later.

What are some signs or actions that have special meaning to a group, such as a club or a team?

Activity

Signs can express different meanings. Some signs or gestures can be used to express more than one meaning. For example, a hug can express love, friendship, reconciliation, or support. Look at this photograph of a gesture that is often used to express inner feelings or commitment. Write three things it could mean to the people involved.

1. _____

   _____

2. _____

   _____

3. _____

   _____

SIGNS OF JESUS

Jesus showed God's love for people through his actions and gestures. In Jesus' time, sitting down and eating with others was a sign of friendship. When Jesus shared a meal with sinners, he was telling everyone that God cares about and forgives sinners.

Healing those who were sick was a sign of love and compassion. When Jesus stopped at Peter's home to heal Peter's mother-in-law (Matthew 8:14-15) and when he healed those with terrible diseases (Mark 1:32-34), he was telling everyone that God cares about those who are sick.

The risen Jesus continues to show us God's love through signs. Daily experiences, world events, people, things, times, and places—all can express God's loving presence with us.

Activity

What objects, gestures, or actions in your daily life reveal Jesus' presence? Name an object, gesture, or action that expresses the following signs.

JESUS EATS WITH SINNERS

One day Jesus was walking along the lakeshore. Near the gate of one of the lakeshore villages, he noticed a man sitting at a tax collector's stand. The man was Levi, a rich tax collector.

Jesus stopped at Levi's stand. He smiled at Levi and said to him, "Follow me!"

Although Levi was surprised at Jesus' invitation, he got up, went with Jesus, and became a follower of Jesus. Soon afterward he invited Jesus to come to his house for dinner.

Levi invited many of his friends to celebrate with him. He wanted them to meet Jesus. Most of the people Levi invited were tax collectors like himself. Because of their work, tax collectors were not popular. They were even considered to be sinners. Other guests were also considered to be sinners. Jesus sat down at the table with Levi and his guests.

Some other people stood outside, watching. They were shocked to see Jesus eating and drinking with sinners.

"Tell us, why does Jesus eat with people like them?" they asked Jesus' disciples.

Jesus overheard their question. Before the disciples could say anything, Jesus spoke up.

"People who are healthy do not need a doctor," he said. "Sick people do. I have come to call sinners, not the self-righteous."

Based on Mark 2:13–17

Discuss

1. How do you know that Jesus cared about Levi and other sinners?

2. Which words were signs of welcome?

3. Which words were signs of forgiveness?

4. Why were some people shocked by Jesus' words and actions?

Christ's Signs to the Church

We've already learned that the Church has special objects and gestures called sacramentals, such as holy water, Bibles, and blessings. Sacramentals help us become more aware of Jesus' presence. The Church also celebrates **seven sacraments**. The seven sacraments are powerful signs and rituals given by Christ to the Church to give grace. The sacraments do more than make us aware of Jesus' presence—they make Jesus present to us in a real way. The seven sacraments are Baptism, Confirmation, Eucharist, Reconciliation, Anointing of the Sick, Matrimony, and Holy Orders.

Vocabulary

seven sacraments: seven powerful signs and rituals given by Christ to the Church to give grace

ritual: a ceremonial act or action

✦ ✦ ✦ ✦ ✦ ✦ ✦ ✦ ✦ ✦

We Believe

The Church celebrates the presence and actions of the risen Jesus in our lives through seven powerful signs and rituals. They are called the seven sacraments.

Activity

When visitors come to your home, what are some things you and your family members do to make them feel welcome? List three of these things.

1. _____

2. _____

3. _____

Jesus Welcomed People

The gospels give us many examples of how warm and welcoming Jesus was. Jesus welcomed everyone—large crowds, children, people who were crippled, people who had diseases, people who were sinners, and many other kinds of people. In this chapter you read Mark 2:13-17 and learned about how Jesus welcomed the opportunity to eat with people who were unpopular—tax collectors and sinners. All of these people were important to Jesus.

On many occasions, great crowds followed Jesus because they were amazed at his teaching and the way in which he healed people. One time a man with a skin disease asked Jesus to heal him. Jesus reached out and touched the man, saying, "Be healed." The man was healed (based on Matthew 8:1-3).

When Jesus arrived at Gennesaret, people ran to him, bringing those who were sick on mats. Wherever Jesus went people brought their sick. They begged Jesus to let them touch his cloak so that they would be healed. And all who touched it were healed (based on Mark 6:53-56).

The crowds followed Jesus to Bethsaida. Jesus welcomed the crowds and spoke to them about the kingdom of God. Late in the day, the disciples asked Jesus to dismiss the crowd so that the people could find places to sleep and food to eat. But Jesus said, "Give them some food . . ." (Luke 9:10-13).

Whenever Jesus met people who were sick, hungry, or ignored by others, he welcomed them and was present to them.

THE SACRAMENTS OF INITIATION

The Church welcomes new members through three **sacraments of initiation**—Baptism, Confirmation, and Eucharist. Through them the Church celebrates the presence and actions of the risen Jesus in our lives and welcomes us into the Christian community. These sacraments bring us to full membership in the Church.

Activity

Look at the photographs on this page. Identify each sacrament of initiation by writing its name on the line provided.

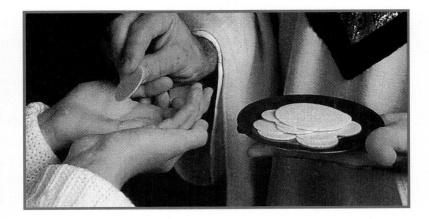

Discuss

1. Which of the seven sacraments have you already received?

2. Which sacrament will you probably celebrate next?

Vocabulary

sacraments of initiation: Baptism, Confirmation, and Eucharist—the Church's three sacraments of welcome and belonging

◆ ◆ ◆ ◆ ◆ ◆ ◆ ◆ ◆ ◆ ◆

Activity

Decide if the following acts are acts of healing or commitment. Some may be both.
Write **H** for healing, **C** for commitment, or **B** for both.

_____ **1.** A husband helps his wife look for a new job.

_____ **2.** A doctor performs emergency surgery.

_____ **3.** A priest spends time with the parish's youth group.

_____ **4.** A husband and wife find time to spend together.

_____ **5.** A physical therapist works with an accident victim.

_____ **6.** A bishop celebrates Confirmation at the parishes in his diocese.

THE SACRAMENTS OF HEALING

We have all experienced healing in many different ways. We have been physically healed with the help of doctors and other medical people and the medication they've given us. We've also been healed emotionally when someone has apologized for hurting our feelings or letting us down.

The Catholic Church continues Jesus' ministry of healing through the **sacraments of healing.** When our relationship with God and others breaks down, we are healed through the sacrament of Reconciliation. When we are very sick, seriously injured, or elderly, we are healed through the sacrament of Anointing of the Sick.

Activity

Identify the sacrament of healing shown in each photograph by writing the sacrament's name on the line provided.

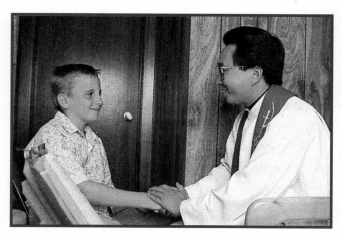

_____   _____

THE SACRAMENTS OF COMMITMENT

The Catholic Church offers us two **sacraments of commitment**— Matrimony or Marriage and Holy Orders.

In the sacrament of Matrimony, a woman and a man promise to love one another through a lifelong commitment. The man and woman promise to commit themselves to each other, in spite of sickness or other difficult circumstances. Married love is an adult commitment of unconditional love, much like the love Jesus has for the Church.

In the sacrament of Holy Orders, a man promises to be faithful to God's call as deacon, priest, or bishop. He promises to serve the Catholic community in a role of leadership and ministry.

Activity

Identify the sacrament of commitment shown in each photograph on this page by writing the sacrament's name on the line provided.

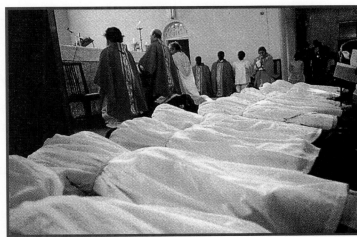

Vocabulary

sacraments of healing: Reconciliation and Anointing of the Sick—the Catholic Church's two sacraments of healing

sacraments of commitment: Matrimony and Holy Orders—the Catholic Church's two sacraments of commitment

PRAYING THE DAYENU

The Dayenu is an ancient form of prayer that praises God. This prayer was probably familiar to Jesus as he was growing up, since it is a Hebrew prayer. In the Dayenu, the person who is praying names the wonderful things God has done and praises God for them. The purpose of the prayer is to think about and name the many ways that God acts in our lives.

Read the examples below to help you get started. Then continue the prayer by completing the sentences.

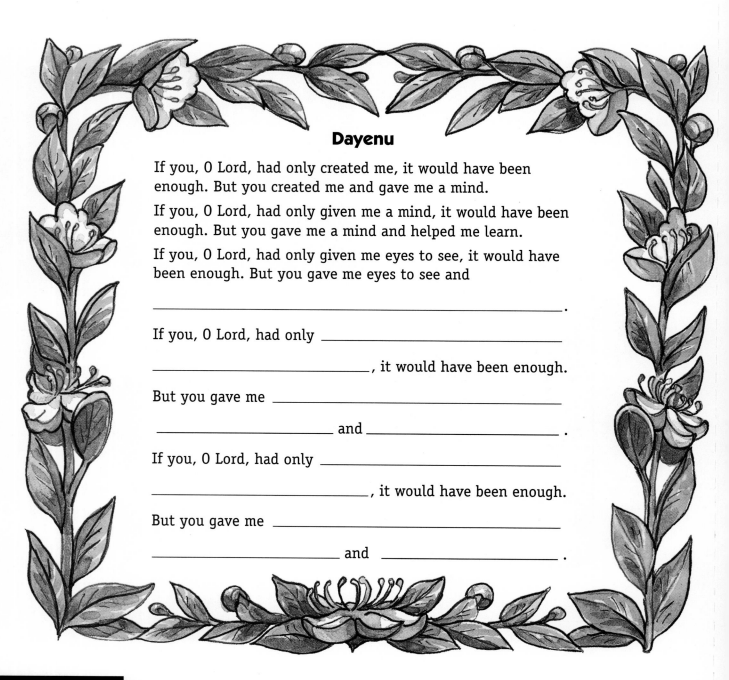

Dayenu

If you, O Lord, had only created me, it would have been enough. But you created me and gave me a mind.

If you, O Lord, had only given me a mind, it would have been enough. But you gave me a mind and helped me learn.

If you, O Lord, had only given me eyes to see, it would have been enough. But you gave me eyes to see and

_____ .

If you, O Lord, had only _____

_____ , it would have been enough.

But you gave me _____

_____ and _____ .

If you, O Lord, had only _____

_____ , it would have been enough.

But you gave me _____

_____ and _____ .

Chapter Review

In Jesus' time, eating with a person was a sign of friendship. Name some signs or actions you show others to let them know that you accept and care about them.

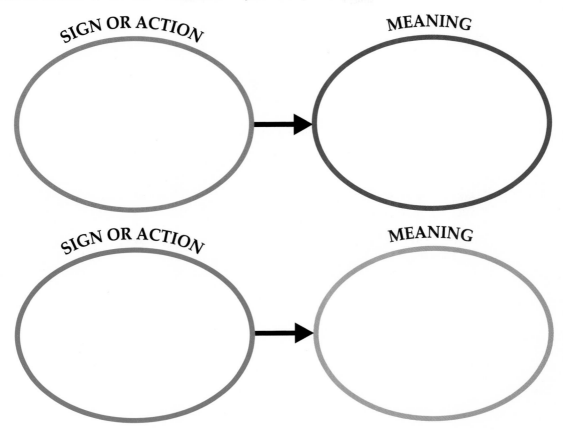

SIGN OR ACTION → MEANING

SIGN OR ACTION → MEANING

Fill in the answers to the first two questions.

1. What is meant by the *seven sacraments*? Name the

   seven sacraments. _____

   _____

   _____

   _____

   _____

2. What does the Church celebrate through the

   sacraments? _____

   _____

3. Discuss what you can do to be more aware of Christ's presence and actions in your life.

My God will supply your needs fully.
Based on Philippians 4:19

14

BAPTISM IS A SACRAMENT OF WELCOME

TONG'S CHALLENGE

Tong stared at the blank sheet of paper on the kitchen table. Father Clarke had asked him to write down his reasons for wanting to join the Catholic Church so that the parishioners of Queen of Peace Parish could read about their newest member in a special Easter bulletin.

(to be continued)

Activity

Imagine that you are asked to write why you would want to become or remain a Catholic. Write your reasons.

I want to become or remain a Catholic because

Tong's Challenge (continued from page 172)

Tong's eyes wandered to the wall where there were several photographs of his family and their home in Vietnam. He tried hard to remember his grandparents, but Tong was very young when they died in the war and it was difficult now to recall them. Tears welled up in his eyes when he looked at his father's picture. It was still hard to believe that his father, too, died in the war.

One photograph showed Tong, his mother, and his sister with a group of "boat people" who also risked their lives in the escape from oppression in their country of Vietnam in Southeast Asia.

Tong trembled as he remembered his family's dangerous and difficult journey to the United States. Since arriving here, Tong has tried to forget that painful, terrifying month. That was 1978, and he was just six years old then.

Tong smiled as he remembered Sister Diane and Father Clarke, who welcomed his family when they arrived in California. Father Clarke even invited them to stay at the parish house until they could find an apartment. Most of all he thought of the Nelson family who were lay leaders in Queen of Peace Parish. They helped his mother find a job in the parish. They also helped Tong's mother enroll Tong and his sister in the local school. The Nelson children, Lexie, Danny, and Michael, welcomed Tong and his sister as friends even though it was difficult communicating at first. With them, Tong began to feel at home in California.

(to be continued)

The Church Welcomes New Members

The Catholic Church welcomes its new members through the sacraments of initiation: Baptism, Confirmation, and Eucharist. New adult members of the Church and older children normally celebrate all three sacraments of initiation during the **Easter Vigil** as part of their catechumenate. The **catechumenate** is a process of formation during which candidates pray, study, and learn about the Catholic faith. It is the Church's way of baptizing adults and initiating them into the Christian community. Young children usually celebrate these sacraments on other separate occasions.

Vocabulary

Easter Vigil: The Easter Vigil is the most important of all the Church's celebrations. On Holy Saturday night we celebrate Jesus' victory over death.

catechumenate: a process of formation during which candidates pray, study, and learn about the Catholic faith. It is the Church's way of initiating adults and older children into the Christian community.

◆ ◆ ◆ ◆ ◆ ◆ ◆ ◆ ◆ ◆

Tong's Challenge *(continued from page 173)*

Now Tong was twenty-five. He, his mother, and his sister were completing the catechumenate at Queen of Peace Parish and were looking forward to the Easter Vigil.

As Tong's memories from the past twenty-five years came back, an answer to the question of why he now wanted to become a Catholic slowly took shape.

He picked up his pen and wrote, "There are many reasons why I want to become a Catholic—the sacraments, the Scriptures, the Mass, and the special beliefs shared by all Catholics around the world. But, most of all, I want to become a Catholic because of the first Catholics my family and I met here in California—Sister Diane, Father Clarke, and the Nelsons. They brought us into their lives and into their hearts and made us feel welcome and important. It is through them that I have come to know Jesus, as well as what it means to belong to a Christian community."

JESUS AND BAPTISM

After Jesus' resurrection his eleven disciples went up to Galilee. They went to a mountain where they had often gone with Jesus. There Jesus met them. He gave them an important mission.

"Go," Jesus told them, "and make disciples of all the nations. Baptize them in the name of the Father, and of the Son, and of the Holy Spirit. Teach them to do everything I have commanded you. And know that I am with you always, until the end of time!"

Based on Matthew 28:16–20

THE SIGNS OF BAPTISM

Baptism is the sacrament through which we are joined to Jesus, welcomed into the Catholic Church, and freed of **original sin**. We begin to grow as followers of Jesus. In Baptism, Jesus gives us new life in the Holy Spirit. Through the Holy Spirit we begin to share in God's loving presence, or **grace**.

The celebration of Baptism includes several signs of Jesus present to us. The signs also help us understand the meaning of the sacrament.

Water

Water, a symbol of life, is the source of all forms of life. All living beings need water. It nourishes life, cleanses, refreshes, cools, warms, relaxes, and stimulates. In the Bible, water is a sign of God's life-giving, saving actions. Pouring water on the new member is a sign of the new life of God's love and grace that comes to us through Jesus and the Church. As the priest baptizes with water, he says "*(Name)*, I baptize you in the name of the Father, and of the Son, and of the Holy Spirit."

Chrism

The priest **anoints** the newly baptized person with **chrism**, a perfumed oil that has been blessed by the bishop. This anointing is a sign of the newly baptized person's special mission as a follower of Jesus.

White Garment

A white garment is placed on the new member of the Christian community. This action symbolizes the new dignity of the Christian. He or she is now expected to live according to the teachings of Jesus.

Lighted Candle

A parent, godparent, or some other family member lights a candle from the Paschal, or Easter, candle. The candle is then given to, or held for, the newly baptized Christian. The lighting of the candle signifies that Jesus, the Light of the World, asks all his followers to let his light shine for all to see.

We Believe

The sacraments of initiation are Baptism, Confirmation, and Eucharist. Baptism celebrates the new Christian's sharing in Christ's life. Baptism is the first sacrament of welcome into the Church.

THE SACRAMENT OF BAPTISM

1. The Catholic community gathers for the Easter Vigil to celebrate Jesus' death and resurrection and to welcome its new members. Tong, his mother, and his sister are excited.

2. After the Liturgy of the Word, those who are to be baptized go with their godparents to the special baptismal pool. Everyone in the church joins together in a litany to the saints. The celebrant then blesses the water that will be used for Baptism. Along with the gathered community, Tong renounces sin and professes his new faith.

3. The celebrant then baptizes Tong, pouring water over his head three times while saying, "Tong, I baptize you in the name of the Father, and of the Son, and of the Holy Spirit."

4. The celebrant anoints Tong on the head with chrism. This anointing is a sign that through the sacraments of Baptism and Confirmation, the Holy Spirit will strengthen Tong as he begins his life as a follower of Jesus.

5. Then the celebrant prays for Tong as his godparents give him a white garment to wear—a sign of his dignity as a follower of Jesus. The garment also symbolizes the new life that Tong is called to live in Jesus.

6. Mr. and Mrs. Nelson, Tong's godparents, light a candle from the Paschal candle and give it to Tong. The lighted candle symbolizes that the risen Christ will be with this new Christian as a light and guide throughout his life. Then everyone sings a hymn.

Activity

With your family's help, fill in these facts about your own Baptism.

CERTIFICATE

Date of Baptism: _____

Church of Baptism: _____

City: _____

Baptizing Minister: _____

Godparents: _____

Activity

The young people below are from countries around the world. Read their ideas about what it means to them to be baptized Christians. Then paste or draw a picture of yourself. Share with your classmates what being a baptized Christian means to you.

◄ My name is Akins. I live in Nigeria. My family and I were baptized last year. We have always believed in God, but we are very happy to belong to Jesus. Now I have lots of brothers and sisters all over the world. I like that!

▲ My name is Ramon. I'm from the Philippines. My family is Christian. My faith is important to me, but it's not easy to live as peacefully as Jesus wants us to live. If you have brothers and sisters, you know what I mean!

▲ My name is Sasha and I live in Russia with my mom and dad. We are Christians. Life is sometimes hard. Maybe it sounds corny but I'm glad that Jesus is a part of my life. I can always tell him what's bothering me. I know that he cares about me because other Christians show me his love all the time. I'm glad to belong to the Christian community.

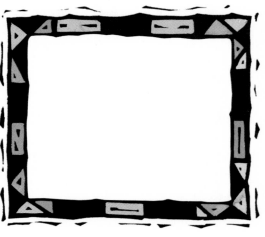

My name is _____

and I live in _____.

UNITED IN JESUS

Each one of you is a child of God because of your faith in Jesus. Everyone who has been baptized into Christ has been united with him. It does not matter whether you are male or female, a slave or free person, a Jew or a Greek. You are all one in Christ Jesus.

Based on Galatians 3:26–28

Through the sacrament of Baptism we are united with every other baptized person throughout the world. We may look different. We may speak different languages. We may belong to different Christian traditions. But we are one in Jesus.

Our Baptismal Call

As baptized Catholics, we have a special call to live as members of Christ's body, the Church. By our words and actions, we show that we are part of the body of Christ, and we bring Christ into the world. Through the anointing with chrism at Baptism, we share in the priesthood of Jesus and his **mission:** the ministry of service and healing, the ministry of teaching, and the ministry of prayer. At Baptism, we received the life of the Holy Spirit. The Holy Spirit helps us imitate Jesus in our words and actions.

In the Scriptures, Jesus tells us, "You are the light of the world. Your light must shine so that everyone will give praise to God in heaven" (based on Matthew 5:14–15).

Activity

Put a ✔ in front of three things that you will try to do to let your light shine as a follower of Jesus.

_____ I will try to go to Mass more often.

_____ I will try to be more patient with my brothers and sisters.

_____ I will try to be less selfish with my time and my things.

_____ I will try to pray every day.

_____ I will try to cooperate at home and at school.

Vocabulary

mission: a sending or being sent out with authority to perform a special service

◆ ◆ ◆ ◆ ◆ ◆ ◆ ◆ ◆ ◆ ◆

PRAYING OUR BAPTISMAL PROMISES

When we were baptized, our parents or godparents spoke the promises of Baptism for us. Now we are able to speak for ourselves. Let us respond with the words *I do* to each of these questions.

Leader: Do you believe in God, the Father almighty, creator of heaven and earth?
All: I do.

Leader: Do you believe in Jesus Christ, his only Son, our Lord, who was born of the Virgin Mary, was crucified, died, and was buried, rose from the dead, and is now seated at the right hand of the Father?
All: I do.

Leader: Do you believe in the Holy Spirit, the holy catholic Church, the communion of saints, the forgiveness of sins, the resurrection of the body, and life everlasting?
All: I do.

Leader: This is our faith. This is the faith of the Church. We are proud to profess it, in Christ Jesus our Lord. Amen.

Rite of Baptism for Children

Chapter Review

Find four words in the word box below that relate to Baptism. Write each word and its meaning in the sacrament of Baptism in the space provided.

lighted candle	wine	black robe	bread
chrism	water	white garment	chalice

Word	Meaning in Baptism
1. _____ _____	1. _____ _____ _____
2. _____	2. _____ _____ _____
3. _____	3. _____ _____ _____
4. _____ _____	4. _____ _____ _____

Fill in the answers to the first two questions.

1. What is *Baptism*?_____
   _____
   _____

2. What does Baptism celebrate?_____
   _____

3. Discuss how we can more faithfully live out our baptismal promises.

> **You are fellow citizens of the saints and members of the household of God.**
> **Ephesians 2:19**

CONFIRMATION IS A SACRAMENT OF THE HOLY SPIRIT

What is one thing you do that might help lead people to recognize you as a Catholic?

TAKING ANOTHER BIG STEP

"Why do I have to do that?" Mark objected. "Peter has always done the chores after school."

"Mark," his mother responded. "You know it's time for us to begin spring planting. Your dad needs Peter in the fields. We feel you are old enough now to take over Peter's responsibilities for the afternoon chores."

"But I want to play on the soccer team," Mark insisted. "And practice starts right after school."

"I did it when I was your age," Peter observed. "I played soccer. I was also in the school play. *And* I did the chores."

There was a moment of silence as the family continued their meal. Mr. Hoffman broke the silence. "Mark, you know how much work there is on the farm when we begin planting. I need Peter in the fields with me after school. And besides, he's getting ready for **Confirmation**. He's taking on new responsibilities himself. Your mom and I need you to be responsible for the chores after school. You can still practice for the soccer team."

Mark knew his dad was right. He actually felt a twinge of pride that his parents trusted him with these new responsibilities. Yet he was still a little angry.

"Why does Peter always get to do what he wants?" he argued. "Now you let him drive the tractor. I never get to do what I want."

"Mark, that's not true, and it's not fair," his mother said. "Your dad and I let you do almost everything you need or want to do. You have rights, too. We know that. Now, you two, it's time to get your homework done."

THE PRESENCE OF THE SPIRIT

Confirmation is another sacrament of initiation into the Church. For those who became brothers and sisters of Jesus at Baptism, the gift of the Spirit is sealed or confirmed in the sacrament of Confirmation. Confirmation celebrates the presence of the Holy Spirit in the Church and in our lives.

The Holy Spirit is the third person of the **Trinity**, the one God who is Father, Son, and Holy Spirit. The Holy Spirit renews God's power within us. We are empowered to grow in our faith and to witness to what we believe as Catholics.

In the sacrament of Confirmation we receive the seven gifts of the Holy Spirit. The gifts of the Spirit are given to us to help us grow as Catholic Christians. The seven gifts are *wisdom, understanding, knowledge, right judgment, courage, reverence, and wonder and awe.*

Wisdom helps us look upon life as a great and remarkable gift from God.

Understanding helps us grasp the meaning of what we believe and act in ways that show that our Christian faith makes a difference.

Knowledge helps us to be certain that God cares for us.

Right judgment helps us see right and good choices to make from among the many choices we make each day.

Courage gives us God's own strength to help us be strong in our beliefs as Christians.

Reverence helps us to honor God as most loving Creator and to treat all people as our brothers and sisters.

Wonder and awe in God's presence helps us respect the goodness and majesty of God. This gift helps us to be grateful to God for the gift of life and encourages us to praise God.

Vocabulary

Confirmation: a sacrament of initiation in which we become fuller members of the Church and in which the Holy Spirit makes us stronger to live and share our faith in Jesus

Trinity: the one God who is Father, Son, and Holy Spirit

We Believe

Confirmation is another sacrament of initiation into the Church. Confirmation celebrates the Christian's growing experience of the Holy Spirit. At Confirmation the Christian is called to grow in faith and to witness to Jesus.

SYMBOLS OF THE HOLY SPIRIT

Symbols help us think about the Holy Spirit and about how the Spirit acts in our lives. Wind, breath, and fire are common symbols of the Holy Spirit.

Wind calls to mind freedom, power, and movement or action. We cannot see the wind, but we can feel its effects. Wind brings a change, the gentle breeze of spring or the gusty gale of winter. Wind blows where it will.

Breath suggests life. The Scriptures tell us in the Book of Genesis that God breathed life into the first human being.

Fire warms us, helps us cook, and provides us with light. Fire is attractive and people tend to gather around it. It sometimes provides a beacon to those who are seeking the way.

Activity

How do the symbols of wind, breath, and fire tell you what the Holy Spirit is like and how the Spirit acts in our lives?

Wind calls to mind the Holy Spirit because _____
_____.

Breath calls to mind the Holy Spirit because _____
_____.

Fire calls to mind the Holy Spirit because _____
_____.

THE SIGNS OF CONFIRMATION

Anointing with chrism and laying on of hands in the sacrament of Confirmation are powerful signs of Jesus' presence in the sacrament. What it means to live and love as Jesus is brought to life in these two signs.

Anointing with Chrism

Anointing with chrism is a special sacramental sign in Confirmation. This tradition, like the laying on of hands, is very old. In ancient Israel the practice had many meanings. Its religious meaning was to signify that a person was being set apart from others and given a special mission. Through our anointing with holy chrism in Baptism and in Confirmation, we share in the mission of Jesus and we are called Christians. Anointing is a sign that tells us we are to become Jesus for others. The use of oil, or chrism, suggests healing, strength, ease of movement, energy, and joy.

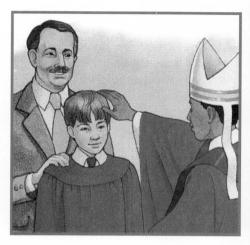

Laying On of Hands

Laying on of hands is an ancient gesture. Both the Old Testament and the New Testament Scriptures tell that the laying on of hands was used when a person was dedicated to God for a certain task. At Confirmation, the laying on of hands signifies that the power of the Holy Spirit is given to each candidate. It is also a sign of the handing over of Christian traditions, rights, and responsibilities to the newly confirmed person.

Activity

1. Anointing with chrism in the sacrament of Confirmation is a sign that we are now called to be a sign of Jesus' presence for others. How can you be a sign of Jesus' presence for others?

   _____

   _____

2. Laying on of hands in the sacrament of Confirmation is a sign that the power of the Holy Spirit is given to the person being confirmed. How do you think the Holy Spirit will empower you to live more like Jesus when you are confirmed?

   _____

   _____

THE SACRAMENT OF CONFIRMATION

It is the night of their Confirmation. Peter and the other six members of his Confirmation class are very excited and a little nervous. For the past two years they have been studying and praying in preparation for this celebration. Now they are saying publicly that they are prepared to accept greater responsibilities as followers of Jesus.

Bishop Arnold has come from Dubuque to celebrate with them. Peter is reading a passage from the Acts of the Apostles.

"It was the feast of Pentecost. Jesus' disciples were gathered together in a house in Jerusalem. Suddenly they heard a noise like a strong, driving wind. It seemed to fill the whole house. Tongues of fire appeared and came to rest above each of Jesus' friends. All the disciples were filled with the Holy Spirit. They began to speak in foreign languages. They bravely said whatever the Spirit urged them to say. The Word of the Lord."

Based on Acts: 2:1–4

1. After Bishop Arnold finishes his homily, he asks Peter and the six other candidates for Confirmation to renew their baptismal promises made for them at their Baptism.

2. Bishop Arnold and Father Lewis, pastor of Saint Martin Parish, extend their hands over Peter and the others who are to be confirmed. This gesture is called the laying on of hands, and as he does so, the bishop prays, "Send your Holy Spirit upon them to be their Helper and Guide."

3. Bishop Arnold pours chrism—perfumed oil that has been blessed—into a small bowl. Peter and Mr. Kurt, his sponsor, walk up to the bishop. Mr. Kurt places his right hand on Peter's shoulder and tells the bishop that Peter has chosen "John" as his Confirmation name.

4. Bishop Arnold dips his right thumb in the chrism and then makes the Sign of the Cross on Peter's forehead with his thumb, and says, "John, be sealed with the Gift of the Holy Spirit." Peter John responds, "Amen!"

5. After the Confirmation rite, the Mass continues. Peter and his six newly-confirmed companions bring the gifts of bread and wine to the altar.

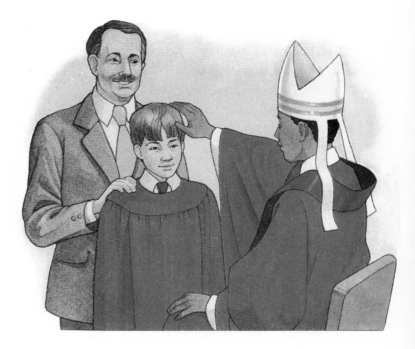

Activity

At Confirmation, the renewal of baptismal promises gives us an opportunity to say aloud what we believe. Think about what you believe about God, Jesus, and the Holy Spirit. Write your beliefs on the lines provided.

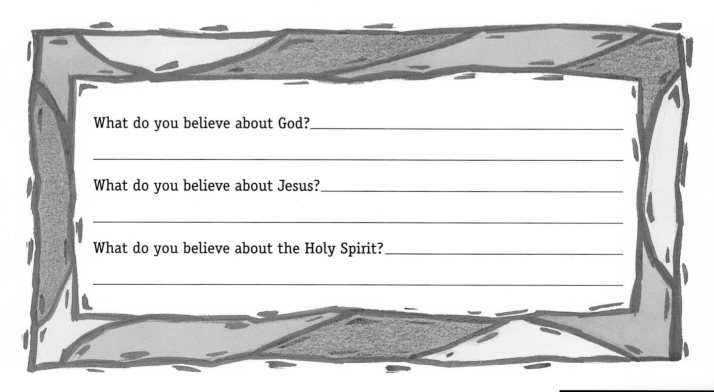

What do you believe about God?_____

_____

What do you believe about Jesus?_____

_____

What do you believe about the Holy Spirit?_____

_____

A MODERN WITNESS FOR CHRIST

All who are confirmed are called to witness to their faith in Jesus by living according to his teachings and example.

Jean Donovan grew up in the suburbs of the United States. She loved life and had almost anything a young girl could want. She especially loved to ride horses. She studied hard and enjoyed traveling.

As a young woman, Jean was very successful. She had a good job and an apartment of her own. She owned a car and a motorcycle. She had many friends. However, she felt something missing in her life. Jean felt that Jesus wanted her to do more for him and for others. She went to Cleveland and began doing volunteer work for the Catholic Church.

One day, Jean saw a story about the sufferings of people in El Salvador, a country in Central America. A civil war was going on there. She learned that volunteers were needed to help the people in the midst of so much suffering. She decided that she would go to El Salvador.

Once there, she sometimes wondered why she gave up such a comfortable life in the United States. Everywhere in El Salvador, Jean saw people who were very poor and very frightened. They had no jobs, no decent homes, no new clothes, no good food. Most of all they had little hope that things would change.

Jean reached out to help the people of El Salvador and quickly came to love them. She learned much about life and about God from those people.

Jean knew that her life was in danger because of her work with the poor. She was often afraid. Two friends were killed outside her home. Her family, her friends, and her boyfriend kept writing to her, asking her to leave El Salvador before she, too, was killed.

Jean was happy that so many people cared about her, but she felt God wanted her to be in El Salvador. She believed that Christ called her to share her faith and love with the poor and suffering.

So she stayed on. She worked hard to change the situations that kept people poor.

Enemies of the poor decided to stop Jean's good work. On December 2, 1980, about ten o'clock at night, they shot Jean Donovan and her three companions. She was twenty-seven years old when she died, a witness for Christ.

FRUITS OF THE HOLY SPIRIT

We give witness to our faith in Christ Jesus by the way we live. The risen Jesus gives us the Holy Spirit to be our helper, our strength, and our guide. The signs of the Spirit's presence in our lives are called the fruits of the Holy Spirit. They are love, joy, peace, patience, kindness, generosity, faithfulness, gentleness, and self-control.

Based on Galatians 5:22–23

Activity

The fruits of the Holy Spirit are life-giving qualities that help us to become the persons God calls us to be. Look carefully at the fruits of the Holy Spirit listed on this page. Then answer the following questions.

1. Which of the fruits of the Holy Spirit do you find most noticeable in Jean Donovan's life?

   _____

2. Which fruits of the Holy Spirit do you feel you demonstrate well?

   _____

   _____

3. What is one thing you do to demonstrate each of the fruits of the Holy Spirit that you listed above?

   _____

   _____

   _____

4. Which of the fruits of the Holy Spirit do you need to demonstrate better?

   _____

   _____

   What is one thing you could do to grow in that sign of the Spirit of Christ?

   _____

   _____

love

gentleness

peace

kindness

patience

generosity

faithfulness

JOY

self-control

PRAYING TO THE HOLY SPIRIT

We pray to the Holy Spirit to help us become aware of the effects of the Spirit's presence in our lives. Create your own prayer to the Holy Spirit by completing the outline below. Remember to pray your prayer often.

Holy Spirit, help me to know your life-giving qualities and to live them each day. With your help,

I can be more loving when _____

_____.

I can be more joyful when _____

_____.

I can be more peaceful when _____

_____.

I can be more patient when _____

_____.

I can be kinder when _____

_____.

I can show your goodness when _____

_____.

I can be more faithful when _____

_____.

I can be more gentle when _____

_____.

I can use more self-control when _____

_____.

Come, Holy Spirit, and fill my heart. Amen.

Chapter Review

Six parts of the Confirmation celebration are listed below. Show the order in which they occur by numbering them from 1 through 6.

peace greeting

_____

renewal of baptismal promises

_____

sponsor presents the candidate by name

_____

anointing with chrism

_____

laying on of hands

_____

pastor presents the candidates to the bishop

_____

Fill in the answers to the first two questions.

1. What is *Confirmation*?

_____

_____

_____

_____

2. What is the Christian called to do at Confirmation?

_____

_____

3. Discuss how you can be a better witness to Christ.

When you receive the Holy Spirit, you will be filled with power to witness for me.
Based on Acts 1:8

16

THE EUCHARIST IS A SACRAMENT OF UNITY AND LOVE

Tell of a time when you did something with people who love you that made you feel even closer and more united.

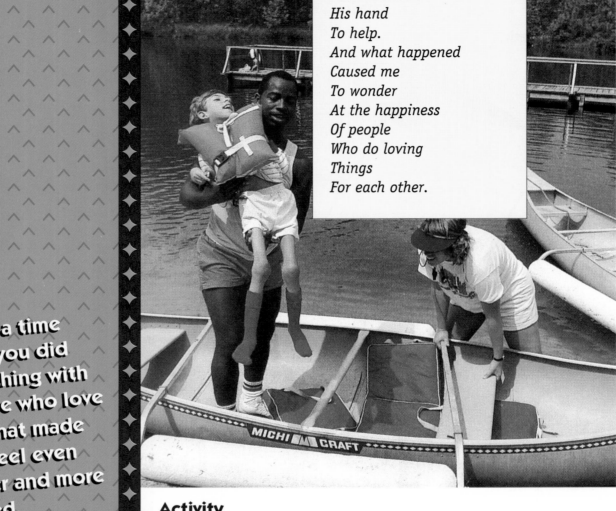

He Reached Out His Hand
He reached out
His hand
To help.
And what happened
Caused me
To wonder
At the happiness
Of people
Who do loving
Things
For each other.

Activity

Think about the poem and photograph on this page. Write about a time when someone reached out and helped you or invited you to join him or her.

_____

_____

_____

HUMAN HUNGERS

Every human being hungers for many different things. When we are physically hungry, we give our bodies food and water to keep them healthy and to give us energy. But we need much more than food and water to be healthy. We need to be loved and wanted. We need to be comforted when we are sad. We need to be forgiven when we have hurt someone. All of these needs are hungers that people of all ages share.

Activity

Think about what kinds of things you hunger for. Then complete the statements.

When I'm lonely, I hunger for_____.

When I'm unhappy, I hunger for_____.

When I'm scared, I hunger for_____.

When I'm discouraged, I hunger for_____.

When I'm sorry, I hunger for_____.

When I'm ignored, I hunger for_____.

When I'm confused, I hunger for_____.

When I'm sad, I hunger for_____.

Hungry for Eucharist

Jesus understands the hungers of every human person. While he lived on the earth, Jesus filled many human hungers. He knew that people were hungry for forgiveness and healing as well as for love and friendship. Jesus also knew that people were hungry for a close friendship with him. Jesus gives himself to us in the Eucharist. We call him the Bread of Life because Jesus in the Eucharist can fill our deepest hungers for all that Jesus is: life, love, peace, forgiveness, and unity.

food

clothing

shelter

love

forgiveness

happiness

peace

compassion

freedom

joy

friendship

SACRAMENT OF UNITY AND LOVE

The **Eucharist** is another sacrament of initiation into the Church. It is a celebration of our unity with each other and with the risen Christ. The Eucharist is an invitation to love Jesus and one another even more. The Mass recalls the Last Supper. The Mass begins as people gather together as a community, greet one another, ask forgiveness for whatever has disrupted their unity with Jesus and with one another, and pray for God's help. The people themselves are a sign to one another of the presence of the risen Christ, uniting them with Jesus and with one another. The **presider**, or the priest leading the eucharistic celebration, is another sign of the presence of Jesus. The Eucharist is sometimes referred to as the Holy Sacrifice of the Mass because it celebrates the sacrifice of Jesus when he gave his life for us on the cross.

Lectors proclaim God's word in the Scripture readings and the priest interprets the readings in a homily. God's word, calling the Church to unity and love, is also a sign of the presence of Christ.

Gathered around the altar, the priest and people bring gifts of bread and wine so that the bread and wine may become the Body and Blood of Jesus Christ. They remember the Last Supper and Jesus' death and resurrection, and offer themselves to God with Jesus. Then they celebrate the breaking of the bread to become more united with Jesus and with one another. The Eucharist is Jesus' real presence with his people.

The priest brings the Mass to a close, blessing the people and sending them back to their homes and to the world to love and serve God and others. The Church, by its unity and love, is to become a sign of the healing, comforting, challenging presence of Jesus in the world.

Activity

Jesus is present to us in four specific ways when we gather for Eucharist. Name them here.

1. _____
   _____
2. _____
   _____
3. _____
   _____
4. _____
   _____

The Last Supper (artist unknown), Courtesy of the S.M.A. Fathers.

THE LORD'S SUPPER

I received from the Lord what I have handed on to you, that the Lord Jesus on the night before he died, took bread, and, after he had given thanks, broke it and said, "This is my body that I give up for you. Whenever you do this, remember me."

In the same way he took the cup and said, "This cup is the new covenant in my blood. Do this, as often as you drink it, in remembrance of me."

For each time you eat this bread and drink this cup, you proclaim the death of the Lord until he comes.

Based on 1 Corinthians 11:23–26

Signs of the Sacrament of the Eucharist

Bread and wine, for Jesus and the people of his time, were a kind of food and drink commonly found in most households. Jesus chose to give himself to us under the appearances of bread and wine.

Catholics believe that after the presider blesses the bread and wine and prays the prayers of **consecration** over them, Jesus becomes really present in them. Although the Body and Blood of Jesus still look like bread and wine, they are no longer bread and wine but rather Jesus, who fills all our hungers.

Activity

At the last supper Jesus told his followers to remember him. When you are at Mass, what do you remember about Jesus?

1. _____

    _____

2. _____

    _____

3. _____

    _____

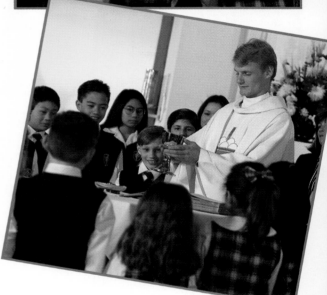

Vocabulary

consecration: prayer and action by which bread and wine become the Body and Blood of Jesus

◆◆◆◆◆◆◆◆◆◆◆◆

THE MASS: A CALL TO SERVE

When we gather to share the Eucharist with the Catholic community, we often say that we gather for Mass. The word *Mass* comes from the Latin word "missa," which means "dismissed" or "sent forth." During the concluding rite of the Mass, the presider tells the community, "Go in peace to love and serve the Lord." He is sending us out into the world. We are challenged to bring with us what we have heard and what we have received.

In the Eucharist, Jesus gives us himself as God's living Word in the Scriptures and as food in the Eucharist. Just as Jesus speaks to us and feeds us, he reaches out to meet the needs of the world. One way Jesus reaches out to those in need is through us.

By our sharing in the Eucharist, we are sent forth to bring Jesus to the world. We continue his mission by teaching others about him, by spending time in prayer, and by serving those in need. Because we share in the Body and Blood of Christ, we bring him to everyone we meet.

Activity

Think about the ways in which you can bring Jesus to others after receiving him in the Eucharist. Write about them here.

_____

_____

_____

_____

_____

_____

_____

_____

_____

A Prayer to Christ in the Eucharist

Lord, Jesus Christ, we worship you living among us in the sacrament of your body and blood.

May we offer to our Father in heaven a solemn pledge of undivided love.

May we offer to our brothers and sisters a life poured out in loving service of that kingdom where you live with the Father and the Holy Spirit, one God, for ever and ever. Amen

From Feast of the Body and Blood of Christ

THE BLESSED SACRAMENT

Another way our Catholic community honors Jesus in the Eucharist is by worshipping him in the **Blessed Sacrament**. This is the name we give to the Eucharist that is kept in the **tabernacle**. The tabernacle is a special container that can be found either in the daily chapel or off to the side of the area where the Mass is celebrated. Although worshipping Jesus in the Blessed Sacrament is important, receiving the Eucharist at Mass is the Church's most important way of honoring Jesus.

Activity

The Eucharist calls us to be united with all people everywhere. Describe what you think unity in Jesus is like.

_____
_____
_____

_____
_____

_____
_____

_____
_____

_____
_____

Vocabulary

Blessed Sacrament: the Eucharist kept in the tabernacle as a continuing sacrament of Christ's presence with us

tabernacle: the special container in church where the Blessed Sacrament is kept

◆ ◆ ◆ ◆ ◆ ◆ ◆ ◆ ◆ ◆

Praying About Service and Unity

Leader: Jesus gives himself to us in the Eucharist and we are challenged to give ourselves to others through service to one another. Let us prepare our hearts for prayer by listening carefully to a reading from one of Paul's letters to the Church at Corinth.

Reader: We give thanks for the cup of blessing, which is a sharing in the blood of Christ. And the bread that we break is a sharing in the body of Christ. Because the loaf of bread is one, we, though many, are one body because we all share that one loaf.

(Based on 1 Corinthians 10:16-17)

Leader: We share in the one bread, who is Jesus, the Bread of Life.

All: Help us, Jesus, to share our bread with the hungry.

Leader: We share in one cup, who is Jesus, who poured out his life for all people.

All: Help us, Jesus, to pour out our talents and gifts in service to others so that they will come to know you and us.

Leader: We who are many are one body, who is Jesus, the One sent by God.

All: Help us, Jesus, to be one with all Christians so that the unity you came to bring will be a visible sign to others of the same unity you share with God, the Father and the Holy Spirit.

Leader: Jesus, we thank you for hearing our prayer. May we always live lives of service, united with all who love you.

All: Amen.

Chapter Review

Find five words in the word box below that relate to the Eucharist. Write each word and its meaning in the sacrament of the Eucharist on the lines provided.

| presider | chrism | water | sending forth |
| bread and wine | consecration | tabernacle | laying on of hands |

Word	Meaning in the Eucharist
1. _____	1. _____
	_____
2. _____	2. _____
	_____
3. _____	3. _____
	_____
4. _____	4. _____
	_____
5. _____	5. _____
	_____

Fill in the answers to the first two questions.

1. What is the *Blessed Sacrament*?

_____

_____

_____

2. What does Christ do for us in the Eucharist?

_____

_____

_____

Because there is one bread, we who are many are one body, for we all eat of the one bread.

Based on 1 Corinthians 10:17

3. Discuss how the Eucharist makes a difference in the way you live your life.

UNIT 4 ORGANIZER

Sacraments of Initiation

Each picture below stands for a chapter in this unit. Complete the sentences about that chapter on the lines provided.

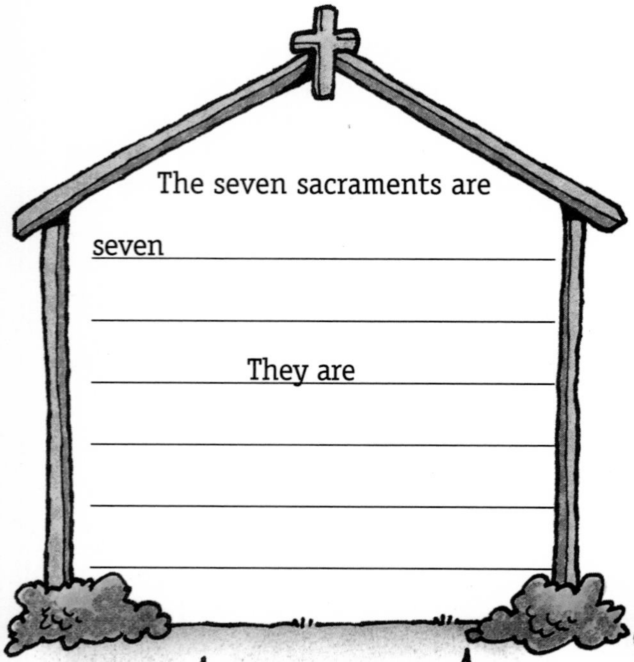

The seven sacraments are

seven ______________________

____

______________ They are ______________

____

____

____

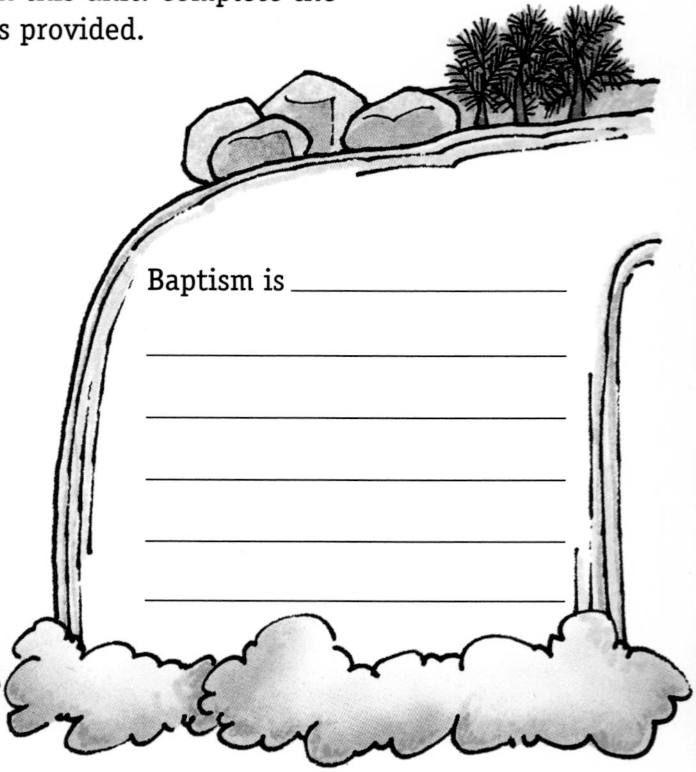

Baptism is ______________________

____

____

____

____

____

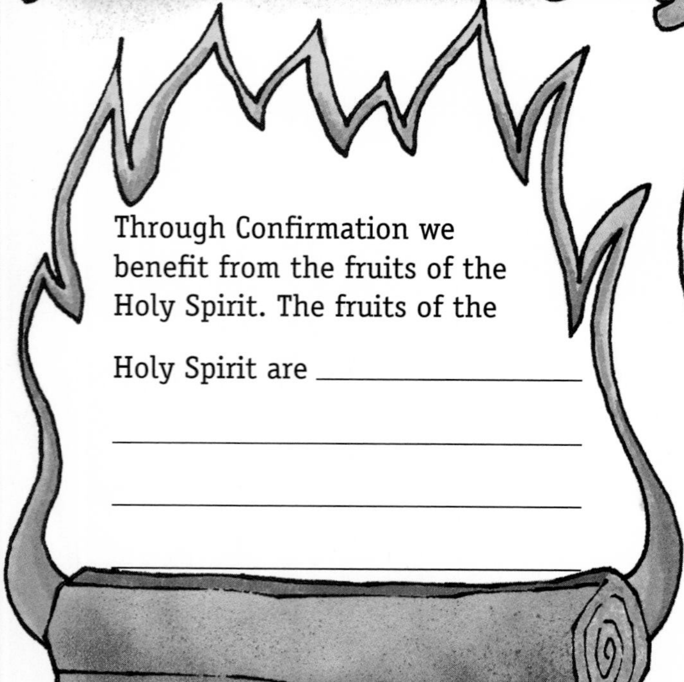

Through Confirmation we benefit from the fruits of the Holy Spirit. The fruits of the

Holy Spirit are ______________________

____

____

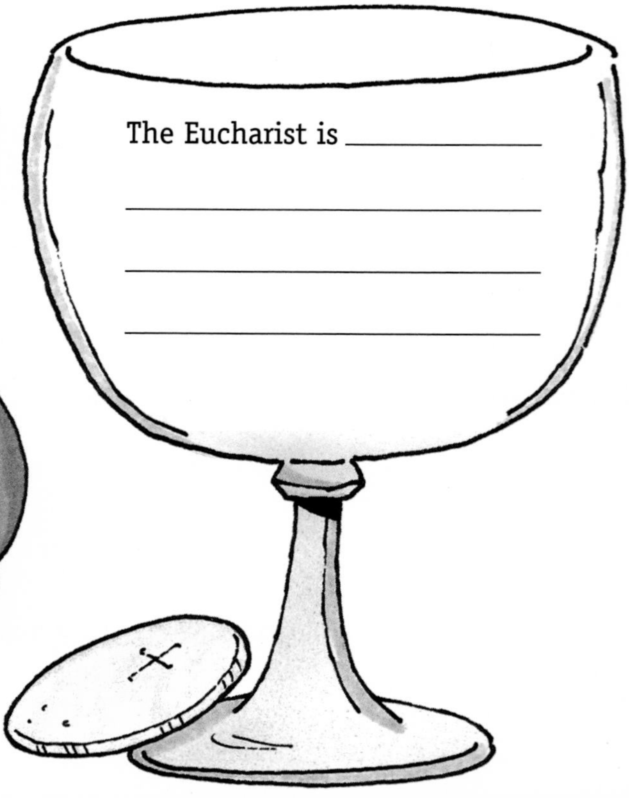

The Eucharist is ______________________

____

____

____

UNIT 4 REVIEW

Answer the following questions.

1. What is meant by the term *seven sacraments*?

_____

_____

2. What are the names of the seven sacraments?

_____

_____

3. What are the three sacraments of initiation?

_____

4. What are two sacraments of healing?

_____

5. What are the two sacraments of commitment?

_____

Write the words that best complete each sentence.

chrism	initiation	members	Christ	welcome

1. Through Baptism, Christ and his Church welcome new _____ into the community of faith.

2. Baptism is one of the sacraments of _____.

3. The lighted candle is a sign that _____ is with the new Christian as a light and guide along the journey of life.

4. The newly baptized person is anointed with perfumed oil called _____.

5. Baptism is also known as the sacrament of _____.

UNIT 4 REVIEW

Use the words in the word box to fill in the acrostic puzzle.

| Pentecost | sacrament | faith | initiation | fire | bishop |
| oil | Spirit | wind | breath | witness | Confirmation |

— — — — — C — — —

O — —

— N — — — — — — —

— — — F — — — — — — —

— I — —

— R — — —

— — — — — M — — —

— A — — —

— — — — T —

— I — —

— — — — O —

— — — N — — —

Match Column A with Column B.

Column A

1. During the Last Supper,

2. One of the sacraments of initiation

3. In the Eucharist, Jesus gives us himself

4. God's word, calling the Church to unity and love, is

5. By sharing in the Body and Blood of Jesus,

Column B

———— as food for life.

———— we bring him to everyone we meet.

———— a sign of the real presence of Christ.

———— Jesus took bread, blessed and broke it, and gave it to his friends.

———— is Holy Eucharist.

BEING a PEACEMAKER WITH MY FAMILY

Reconciliation is a sacrament of forgiveness. Forgiveness brings peace where there is hurt. As peacemakers, we are called by Jesus to forgive those who have hurt us and to ask forgiveness of those we may have hurt.

Some hurts such as cuts, sprains, and broken bones are physical; others are emotional and occur on the inside of the person. Our feelings are hurt when someone says or does something that makes us feel badly. When we use important peacemaking words such as "I'm sorry" and "It's okay, I understand," we are signs of Jesus' love. Acts of reconciliation are not always easy to do. Reconciling may be the most challenging part of our call to be peacemakers.

Activity

Read the following stories. Write responses for the characters in each story. Use words that encourage forgiveness and a sense of peace.

Josh and Mike are brothers. Josh is ten and Mike is seven. Each seems to get a lot of enjoyment from teasing the other. Today has been a long, rainy day, and both boys are bored. Several arguments, usually sparked by teasing, have taken place between the brothers. Now Josh says something that really hurts Mike's feelings, and Mike bursts into tears. Josh realizes he's gone too far and feels badly.

What should Josh say to Mike? Write some words that might bring peace to Josh's relationship with Mike.

_____

Let's assume that Josh has told Mike that he is sorry. How might Mike respond to Josh's apology?

_____

What do you think needs to happen next?

_____

_____

ichelle arrives home from school, excited about the plans she has made to go to the movies with her friends on Saturday. When her mother gets home from work, Michelle tells her about the plans. Unfortunately, her mother doesn't agree with the plans and tells Michelle that she will have to miss out on the activity. She reminds Michelle that she was counting on her help with her younger brother, Tommy. Tommy's friends are coming to play that day. Michelle is angry and shouts at her mother, "You never let me do anything that I want to do. I always have to take care of Tommy." Michelle then runs to her room and slams the door.

What is causing the disagreement between Michelle and her mother?

_____

_____

Who needs to ask forgiveness in this story?

_____

What might Michelle's mother say to Michelle?

_____

What do you think needs to happen next?

_____

3

POINTS TO REMEMBER

A sincere apology

- includes thoughtful words.
- uses a pleasant tone of voice.
- is followed by a change in behavior by those who have been hurtful.

Following Jesus

We follow Jesus when we offer words of forgiveness to those who have hurt us. Forgiving isn't an easy thing to do, particularly when the hurt is still very much a part of us. Yet, as peacemakers, we are called to let go of our hurt. As followers of Jesus we trust that Jesus is with us and will give us strength.

PRAYER

Jesus, I know you are with me as I struggle to let go of hurt feelings and to be open to the experience of your peace and love. Help me to forgive those who have hurt me. Amen.

OPENING DOORS

A Take-Home Magazine™

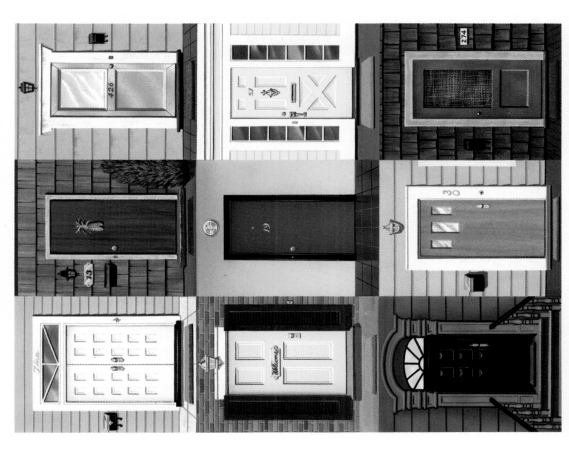

THIS IS OUR FAITH

Growing Closer

USE THE ILLUSTRATION on this page as a model for a welcome wreath for your family. Place it on one of the doors which everyone uses frequently. Hang a pen close by, too, so it will always be available. For the next week, ask all family members to write on slips of paper words that express love and concern obvious in your home. Have them tape the slips to the wreath. At the end of the week, discuss how the love experienced in your home can be shown to all your relatives, family friends, and neighbors.

Looking Ahead

Your child will also learn about the sacraments of vocation, Holy Orders and Marriage, or Matrimony. These sacraments involve a lifelong commitment of love or service in the Christian community.

New Life

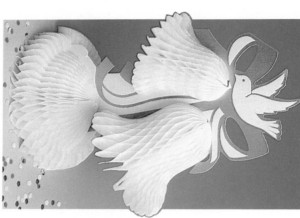

Do you remember 4 A.M. feedings and diaper duty at all times of the night and day? Do you also remember the goos and giggles, the delight in baby's first rolls, crawls and steps, and the angelic look of a sleeping infant? A new baby brings new life and a new way of living into a home. A baby changes things not only for Mom and Dad but also for your entire family.

Also, how will you feel when your son or daughter brings home a very special young man or woman to meet? You'll probably be a little nervous yourself, anxious to make a good impression, and you'll go out of your way to make him or her feel comfortable and welcome. A wedding in the family brings new life and new ways of doing things.

The third step, the illumination, is a period of immediate preparation for the sacraments of initiation. This step usually takes place during Lent and culminates in the reception of Baptism, Confirmation, and Eucharist (in that order) at the Easter Vigil service. This change from former practice restores the original way the early Church welcomed new members.

The last step, the *mystagogia* (a word that means "teaching of the mysteries"), takes place between Easter and Pentecost. During this time, the new Catholics participate fully in the life of the parish. They experience community and give service. This last step stresses that conversion in faith is a lifelong process, something that does not end with Baptism.

Under the guidelines of the RCIA, every Catholic shares the responsibility of preparing, educating, and welcoming the new Catholics. Every Catholic is also called to ongoing growth in faith and friendship with Jesus and the other members of the community.

Brothers and Sisters in Christ

A new baby or a new son or daughter-in-law can make us more loving, more patient, more open, more accepting, more hospitable. New members in the parish family can do that, too. Whether they have just joined the Church or have moved into the city, newcomers to a parish are like new members in a family.

Instead of thinking of your children as your children, sometimes try to think of them as fellow Christians, your brothers and sisters in Christ. Through Baptism and Eucharist, they are building a faith relationship with Christ that deserves to be recognized, respected and nurtured.

What Exactly Is the RCIA???

First and foremost the RCIA is a community process, a journey of faith. Together with members of the parish, converts embark on a journey toward Church membership. This journey includes the following four steps:

In the first step, the pre–catechumenate, the person has a chance to listen to God's word in Scripture and to ask questions about the Church and its teachings. This is a time of inquiry, of finding out more about the Church and what it means to live as a Catholic.

In the second step, the catechumenate, catechumens (as they are now called) are joined by sponsors from the parish, who serve as guides and companions in faith. This step may last several months to three years. During this time, the catechumens study the Catholic faith, join the community in prayer and worship, and begin to participate in parish activities.

A Time of Learning

The initiation of catechumens is a gradual process that takes place within the community of the faithful. By joining the catechumens in reflecting on the value of the mystery and by renewing their own conversion, the faithful provide an example that will help the catechumens to obey the Holy Spirit more generously. (Rite of Christian Initiation of Adults).

The entire parish community shares in the richness of the process of preparing adults for initiation into the Church through the sacraments of Baptism, Confirmation and Eucharist. In the not-too-distant past, a person who wanted to become a Catholic was privately instructed and received into the Church. However, such practices have changed since 1964, when the bishops of Vatican II reinstated the adult *catechumenate* (a word that means "time of learning"). Today the process of a person becoming Catholic is called the Rite of Christian Initiation of Adults (RCIA). All dioceses were required to implement the RCIA by September 1, 1989.

On the opposite page, are the reactions of parishioners who have just witnessed the Rite for Sending when candidates and catechumens are formally enrolled in the "book of the elect" and chosen for sacramental initiation in the Catholic Church. The parishioners were interviewed during the hospitality hour after the 10:00 A.M. Mass at Saint James Parish. The parish community has participated in the RCIA process for six years.

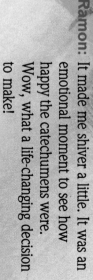

Roger: I've noticed a big difference in the parish since we started the RCIA. Those of us who have come to the 10:00 o'clock Mass for years are more open and welcoming. More people are involved in planning to make Sunday Eucharist a special occasion.

Audrey: Every week, I feel a little pull when the catechumens leave the church after the Prayer of the Faithful. I can hardly wait for the Easter Vigil when they will finally participate fully in the celebration of the Eucharist.

Ramon: It made me shiver a little. It was an emotional moment to see how happy the catechumens were. Wow, what a life-changing decision to make!

Jenny: I think having the RCIA group at Mass with us helps me appreciate what I have and what I'm doing here every Sunday.

Dan: It brought me back to the three years ago when I was catechumen. So many people were supportive. I do what I can now to help. I tell everyone I know what a great experience it is to participate in the RCIA process.

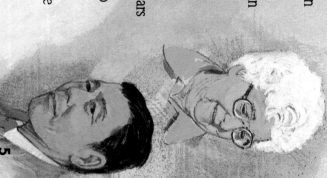

UNIT 5

SACRAMENTS OF HEALING AND COMMITMENT

Has someone helped you heal after an injury or illness?

RECONCILIATION IS A SACRAMENT OF FORGIVENESS

Activity

Study the picture story. Imagine what might be happening. Then write whatever you think each person could be saying.

_____

_____

_____

_____

Tell about a time when someone hurt you and you forgave him or her.

Jesus Passes on the Spirit of Reconciliation

On the evening of the day Jesus rose from the dead, his disciples were together in a locked room. They were afraid that Jesus' enemies might attack them, too.

Suddenly, Jesus was there with them. "Peace be with you," he said. He showed them his hands and his side. His friends were overjoyed to be with Jesus again.

"Peace be with you," Jesus said a second time. "As the Father has sent me, so I send you."

He breathed on them and said, "Receive the Holy Spirit. If you forgive people's sins, they are forgiven."

Based on John 20:19–23

The Challenge of Reconciliation

The act of **reconciliation** involves making up with someone and being at peace. Reconciliation means to forgive someone for having hurt us, and it means to ask forgiveness when we have hurt someone else.

It is from Jesus that we receive the challenge of reconciliation. Jesus teaches us in the gospel story on this page that the only way to be at peace is to be reconciled with one another through forgiveness.

Activity

Below is a situation in which reconciliation is needed. On the lines provided, tell how you think the boys can be reconciled with one another.

Duane and James are best friends. Duane invited James to go to the movies with him and his family on Saturday. James was very happy about the invitation and said that he would like to go with them. In the meantime, James's other friend, Adam, asked James to go skating with him on Saturday. James decided to go skating with Adam instead of going to the movies with Duane. Duane was very hurt and disappointed.

Vocabulary

reconciliation: making up with someone through sorrow and forgiveness

✖ ✖ ✖ ✖ ✖ ✖ ✖ ✖ ✖ ✖ ✖ ✖

To be reconciled, we must first have a change of heart. Here is a gospel story about how one man had a change of heart because of his new friendship with Jesus.

ZACCHAEUS HAS A CHANGE OF HEART

Jesus entered Jericho and was passing through it. A man was there whose name was Zacchaeus. He was a chief tax collector and a wealthy man. He was trying to see who Jesus was, but the man was very short, and the crowd was very large. So he ran ahead and climbed a sycamore tree to see Jesus, because Jesus was going to pass that way.

When Jesus came to the place, he looked up and said to him, "Zacchaeus, hurry down. I want to stay at your house today."

So Zacchaeus hurried down and was happy to welcome Jesus to his home. All who saw this began to grumble, complaining, "Jesus has gone to be the guest of one who is a sinner."

Zacchaeus was as surprised as everyone else that Jesus should want to come to his house. He said to Jesus, "I will give half of everything I own to the poor, Lord. And if I have cheated anyone, I will pay that person back four times as much as what I stole."

Jesus said to Zacchaeus, "Today salvation has come to your house. I have come to save those who are lost."

Based on Luke 19:1–10

CALLED TO CONVERSION

Just as Zacchaeus experienced a change of heart, or **conversion**, we are also called to turn away from our selfish ways of living and turn back to God. It is Jesus who forgives us and heals us when we are sorry for being selfish and unkind.

In the sacrament of Reconciliation, Catholics have a special way of celebrating a change of heart and receiving the forgiveness and peace of Jesus. Through the sacrament of Reconciliation, the Church continues to share in Jesus' mission to forgive, to heal, to reconcile, and to call all people to conversion and peace. Reconciliation is one of the sacraments of healing.

Activity

Write an ending that shows a change of heart, or conversion, for each situation listed below.

1. Trisha made false statements to Jessica about one of their friends.

_____

_____

_____

_____

2. Bob took a baseball card from Mario's prized collection.

_____

_____

_____

_____

3. Alex spent the change from the store without his parents' permission.

_____

_____

_____

_____

Vocabulary

conversion: to turn away from our selfish ways and turn back to God

✕ ✕ ✕ ✕ ✕ ✕ ✕ ✕ ✕ ✕ ✕ ✕

Activity

Consider how important forgiveness and reconciliation are in your life. Complete the sentences below as honestly as you can.

1. When someone hurts me, the first thing I want to do is _____

_____.

2. Being hurt feels like _____

_____.

3. Usually I forgive someone who hurts me by _____

_____.

4. Forgiving someone feels like _____

_____.

5. Being forgiven feels like _____

_____.

6. I participate in the sacrament of Reconciliation because _____

_____.

You Must Forgive Others

"As I have loved you, in the same way, then, you must love one another" (based on John 13:34).

With those words, Jesus passes on to every Christian the command to love others in the same way that he loves us. Part of loving others as we are loved is through forgiveness.

And how does Jesus forgive us? Jesus forgives us completely. Jesus forgives us without limit. Jesus forgives us each time we ask forgiveness.

Jesus' disciples were trying to understand the way that Jesus was asking them to forgive, and so one day they asked him, "How often must we forgive someone who has hurt us? Seven times?" Jesus answered them by saying, "Not seven times, but rather seventy times seven times" (based on Matthew 18:22). The disciples were amazed because to them "seventy times seven" meant a number so large that it couldn't be counted.

Activity

We forgive one another in many different ways. Look at the people in the photographs below. What seems to be happening? How can forgiveness be shown in each situation? On the lines provided, write about how forgiveness and reconciliation can take place.

_____

_____

_____

_____

_____

_____

_____

_____

_____

THE SACRAMENT OF RECONCILIATION

Through the sacrament of Reconciliation, the Church continues to carry on the ministry of forgiveness that Jesus entrusted to his followers. The risen Jesus continues to forgive our sins through the power of the Holy Spirit. The sacrament of Reconciliation celebrates Christ's forgiveness and our sorrow for sin. Our most symbolic actions and words in the celebration of this sacrament concern being sorry for our sins, confessing them, and doing the penance the priest gives us.

The important symbolic actions, as well as words we use, help us understand the meaning of this sacrament.

- After examining our conscience, we go to the reconciliation room. Approaching the priest is itself a sign of sorrow. The priest's welcome is a sign of Jesus' eagerness to forgive.

- Telling the priest our sins is another sign of our sorrow and willingness to change. We **sin** when we make a free decision to do what we know is wrong or when we fail to do what we know is right. We tell the priest our sins because the priest represents Jesus and the Christian community. Our sins hurt the whole community.

A **mortal sin**, a very serious refusal to follow the teachings of Jesus, turns us away from God. There are three conditions that make a sin mortal: the act must be seriously wrong, we must know that the act is seriously wrong, and we must make a free choice to commit the sin. Mortal sins must be confessed. A **venial sin** is a less serious act of selfishness; this type of sin weakens our relationship with God. Even when we sin, God's mercy and love never leave us.

- The priest listens and gives us a penance. The penance is usually some prayer or action related to what we have confessed. Accepting the penance is another sign of our sorrow and our desire to grow in God's love.

- Then we express our sorrow in the words of a prayer called the Act of Contrition. Included in the Act of Contrition is a firm purpose of amendment—our sincere intention to try not to sin again.

- The priest places his hands over our heads. He says the words of **absolution**, the prayer and declaration of forgiveness for sins. It is a prayerful act of forgiving. The priest's absolution is the sign that makes Christ's forgiveness real. It is also a sign that the Church, the community we have hurt, forgives us, too.

Vocabulary

sin: a free decision to do what we know is wrong or not to do something we know is right

mortal sin: a very serious refusal to follow the teachings of Jesus, one which turns us away from God

venial sin: a less serious act of selfishness, one which weakens our relationship with God

absolution: the prayer and declaration of forgiveness for sins prayed by the priest in the sacrament of Reconciliation

✖ ✖ ✖ ✖ ✖ ✖ ✖ ✖ ✖ ✖ ✖ ✖

We Believe

The sacrament of Penance or Reconciliation is one of the sacraments of healing. Penance is a sacrament of our sorrow and God's forgiveness. The risen Jesus brings us God's mercy through the Church, which the priest represents.

PRAYING FOR A CHANGE OF HEART

Leader: Help us to have a change of heart.
    All: Lord, hear our prayer.

Leader: Help us to forgive others for having hurt us.
    All: Lord, hear our prayer.

Leader: Help us to turn away from our selfish living and to turn back to you.
    All: Lord, hear our prayer.

Leader: Help us to love others in the same way that Jesus loves us.
    All: Lord, hear our prayer.

Leader: Quietly reflect on someone you would like the Lord to help you forgive. *(pause)*
    All: Lord, hear our prayer.

Leader: Help us to be reconciled with one another through forgiveness.
    All: Lord, hear our prayer.

Leader: Let us now pray together the Act of Contrition.

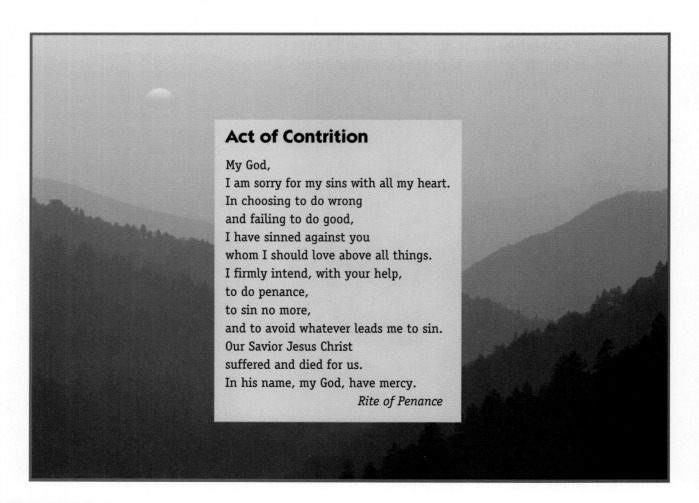

Act of Contrition

My God,
I am sorry for my sins with all my heart.
In choosing to do wrong
and failing to do good,
I have sinned against you
whom I should love above all things.
I firmly intend, with your help,
to do penance,
to sin no more,
and to avoid whatever leads me to sin.
Our Savior Jesus Christ
suffered and died for us.
In his name, my God, have mercy.

Rite of Penance

Chapter Review

Solve the puzzle to review words that apply to reconciliation.

Across

1. What most leads to hurting others
3. Another word for making up
8. Another word for sorrow
10. What we give to someone who has hurt us and is sorry

Down

1. What we feel when we wish we had not hurt someone
2. What the priest tells us to do to make up for our sins
4. Our inner ability to judge right and wrong
5. The words the priest says in bringing us Christ's forgiveness
6. Telling our sins to the priest
7. Choosing to act selfishly
9. What God feels for sinners

Fill in the answers to the first two questions.

1. What is meant by *sin*?

   _____

   _____

   _____

2. What are the three most symbolic actions of someone celebrating the sacrament of Reconciliation?

   _____

   _____

   _____

3. Discuss how you can make up with those you have hurt or who have hurt you.

> **Merciful and gracious is the Lord, slow to anger and abounding in kindness.**
> Psalm 103:8

18

ANOINTING OF THE SICK IS A SACRAMENT OF HEALING

Have you—or has anyone in your family—been seriously ill or injured? What happened?

A HEALING PRESENCE

Molly was very sick. For almost a week she had a high fever.

"I hurt all over," she told her mother. "What's wrong with me?"

Dr. Flynn examined Molly. He gave her medicines. Molly stayed in bed, but nothing seemed to help.

The next day, Molly felt even worse. She was afraid. Her mother called Dr. Flynn.

"Take her to the hospital right away," he directed. "I'll be there in half an hour."

"Let me go with you and Molly," her brother Tom begged. His mother explained that she and Molly might have to stay overnight in the hospital and it would be better if he stayed home with his Grandpa.

On the way to the hospital, Molly began to cry. "I'm scared," she told her mother.

Dr. Flynn called in other doctors. They were not sure what was wrong with Molly. Molly felt worse and worse.

"Your daughter is very sick," Dr. Flynn told Molly's mother. "We're doing everything we can."

Molly's mother called Father Malovetz. He came to the hospital, anointed Molly, and prayed with her. Afterward, Molly seemed to be calmer and soon fell asleep.

All night, Molly's mother sat by the bed. She held Molly's hand and wiped her face with cool cloths. And she prayed.

As the sun began to lighten the darkness, Molly was sleeping peacefully. "Now she'll be all right," her mother thought to herself hopefully.

Dr. Flynn came by early and examined Molly. "She's better," he told her mom.

Just then the phone rang. It was Tom. "How's Molly?" he asked anxiously.

"She's still very sick," his mother answered, "but Dr. Flynn says she's better. I'm sure she'd like it if you made her a get-well card. You can bring it over to the hospital at lunch time."

Discuss

1. Do you think that Molly's mother helped Molly get well?

2. Who else in the story helped Molly get well?

3. How do you think Molly's brother felt when Molly was sick?

4. What do you want most when you are sick?

5. What can you do for someone who is sick?

THE HEALING PRESENCE OF JESUS

We experience the healing presence of Jesus in many ways and through many people. From the beginning of the Church, we have cared for one another and continued the healing ministry.

We who are Catholics celebrate Jesus' healing presence when we celebrate one of the seven sacraments, Anointing of the Sick. Anointing of the Sick is another sacrament of healing. Jesus sometimes brings physical or emotional healing through this sacrament. He *always* brings love, strength, and support to the sick person.

THE EARLY CHRISTIANS CARED FOR THE SICK

Much of what takes place in the sacrament of Anointing of the Sick is described in the Letter of James. In your Bible, read James 5:14–16.

The following Scripture play is fictional. It puts into dialogue what James is teaching us about how we as Christians should care for the sick among us. Now read this play with your class.

Narrator: It is about A.D. 38. The presbyters of the Christian community are gathered at Miriam's house, discussing how they can better serve the needs of their community.

James: We've gathered here to discuss how we can better serve the members of this Christian community. My dear friends, what are some of the needs you see in our group?

Miriam: I've noticed that some members of our group don't always have enough to eat nor do they have enough clothes to wear. Some are even living in our streets. We cannot allow our brothers and sisters in Jesus to have so little. We must share what we have with them.

James: Miriam, you have brought up important needs in our community. Before we find solutions, let me ask if anyone else has a concern to put before our leaders.

Benjamin: Yes, James. My mother-in-law is very ill, and my neighbor's child is sick, too. There are many members of our community who are elderly and frail. The Lord Jesus always

showed special care for those who were sick or weak. He healed many of them of their illnesses and many from their fears. He gave them courage and hope. Then his apostles were given the gift of healing so that Jesus' healing power would continue to touch his people. What can we do for those who are sick?

James: You are right to care about the sick, Benjamin. This is what we should do: Those who are sick among us should call for us, the presbyters of the Church. We should pray over them, lay our hands on them in the name of the Lord Jesus and the entire Christian community, and anoint them with oil. Then this prayer prayed in faith will strengthen the one who is ill, and the Lord will restore the person to health. If the person has committed any sins, the person's sins will be forgiven.

Benjamin: I will take the responsibility of telling the community about our plan for carrying on Jesus' healing. But first, my friends, come home with me and anoint and pray over my mother-in-law and my neighbor's daughter.

Narrator: The presbyters finished their meeting and then walked to the home of Benjamin to anoint the sick.

Signs of Anointing of the Sick

In the early days of the Church, special signs were used to bring the healing presence of Jesus to those who were sick. Today the Church still uses the same signs to show to the sick that Jesus is present to them and wants to heal them.

- **Anointing with oil** in this sacrament is a sign of the Holy Spirit, of strength, and of health. Jesus' disciples anointed sick people with oil and cured many of them.

- **The laying on of hands** in this sacrament is a sign of the healing touch of Jesus and the sharing of the Holy Spirit. This action is also a sign of the care of God and the Church for whoever is sick.

JESUS HEALS A SICK BOY

One day a man came and knelt before Jesus. "Lord," he pleaded, "take pity on my child. He suffers strange seizures. Sometimes he falls into the fire or water. He could be killed. Even your disciples could not help him."

"Bring the boy to me," Jesus told the man.

Jesus felt sorry for the boy. He gave a command, and immediately the sick boy was cured.

When Jesus was alone, his disciples went to him. They wanted to know why they could not cure the child.

Jesus said "If your faith is no larger than a mustard seed, you could tell this mountain, 'Move from here to here,' and it will move. Everything will be possible for you."

Based on Matthew 17:14–21

THE SACRAMENT OF ANOINTING OF THE SICK

The sacrament of Anointing of the Sick may be celebrated anywhere. It is sometimes celebrated in a hospital or at home, where family members can be present. An ideal time and place for this sacrament is during the celebration of the Eucharist. When Anointing of the Sick is celebrated at a parish Mass, many people are usually anointed. Some people may be seriously ill. Others may be preparing for surgery or they may be suffering from a lifelong illness.

The important symbolic actions and words of Anointing of the Sick can help us understand the meaning of this sacrament.

- The coming of the priest to visit the person who is sick is a symbol of the Church's concern for the sick. So, too, is the gathering of family and friends around the sick person. They all pray for the one who is suffering.

- The priest places his hands on the head of the sick person. The priest then anoints the sick person on the forehead and on the hands with blessed oil. As he anoints the sick person, he prays these words.

> Through this holy anointing
> may the Lord in his love and mercy help you
> with the grace of the Holy Spirit.
>
> May the Lord who frees you from sin
> save you and raise you up.
>
> *Pastoral Care of the Sick: Rites of Anointing and Viaticum*

- After the anointing with oil, the priest prays to the risen Jesus. He prays for three things for the person who is sick: (1) the easing of suffering, with strength to cope with it; (2) the physical healing of mind and body; and (3) the forgiveness of sins. Everyone present then prays The Lord's Prayer together. The person who is sick may receive the Eucharist. The Eucharist given when a person is in danger of dying is called **Viaticum**. The word *viaticum* means "food for the journey."

Vocabulary

Viaticum: the Eucharist given to a person in danger of dying

✖ ✖ ✖ ✖ ✖ ✖ ✖ ✖ ✖ ✖ ✖

We Believe

Anointing of the Sick is another sacrament of healing. It celebrates Christ's healing presence in our lives. Through this sacrament the risen Jesus also reaches out to bring strength, healing, and forgiveness to people who are ill.

Activity

Unscramble these words to discover some of the many people who work to help those who are sick. Then write something each person does to care for those who are sick.

1. SURNE _____

_____

_____

2. RATPEN _____

_____

_____

3. STIRPE _____

_____

_____

4. TOCROD _____

_____

_____

5. ASCIMTRAPH _____

_____

_____

6. RAPTSITHER _____

_____

_____

CALLED TO BE HEALERS

Jesus had great compassion for those who were sick. He taught this same compassion to his disciples. The Church continues to teach the compassion of Jesus today. Not everyone can be a doctor, a nurse, or a priest, but all followers of Jesus are called to be compassionate healers.

Christians can be healers in many ways. We can comfort those who are ill by visiting them or sending them get-well cards. We can give of our time to help someone in our family who is sick. We can also show our compassion by being sensitive to people who are suffering from emotional problems by encouraging them with kind words or by simply being a good friend to them. Another important way to bring healing into the lives of others is by praying for them. Our prayers can bring the healing presence of Jesus to others.

NEEDING TO BE HEALED

At different times in our lives, we all need healing. This has always been true. In the Bible, there are stories of Jesus healing people who came or were brought to him. Jesus continues to heal through people who help us when we are sick and suffering. We can't always change what is happening to us but with Jesus' help and the help of others we can accept our suffering. Catholics believe that when we are physically or emotionally sick, or when we suffer from loneliness, discouragement, or prejudice, Jesus is always near us in our suffering.

The Church has many formal prayers for use with those who are sick. Read the prayer below which is from *The Rites of the Catholic Church*. This prayer is suggested to be prayed with a child who is ill.

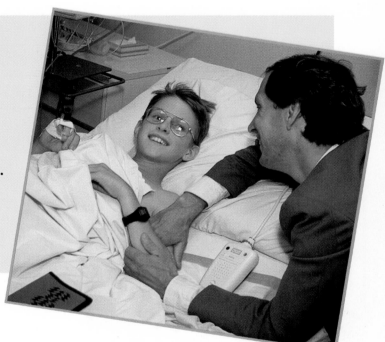

God of love,
ever caring
ever strong,
stand by us in our time of need.
Watch over your child (N.) who is sick,
look after him/her in every danger,
and grant him/her your healing and peace.
We ask this in the name of Jesus the Lord.
Amen.

Pastoral Care of the Sick: Visits to a Sick Child

Activity

Write a short prayer in your own words for someone you know, or someone you have heard or read about, who is sick.

_____

_____

_____

_____

_____

_____

PRAYING FOR HEALING AND FOR HEALERS

Teacher: Lord Jesus, we come to you now with our prayers for those who need healing and for those whose entire lives are devoted to healing others.

Leader #1: Lord, give your strength to those who need the comfort of your healing presence, especially to

_____ .
(*Name*)

Help them to _____

_____

_____

_____ .

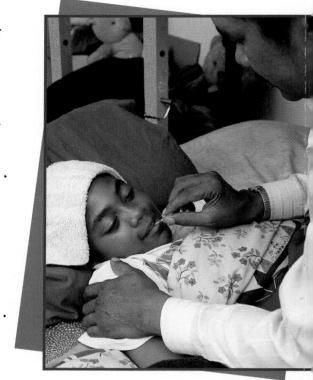

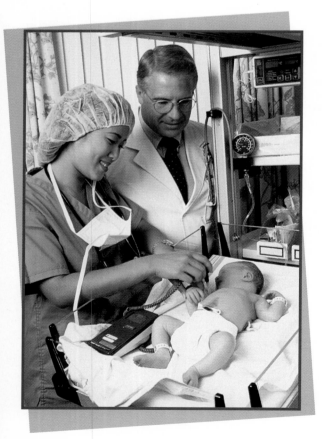

Leader #2: Lord, give your strength to those whose entire lives are devoted to healing others, especially to

_____ .
(*Name*)

Help them to _____

_____

_____

_____ .

Teacher: We ask our prayers in the name of Jesus, who is our Healer.

All: Amen.

Chapter Review

Turn back to pages 224 and 225. Reread the Scripture play. Compare the actions described in the play with Anointing of the Sick as we know it today. List three things that are the same.

1. _____

_____

2. _____

_____

_____

3. _____

In the sacrament of Anointing of the Sick, the priest prays three main blessings for the sick person. What are the three blessings?

1. _____

_____

2. _____

3. _____

◆◆◆◆◆◆◆◆◆◆◆◆◆◆◆◆◆◆◆◆◆

Fill in the answers to the first two questions.

1. What is *Viaticum*?

_____

_____

2. What can sick or elderly people hope for in celebrating the sacrament of Anointing of the Sick?

_____

_____

3. Discuss what you can do for people who are sick.

I, the LORD, am your healer.
Exodus 15:26

HOLY ORDERS IS A SACRAMENT OF COMMITMENT

Activity

Think of any group or community to which you belong. Pretend that you have to select a leader for your group. What qualities would you look for in a leader? What would you want a leader to do for the group? Make two lists under the headings below.

Leadership Qualities

_____

_____

_____

_____

Leadership Responsibilities

_____

_____

_____

_____

Tell about a time when you were chosen to lead a group or an activity.

Jesus knew that the communities of believers would need leaders to serve all the needs of the members.

JESUS SELECTS LEADERS

Jesus chose a group of special followers. He taught them and sent them out to preach his good news. He wanted them to help the sick and to teach people his way of happiness (Mark 6:7–13). He wanted them to forgive sinners as he had (John 20:23). He wanted them to baptize people and make them his disciples (Matthew 28:19). He told them to celebrate in his memory the special meal he left them (Luke 22:14–20). He chose Peter to strengthen and support the others (John 21:15–17).

Activity

Reread the paragraph above to determine some of the ministries that Jesus asked of his followers. Then complete each sentence below.

1. In Mark 6:7–13, Jesus asked his special followers to serve others by

   _____.

2. In John 20:23, Jesus asked his special followers to serve others by

   _____.

3. In Luke 22:14–20, Jesus told his followers to

   _____.

4. In John 21:15–17, Jesus told Peter to

   _____.

Ordained to Special Service

Jesus chose some of his followers to serve the others in special ways. Catholics believe the risen Jesus continues to call some members of the Church to a special service of leadership to the community. These members serve by helping people carry out the mission of Jesus in the world. We know them as bishops, priests, and **deacons**. They are **ordained** in the sacrament of Holy Orders to lifelong service to the Catholic Church.

The word *deacon* comes from a Greek word that means "to serve." When a deacon is ordained, he is ordained to specific responsibilities of service. Deacons are ordained to baptize, to witness marriages, to preach, and to conduct funerals. They cannot, however, lead the community celebration of the Mass, Anointing of the Sick, or Holy Orders. They are not able to confirm, or give absolution in the sacrament of Reconciliation. A deacon can either be married or unmarried.

A priest is ordained as the leader of worship for the Christian community. He also serves in a wide variety of ministries in the Church. In the Roman Catholic Church, the priest, like the bishop, remains unmarried.

A bishop is ordained to be the chief teacher and leader of his diocese. As the bishop of Rome, the pope is the head of all the bishops and the leader of all Catholics.

Discuss

Look at these three photographs. Then tell how the ordained minister in each photo is carrying out his special role of leadership and service.

POPE JOHN PAUL II

Karol Wojtyla grew up in a small town in Poland. When Karol was nine years old, his mother died, so his father raised him. Karol was an energetic, likable boy, who loved sports. His favorite sport was soccer. He also liked to ski. However, life was not all play for him. As a teenager he had to go to work to help his father support the family.

He decided to become an actor, but the war put an end to his acting classes. He went to work in a chemical factory. At the time, enemy soldiers occupied Poland. The people in Karol's country were no longer free.

Karol and his friends tried to improve conditions for the factory workers. They met secretly, planning ways to resist the enemy. They risked great danger each time they met.

During this time, Karol decided to become a priest instead of an actor. He had to study in secret until after the war. He was ordained a priest in Krakow, Poland, on November 1, 1946. Then he studied in Rome.

After his studies he returned to Poland. The young priest preached Christ's message, celebrated the sacraments, taught, and wrote books. He did all that he could to help the poor, especially the factory workers.

The pope named Father Wojtyla a bishop. As a bishop he stood up for the rights of all people. He was a leader among the bishops during the Second Vatican Council in Rome.

In 1978, Bishop Wojtyla was elected pope. He took the name John Paul II. No pope has traveled as much as he has to unite and strengthen the Church all over the world. Pope John Paul II has risked his life to travel to places where Catholics are suffering most. During his travels he speaks out everywhere against injustice, always taking the side of the poor. His life shows us what the sacrament of Holy Orders is all about.

Vocabulary

deacon: a person ordained to assist in the ministry by preaching, baptizing, distributing the Eucharist, visiting the sick, and witnessing marriages

ordain: to give someone the special role and dignity of bishop, priest, or deacon

✖ ✖ ✖ ✖ ✖ ✖ ✖ ✖ ✖ ✖ ✖ ✖

We Believe

Holy Orders is a sacrament of special service and commitment to the community. Bishops, priests, and deacons are ordained to preach and teach, to celebrate the sacraments, and to build up the community of Christ's Church.

Activity

Complete the sentences below with the names of Church leaders.

1. Our pope is _____.

2. Our bishop is _____.

3. Our pastor is _____.

4. Other priests in our parish are _____

_____

_____

_____.

5. Deacons in our parish are _____

_____

_____

_____.

THE SACRAMENT OF HOLY ORDERS

Ordination, or the celebration of the sacrament of Holy Orders, always takes place during a Mass. The families and friends of those to be ordained gather with the bishop and several other priests to celebrate this sacrament.

After the Liturgy of the Word, each person to be ordained a priest kneels before the bishop. The bishop places his hands on the head of each one. The laying on of hands is a sign that the bishop shares his special ministry with the new priests.

Then the bishop extends his hands over those being ordained and prays that God will help them live up to their special ministry of leadership.

The priests who are assisting the bishop help the new priests with their **vestments**—the **stole** and **chasuble**.

The bishop then anoints with chrism the palms of the hands of each new priest. This is a sign that the Holy Spirit is with them to help the new priests in their special role in the Church.

Then the bishop presents the new priests with the community's gifts for the Eucharist—the bread on a paten, or plate, and the wine and water in a chalice. The new priests go to the altar and, with the bishop, lead the gathered community for the first time in the concelebration of the Liturgy of the Eucharist.

Activity

Some of the things that bishops, priests, and deacons do are found in the word box below. They are also hidden in the word puzzle. Find the twelve hidden words and circle them. You may circle across or up and down.

pray	encourage	bury
ordain	forgive	organize
confirm	teach	anoint
baptize	counsel	bless

```
P R A Y X Q O R D A I N
L I R Z E S B U R Y R K
A T E A C H U A K U R E
B A P T I Z E P T C U N
E A F Y C Q U T I C M C
A N O R O H E I N O M O
N U R M U N A Z E F O U
O R G A N I Z E L I R R
I N I W S V A I L R N A
N U V A E X A L I M O G
T E E B L E S S N A V E
```

Vocabulary

vestments: the special clothes that symbolize the various ministries of those who are ordained

stole: a narrow strip of cloth worn by bishops, priests, and deacons as a sign of their service to the community

chasuble: a garment worn by bishops and priests during the Mass

✗ ✗ ✗ ✗ ✗ ✗ ✗ ✗ ✗ ✗ ✗ ✗

The body is one and has many members. But even though the body has many members, we are all one body, and so it is with Jesus Christ. It was in one Spirit that we were baptized into the one body.

Now the body is not one member, it is many members. If the foot would say, "Because I am not a hand, I do not belong to the body," that would not make it any less a part of the body. If all were a single member, where would the body be?

God has made the body so that all members may be concerned for one another. If one member suffers, all suffer together. If one member is honored, all rejoice together.

You, then, are the body of Christ, and every one of you is a member of it.

Based on 1 Corinthians 12:12–14, 26–27

Sharers in Christ's Priesthood

Through the sacrament of Holy Orders, some members become ministers to the community in special ways. They are our priests, bishops, and deacons. They promise to spend their lives in loving service to the Church. We who are the Church, the Body of Christ, support them and work with them.

By our Baptism, we are all sharers in Christ's priesthood. We are not ordained ministers, but we are called to share God's word, to celebrate the sacraments, and to pray. We are also called to serve the Church according to the talents and gifts that God has blessed us with.

Activity

The photographs below show Catholic Christians using their unique talents and gifts in service to the Christian community. On the lines provided, tell how the community in each photograph is being served.

_____

_____

_____

_____

_____

_____

_____

_____

_____

Now think about your talents and gifts. As a fifth grader, how can you use some or all of your talents to serve your parish community?

_____

_____

As an adult, how might you be able to serve your parish community?

_____

_____

PRAYING FOR CHURCH LEADERS

Complete this prayer by writing in the names of the
Church leaders and the special help you ask of God for
each leader. Include in your list some leaders in your
parish who are not ordained.

I pray for our pope, _____,

that _____.

I pray for our bishop, _____,

that _____.

I pray for our pastor, _____,

that _____.

I pray for other priests or deacons, _____,

that _____.

I pray for _____,

that _____.

I pray for _____,

that _____.

I pray for _____,

that _____.

God, I thank you for calling us to share in the mission and
priesthood of your Son, Jesus. Help us to do what we can do
best to serve others and to continue Jesus' work in the world.
Amen.

Chapter Review

Some of the sentences below are true. Others are not. Put a ✔ in front of each true statement. Correct any false sentences by rewriting them on the lines provided.

_____ **1.** All who are baptized and confirmed share in the ministry and priesthood of Jesus.

_____ **2.** Priests are ordained by a deacon.

_____ **3.** A chasuble is the oil that is used to anoint the new priest.

_____ **4.** The stole is a narrow strip of cloth placed around the neck of a new priest.

_____

_____

_____

Complete the sentences below.

1. _____ is one sign of the sacrament of Holy Orders. In this sacrament, the sign means

_____

_____ .

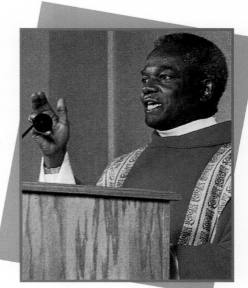

2. _____ is another sign of the sacrament of Holy Orders. In this sacrament the sign means

_____

_____ .

Fill in the answers to the first two questions.

1. What is the meaning of *ordination*?

_____

_____ .

2. What are bishops, priests, and deacons ordained to do?

Whoever wants to rank first among you must serve the needs of all.
Mark 10:44

_____

_____ .

3. Discuss how you as a fifth grader can serve others.

MARRIAGE IS A SACRAMENT OF LOVE

BEST FRIENDS

"Tomorrow's Saturday!" Tom said happily. He was walking home from school with his friend, Michael.

"That means we can work on our boat!" Michael said, excited at the thought of working with Tom on their model boat.

"I'll call you right after breakfast," Tom said as they came to the corner where they had to split up.

Tom ran the rest of the way home. His dad was parking his car in front of the house just as Tom arrived.

"Hi, Dad!" Tom called out. "Michael's coming over in the morning. We're going to work on our boat."

"You and Michael are getting to be good friends, aren't you?" his dad observed. "What do you like about Michael? Why is he your best friend?"

Tom was a bit puzzled. He knew he liked Michael, but he found it hard to put into words. "I don't know," Tom hesitated. "We like doing things together, I guess. He tells me things he can't tell anyone else. I don't know—we're just friends."

"Who's your best friend, Dad?" Tom asked.

His dad smiled. "Your mom. She's been my best friend for the last twenty years!"

Just then Tom's mother came home. She kissed Tom and his dad.

What would you say if someone were to ask you to finish the sentence "A friend is . . ."?

Qualities of Friendship

What makes you and another person best friends? Perhaps you like to do some of the same things, and doing them together makes them even more fun. Perhaps you admire talents in each other. You probably respect each other, too. If one of you does something that hurts the other, you can forgive each other and forget the hurt.

With true friends, all of this is possible because the two of you bring out the very best qualities in each other. This kind of friendship is truly special, and usually it is just that—a special friendship between two people. But sometimes it can become the basis for the love and friendship that develops into the lifelong relationship between a man and a woman that we call marriage.

Activity

Think about YOU. What qualities do you have that make you a good friend?
Write an advertisement that promotes you as a good friend to someone who needs one.

JESUS ENJOYS A WEDDING

Jesus was invited to a wedding in the town of Cana. His mother, Mary, was there, too.

Everybody seemed to be enjoying the party. Then they ran out of wine.

"They have no more wine," Mary mentioned to Jesus. She told the servants to do whatever Jesus told them.

"Fill those jars with water," Jesus told them, pointing to six large stone jars. The servants quickly filled each of them to the brim.

"Take some to the waiter in charge," Jesus instructed the servants.

The headwaiter tasted it. It was wine. He had no idea where they had found more wine. He shared it with the groom. "Most people serve their best wine first, but you have saved the best wine until now!"

Based on John 2:1–11

A Sign of God's Covenant of Love

Jesus began his ministry at the wedding feast in Cana, a village not far from Nazareth. For Jesus, marriage was not only a sign of love between a man and a woman. For him, and for devout Jews then and now, marriage was and is a sign of God's **covenant** of love with his people. After Jesus' resurrection, his followers came to see marriage as a sign of the bond of love between the risen Jesus and the Church. That is why Catholics believe that Marriage, or **Matrimony**, is a sacrament.

Marriage is a sacrament of love and commitment. The sacrament of Marriage is a celebration of the commitment of a lifelong love made between a man and a woman. It is a sacrament of love that God shares with them. The sacrament of Matrimony symbolizes the love Jesus has for the Church.

Activity

Use the words in the word box to complete Paul's thoughts about marriage, which he wrote to the Church at Ephesus. Some of the words need to be used more than once.

Church	same	love
Christ	husbands	wife
wives	respect	husband
care	himself	loves

"Husbands, love your _____, in the _____ way that _____ loves the _____. In the same way, _____ should love their _____ as they love their own bodies. He who _____ his _____ loves himself. Just as Christ cares for the _____, husbands and wives must _____ for one another. Each one of you must _____ his wife as he loves _____ and a wife must _____ her _____."

Based on Ephesians 5:25, 29

Vocabulary

covenant: an agreement or a contract between two people or groups

Matrimony: another name for the sacrament of Marriage, in which a man and a woman promise to love one another for the rest of their lives as husband and wife

✖ ✖ ✖ ✖ ✖ ✖ ✖ ✖ ✖ ✖ ✖

We Believe

Marriage is a sacrament of lifelong love. Marriage is a sign of God's love for his people and Christ's love for the Church.

Activity

Think about a wedding that you have attended, heard about, or read about. Or, ask a family member about a wedding he or she has attended. Then answer the questions below.

1. Who was married?

   _____

2. What was most memorable about the ceremony?

   _____

   _____

THE SACRAMENT OF MATRIMONY

The sacrament of Marriage is normally celebrated during Mass. In the Liturgy of the Word, we hear of God's love for us and his call for us to love one another. In the Liturgy of the Eucharist, we celebrate the bond of love, the covenant between God and us.

■ The woman and man stand before the priest and the whole gathering. They join their hands. They give themselves totally to each other for life with these words, or words that are similar.

> "I, (Name), take you, (Name), to be my (wife or husband). I promise to be true to you in good times and in bad, in sickness and in health. I will love you and honor you all the days of my life."
>
> *Rite of Marriage*

These words, called the exchange of **vows**, or promises, are the most important part of the sacramental celebration and one of the signs of the sacrament. They express the covenant, or bond, of love between the husband and wife. The man and woman being married are the ministers of the sacrament. The priest is present as the official witness to their marriage.

The Holy Spirit, the Spirit of Love, will help and guide them as they try to be faithful to their promise of lifelong love.

■ Then the couple place wedding rings on each other's fingers. The rings are another sign of the sacrament of Matrimony, expressing the bond of love and faithfulness between the husband and the wife. The rings also tell others that the two are married.

■ After The Lord's Prayer, the priest faces the bride and groom who join hands again. The priest extends his hands over the couple. He prays that God will bless them and keep them together in love. This blessing is called the **nuptial blessing.**

■ The couple usually receive the Eucharist. Jesus gives himself to them just as they have given themselves to each other. He is with them to help them live together in a true communion of love.

THE STORY OF BRIAN AND JULIE

as told by Julie

Brian and I met when we were in college and got married just after graduation. In the first years of marriage, we worked hard at our jobs. I taught school and Brian worked for a computer company. After two years, Brian lost his job when his company was sold. It took awhile for Brian to find another job that would use his computer skills, but eventually he did. That was a difficult time in our young married life.

Soon after Brian started his new job, I became very ill and had to have surgery. The doctor told us that because of the surgery, I wouldn't be able to have children. This was very sad news for us because we always wanted to have children. When I was well again, Brian and I decided that we could still have children—we could adopt! And we did! We adopted a beautiful baby boy whom we named Joshua, and a few years later, a beautiful baby girl named Sarah. What a miracle they are in our lives!

Now we are a busy, growing family. Some days there is so much work to do just to keep our family going that Brian and I hardly have any time for ourselves. Sometimes it's hard to make ends meet because it costs so much to feed and clothe our children. Brian and I often give up things that we would like to have so that our children can have what they need. Yet through the good times and the hard times, we are thankful that the Holy Spirit is with us to help us remember the promises we made to each other when we were married. The presence of God in each day gives us the strength we need to be loving, faithful spouses and parents.

A Promise of Love

In marriage a man and a woman promise to love one another as husband and wife for the rest of their lives. The Holy Spirit helps them remain faithful to their promises to each other. Many married couples grow in love as the years go by. Their love may create children who will share their love and return it.

It is not always easy to love. Some couples experience difficulties they cannot overcome. They may not be able to live together in love all their lives. Even though they may try hard to love one another, they may someday decide that it is better for them not to live together any longer. When a couple's best efforts at marriage fail, the Church allows them to separate for their own good and for the good of their children. God continues to love them. The Holy Spirit stays with them to help and guide them.

Activity

On the lines below, write some things you think might be difficult for married couples. Then write some things you think might help couples deepen their love and overcome difficulties.

PRAYING FOR MARRIED COUPLES

Paul wrote a letter to Christians living in the city of Corinth, in the country of Greece. They were having many arguments and fights. They were finding it very hard to live together as followers of Jesus.

Paul's letter explained to them how important love is. He painted for them a word picture of what real love is like—not only for married couples but for all Christians. A part of Paul's letter is printed here. Read it slowly and think about its meaning for your life as a young Christian.

Love is patient and kind.
Love is not jealous or boastful;
  it is not arrogant or rude.
Love does not insist on its own way.
  It is not irritable or resentful.
Love does not rejoice at what is wrong,
  but rejoices at what is right.
Love bears all things,
  believes all things,
  hopes all things,
  endures all things.
Love never ends.

Based on 1 Corinthians 13:4–8

Write a prayer for a married couple you know.
Share your prayer with them.

_____

_____

_____

_____

_____

Chapter Review

Complete the sentences by using the words from the word box.

rings	groom	witness of the Church	vows
bride	nuptial blessing	Matrimony	

1. Another name for the sacrament of Marriage is the

   sacrament of _____.

2. There are two ministers of the sacrament of Marriage.

   They are the _____ and the _____.

3. The priest or deacon is present because he is the

   _____.

4. The sign of the sacrament of Marriage is the exchange of

   _____.

5. The couple also exchange _____ which symbolize the bond of love between the husband and wife.

6. The prayer in which the priest prays that the couple will become one in mind and heart is called the

   _____.

Fill in the answers to the first two questions.

1. What is meant by *Matrimony*?

   _____

   _____

   _____

2. What is marriage a sign of?

   _____

   _____

3. Discuss what you can do to be a better friend to others.

God says, "I have always loved you. My love for you will never change."
Based on Jeremiah 31:3

Complete the organizer with information provided in Chapters 17-20.

Five symbolic actions in the sacrament of Reconciliation are

1. _____
2. _____
3. _____
4. _____
5. _____

Five symbolic actions in the sacrament of Anointing of the Sick are

1. _____
2. _____
   _____
   _____
3. _____
   _____
   _____
   _____
   _____
4. _____
   _____
   _____
5. _____
   _____

Bishops, priests, and deacons are ordained to

_____
_____
_____
_____
_____

A man and woman promise one another two things in marriage. They are

1. _____
   _____
   _____
2. _____
   _____
   _____

UNIT **5** REVIEW

Number the four parts of the sacrament of Reconciliation listed below from 1 to 4 to show the order in which they occur. Then answer the question.

_____ We receive absolution from the priest.

_____ We pray the prayer of sorrow.

_____ We confess our sins.

_____ We accept a penance.

Who is the minister of the sacrament of Reconciliation? _____

What is a mortal sin? _____

_____

Find four words in the word box that relate to the sacrament of Anointing of the Sick. Write each word on the lines provided. Then write their meanings.

| anointing with oil | laying on of hands | nuptial blessing | music |
| baptismal promises | coming of the priest | sponsor | Viaticum |

Word	Meaning
1. _____	1. _____
	_____
2. _____	2. _____
	_____
	_____
3. _____	3. _____
	_____
4. _____	4. _____
	_____

UNIT **5** REVIEW

Find four words in the list below that relate to the sacrament of Holy Orders. Write each word on the lines provided. Then write their meanings.

laying on of hands anointing with chrism	baptismal promises vows	sponsor ordain	Viaticum deacon

Word	Meaning
1. _____	1. _____ _____
2. _____	2. _____ _____
3. _____	3. _____ _____
4. _____	4. _____ _____ _____

Complete the sentences below by placing the number of the phrase in Column A before its ending phrase in Column B.

Column A

1. Jesus was invited to a wedding

2. The sacrament of the love between two people who are marrying is called

3. The wedding rings are signs of

4. To help a couple remain faithful to their promises, Christ sends

5. The ministers of the sacrament of Marriage are

6. The solemn promises the couple make to each other are

Column B

_____ the sacrament of Matrimony.

_____ love and faithfulness.

_____ in the town of Cana.

_____ the marriage vows.

_____ his Holy Spirit.

_____ the couple.

BEING a PEACEMAKER WITH MY FRIENDS

Good times and happy feelings are important parts of friendship. Conflicts sometimes enter relationships, and sometimes our response to such conflicts can be hurtful. We may act in hurtful ways because we ourselves have been hurt. It is during these times that the call to be a peacemaker may be most difficult.

Activity

Read the following story. Then answer each question.

Suzy always borrows things from Tara without asking permission. Once Suzy took Tara's new pen before Tara had a chance to use it herself. Tara tells Suzy to stop taking her things, but Suzy just keeps on doing it. Today, while Suzy is at tutoring, Tara decides to get back at her by borrowing Suzy's markers. Suzy is angry when she returns and discovers Tara using her markers. She says to Tara, "It's not fair to take things without asking." Tara replies, "Now you know how it feels to have someone use your things without permission." Tara tosses the markers to Suzy.

1. Who needs to be a peacemaker in this situation? _____

2. What might Suzy say to Tara? _____

3. Was it okay for Tara to take Suzy's markers without asking her permission to use them? _____

4. Let's assume that Tara apologizes. How might Suzy respond? _____

5. What might Tara say to Suzy to restore peace to the relationship? _____

6. What do you think needs to happen next? _____

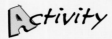
Activity

In the first space below, represent a time when you were in conflict with a friend. In the second space, represent what you did to restore peace to the relationship. Draw a picture or write a short paragraph to represent each situation.

POINTS TO REMEMBER

- Peace begins when I experience God's love and because of that experience I feel a desire to share God's love with others.

- I can be a peacemaker for myself by being open to God's love even when I'm unhappy or upset.

- I can be a peacemaker for others by acting in ways that are loving, not hurtful.

- I can be a peacemaker for others by forgiving those who have hurt me and by asking forgiveness from those I may have hurt.

- I can be a peacemaker for others by trying to find ways, however small, to bring about equality and fairness.

Following Jesus

As followers of Jesus, we need to be peacemakers with our friends, especially during conflicts. We follow Jesus when we share God's love with others and are open to God's love when we are unhappy or upset. We are called to be loving, forgiving, and fair during these times.

PRAYER

Pray a class peace prayer. Read aloud each of the "Points to Remember" above, responding after each, "Lord, help me be an instrument of your peace."

OPENING DOORS

A Take-Home Magazine™

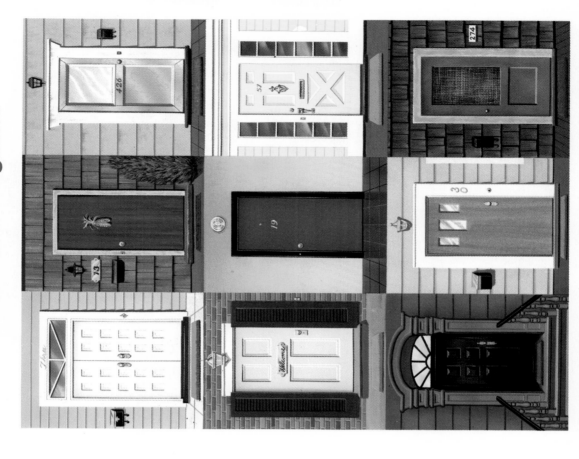

Growing Closer

DISARM YOUR FAMILY

- Discuss the present state of family relationships: What major happenings or crises has our family enjoyed or endured? How did we handle it? How have we hurt or wronged one another? How can we make up with those we have hurt or who have hurt us? How have we helped and supported one another? How can we be more understanding in the future?

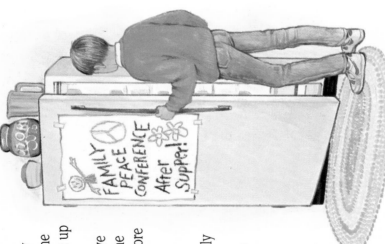

- Extend a sign of peace: whatever gestures your family is comfortable with—hugs, kisses, smiles, or pats on the back.

Looking Ahead

You and your child will have the opportunity to share some leisure hours together. Make the most of these summer months by improving family communication as you work and play together.

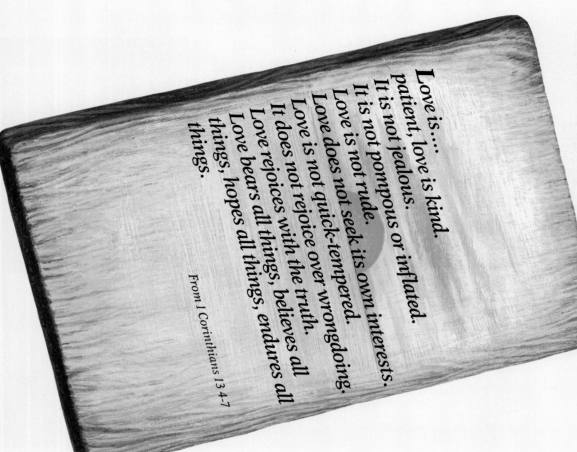

Love is…
patient, love is kind.
It is not jealous.
It is not pompous or inflated.
It is not rude.
Love does not seek its own interests.
Love is not quick-tempered.
Love does not rejoice over wrongdoing.
It does not rejoice with the truth.
Love rejoices all things, believes all
things, hopes all things, endures all
things.

From 1 Corinthians 13 4-7

---

some ministerial roles that can only be filled by a priest (consecrating bread and wine at Mass and absolving sins in Reconciliation), other roles once reserved for priests will soon be filled by trained lay people.

According to the *1983 Revised Code of Canon Law*, lay people can minister in the Church in the following ways:

★ assist pastors as experts or advisors

★ teach theology

★ serve as diocesan chancellors, judges, and auditors

★ participate in the pastoral care of the parish

★ serve as lectors, acolytes, commentators, and cantors at Mass

★ preach

★ preside over liturgical prayers, especially the Liturgy of the Hours

★ baptize

★ distribute the Eucharist

★ conduct funeral services and burials

★ officiate at marriage

Chances are, as the number of priests declines in your diocese, you'll see more lay people serving the Church in these ways.

family *forgiveness*

The Corinthian community may well have used St. Paul's words to examine their family relationships. When you have time with your family, rewrite the passage on the plaque. Replace the words "Love" and "It" with your family's surname (The Smith Family). Then discuss the meaning of the passage for your family relationships.

Life's hurts, pain and disappointment come home with all of us at times. Your fifth grader is very much aware of the need to forgive and to be forgiven. He or she has been hurt and wronged in various ways, and is familiar with your shortcomings and failures, as well as those of teachers, classmates, friends and siblings. He or she has experienced the inner struggle of choosing between what is right and what is wrong, the good feelings that come with choosing what is loving and the guilt and disappointment that come with making poor choices. He or she has experienced feelings of sorrow and repentance. Your example and the way you handle problem situations in your home go a long way toward helping your child deal with resolving conflicts, accepting the faults of others, letting go of hurts and grudges, building friendships, and working to preserve peace and unity in the family.

A TIME TO LOOK AHEAD

What will the United States Church be like in the 21st century? A look at a few statistics may provide some clues.

According to the 1988 *Official Catholic Directory*, there are about 50,000 priests working in the ministry in the United States. The median age of those priests was 60. Because more priests will soon retire and because there are fewer seminarians (9,000 listed in the 1988 *Official Catholic Directory* compared to 50,000 in 1965), the number of priests is expected to drop by half in the next ten years.

This means we can expect to see more and more priestless parishes in the future. Although there will always be

4

SIGNS OF HEALING

There is a very natural correspondence between the flow of human experience and the liturgy. Through the sacraments of the Church, we celebrate the loving presence of Christ at key moments in our lives. This includes the excitement of birth and new life in Baptism and the profound joy and completion achieved in the union of man and woman in marriage or the unity of Christ in us and among us in Eucharist. It also includes the "down side" of life: the Church recognizes and responds to our need for healing, forgiveness, and salvation through the sacraments of Anointing of the Sick and Reconciliation.

We are called to share in the fullness of Christ's life—this means sharing in his pain as well as in his glory. We experience the paschal pattern of death and resurrection—the broken, painful times that call for healing, that keep us humble, and the little Easters that keep us hopeful.

ONE BREAD ONE BODY

The Communion Rite of the Mass incorporates many signs, words and gestures to express the healing and reconciliation and unifying that is taking place. Take a few moments right now to recall and think about some of the words we use.

The Lord's Prayer: "Our Father . . ." by calling God our Father we acknowledge that we are brothers and sisters in Christ.

After the Lord's Prayer, the priest prays:
. . . grant us peace in our day.
. . . protect us from all anxiety.

Before we offer each other the sign of peace, the priest prays:
Look not on our sins, but on the faith of your Church, and grant us the peace and unity of your kingdom where you live forever and ever.

The priest begins Communion:
This is the Lamb of God
who takes away the sins of the world.

Eating and drinking together is a universal sign of unity and love. We partake of the one bread and one cup, and become one body in Christ.

Celebrating the Journey

OPENING PRAYER

Leader: We have learned that the Church recognizes and celebrates the many signs of God's presence with us, especially in the seven sacraments. Having completed this year's journey of faith, we come together now to celebrate the many signs of God's presence in our Church community and in our world.

Reader: This is a reading based on Paul's First Letter to the Corinthians 12:7-11.

To each of us the Spirit has given a special way of serving others. Some people have the ability to speak with understanding; others can speak with knowledge. These gifts come from the Holy Spirit. The same Spirit gives others the gift of faith or the power to heal the sick or the power to work miracles. To another the Spirit has given the ability to be a prophet and to another the ability to know the difference between good and bad. Some can speak in tongues, while others can interpret tongues. The Holy Spirit does all these things and decides which gifts to give to each of us.

CLOSING PRAYER

Leader: Jesus, we thank you for all the signs of your presence in our lives. Help us show your love and presence to all the people who journey with us in faith and in life. We ask these things in your name.

All: Amen.

Our Church Celebrates Advent

A TIME TO GET READY

The first Christians did not celebrate the birth of Jesus. Until the fourth century, Christians celebrated only Easter, the Feast of the Resurrection of Jesus. The celebration of Christmas came about because some people were saying that Jesus did not have a human nature. To stress their belief that Jesus had a human nature as well as a divine nature, Christians began to celebrate his birth.

The pagans of the time believed in a sun god. Every year on December 25, near the time when the days begin to get longer again, the Romans celebrated the feast of the Unconquered Sun—the victory of the sun god over darkness. Christians chose that day as a celebration of Jesus' victory over the darkness of death. Just as the sun was reborn on December 25, Jesus, the Light of the World, was born.

For the Christians of the fourth century, Christmas was a celebration not only of the birth of Jesus but also of his entrance into their lives. They celebrated his coming into their lives and his continued presence among them. They also celebrated his coming again at the end of time. Because the feast of the coming of Jesus was really a celebration of three comings, Christians began to take a long time to prepare for Christmas. That is the origin of the season of Advent. The word *advent* means "coming."

Today, Advent is a season that lasts four weeks. During Advent we actively prepare for Christmas by thinking about the three comings of Jesus. At Christmas we celebrate his first coming, his birth. We also celebrate Jesus' coming to us each day. Finally, we celebrate his coming again at the end of time. During Advent we try to create in ourselves the right attitudes to celebrate Jesus' comings. In the following activity, we will think about what we can do to prepare ourselves for Christmas.

Activity

In each candle, write one way that Jesus comes to you now. Then on the first line next to each candle, write the name of an attitude that helps you recognize Jesus' presence. On the second line, write an activity you will do that will put that attitude into practice.

On each Sunday of Advent, "light" one candle by drawing a flame on top of it.

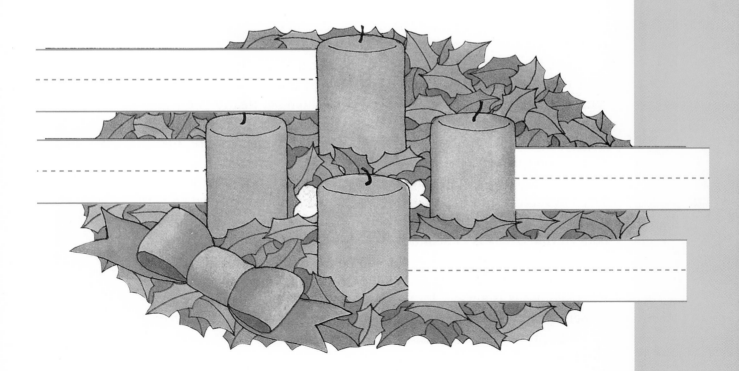

THE THREE COMINGS OF JESUS

During Advent we reflect on the three comings of Jesus into our lives and into the world.

- Jesus came to us when he was born in Bethlehem.
- Jesus comes to us each day.
- Jesus will come to us at the end of time.

We think in a special way about the coming of Jesus, whom we call Emmanuel. *Emmanuel* means "God with us."

Jesus first comes to us in *history*. The Gospels of Matthew and Luke describe the birth of Jesus. They tell us that a male child was born to the Virgin Mary, in the town of Bethlehem, nearly two thousand years ago. From the accounts in the Gospels of Matthew, Mark, Luke, and John, we know about Jesus' life, his ministry, his death, and his resurrection. We know that Jesus, the Son of God, became man and lived among us. Advent is a time to remember the Jesus of history and to thank God for sending his only Son to be with us. We thank God for the gift of faith that makes it possible for us to believe that Jesus is Emmanuel.

Christ also comes to us in *mystery*. A mystery is something we cannot fully explain. One of the great mysteries of our faith is that the risen Jesus is always with us. In Advent we celebrate Christ's presence among us today and always. We cannot explain the mystery of Jesus' presence among us, but we believe because we have faith in all of God's promises.

The risen Jesus is with us in many ways. We celebrate the presence of Jesus in the Christian community. We remember the words of Jesus: "Whenever two or three are gathered in my name, I am there among them" (based on Matthew 18:20). Jesus is also with us when we pray, when we read the Scriptures, and when we listen to the Scriptures proclaimed at Mass. We celebrate Christ's presence in the sacraments, especially in the Eucharist.

In Advent we await Jesus' promise to come in *majesty*. Catholics call this the second coming, when Jesus will return to us in glory at the end of time. The Gospel of Mark tells us that we should always be ready for Jesus' second coming: "Watch, therefore; you do not know when the lord of the house is coming, whether in the evening, or at midnight, or at cockcrow, or in the morning. May he not come suddenly and find you sleeping. What I say to you, I say to all: 'Watch!'" (Mark 13:35–37).

We do not know when the second coming of Jesus will be. Jesus calls us to prepare for his coming in glory. Advent is a special time to look for ways to bring peace, love, and justice into our homes, schools, and communities.

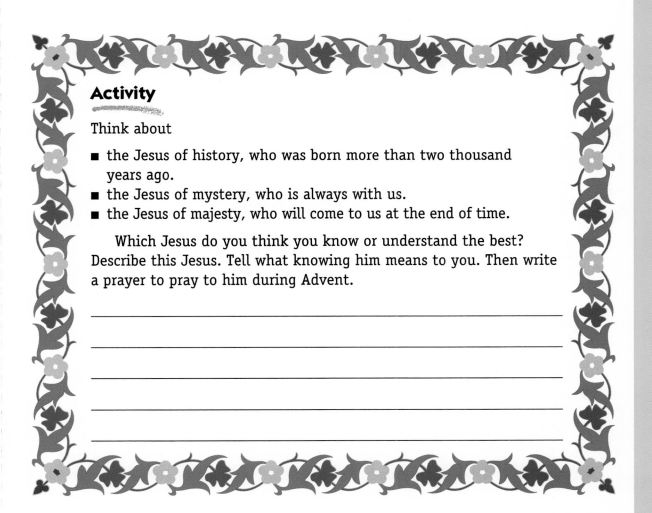

Activity

Think about

- the Jesus of history, who was born more than two thousand years ago.
- the Jesus of mystery, who is always with us.
- the Jesus of majesty, who will come to us at the end of time.

Which Jesus do you think you know or understand the best? Describe this Jesus. Tell what knowing him means to you. Then write a prayer to pray to him during Advent.

_____

_____

_____

_____

_____

ADVENT CUSTOMS

Through the centuries, Christians around the world have celebrated different customs during Advent. Celebrating these customs can help us prepare for the coming of Christ at Christmas.

In the Netherlands, as in many countries of Europe, the Feast of Saint Nicholas is a special day. On that day, a man dresses up as Saint Nicholas and visits children in their homes. Wearing a long white beard and the vestments of a bishop, he asks the children if they have been good. Then he gives them gifts of candy and fruit.

This custom is performed in memory of Saint Nicholas, who was a bishop in the fourth century. Because he had been an orphan, Saint Nicholas had a special love for children. He used to help poor families by secretly putting gifts of money through their windows at night.

The Feast of Saint Nicholas is celebrated on December 6. We can celebrate it by being generous with those around us, especially the poor.

In Sweden, people observe a special custom for the Feast of Saint Lucy. Her feast day is celebrated on December 13, which used to be the shortest day of the year. On the night before the feast, people burn "Lucy fires." These fires are a joyful sign that the days will now grow longer. The people write the name *Lucy*, which means "light," on their doors.

Then early in the morning, a young girl dresses as Saint Lucy. She wears a white dress and, on her head, a wreath with lighted candles. She awakens her family and serves them coffee and cakes.

Today this custom can remind us that, like Saint Lucy, we should point others to the light of Christ.

In Mexico, people celebrate the last week of Advent with the custom of *posadas*. Several families gather together to imitate Joseph and Mary's search for a place to stay. They go from house to house and sing a song asking for shelter. The family in each house turns them away, and then that family joins the procession. Finally, the last family welcomes them. Everyone goes into the house and participates in a prayer service.

Afterward, the children play a game with a *piñata*, which is a clay jar or a cardboard figure filled with candy. Each child is blindfolded and tries to break the piñata with a stick so that all can share the candy. The custom of *posadas* is a way of remembering that Mary and Joseph had no place to stay when Jesus was born. It is up to us to welcome Jesus when he comes to us at Christmas.

Activity

List three customs your family uses to prepare for Christmas. Next to each custom, explain its meaning.

Custom

_____

_____

_____

Meaning

_____

_____

_____

_____

_____

_____

_____

Advent Posters

Jesus is the Light of the World. We celebrate the coming of Jesus at Christmas by lighting candles on our Advent wreaths.

We, too, can be lights in the dark places of our world. We can imitate Jesus by bringing our light to others. We can feed the hungry, help the poor, heal the sick, work for peace, and clean up polluted parts of our environment.

Think of one dark area in which the world needs light. On the lines provided, describe that group of people or part of nature that needs help.

_____

_____

Think of one way that you can be a light to that dark area. What can you do to help this group of people or part of nature? Write it on the lines below.

_____

_____

Create a class Advent poster. Look through newspapers and magazines for photographs that describe the dark area of the world you listed. Cut out the photographs and paste them to a large piece of posterboard or newsprint. If you cannot find any photographs, draw a picture that illustrates the area of darkness.

Hang the poster on a wall in your classroom, and place an Advent wreath on a table in front of the poster. When the Advent wreath is lighted each day, let it remind you of your pledge to be a light to those in darkness.

Let It Shine!

Opening Song: "O Come, O Come, Emmanuel"

Advent Prayer

Leader: Let us pray.

(*pause*)

Loving God, you have given us this season of Advent as a time to prepare for the coming of Jesus. Help us to see this Advent wreath as a sign of his coming. May these green branches remind us of the life that comes to us in Jesus, even in the cold of winter. May these candles remind us to prepare each day during these four weeks for the coming of Jesus. And may the flame that lights these candles enlighten us to see you, our true Light, that we may share our light with those in darkness. We ask this through Christ, our Lord.

All: Amen.

Gospel Reading

Reader: The Lord be with you.

All: And also with you.

Reader: A reading based on the Gospel according to Matthew 5:14–16.

All: Glory to you, Lord.

Reader: Jesus said to his disciples, "You are the light of the world. A city set on a hill cannot be hidden. People do not light a candle and then put it under a basket. They set it on a table where it gives light to all in the house. In the same way, your light must shine before all so that they may see goodness in their acts and give praise to your heavenly Father."

The gospel of the Lord.

All: Praise to you, Lord Jesus Christ.

Prayer of the Faithful

Leader: My brothers and sisters, God is always with us. God loves each of us and holds us close. We now present our prayers to God, our Father. (*Students present the petitions. The response is, "Lord, enlighten us."*)

Leader: Loving God, we thank you for hearing the prayers we make in Jesus' name.

All: Amen.

Closing Song: "This Little Light of Mine"

Our Church Celebrates Christmas

THE BIRTH OF JESUS—THE CHRISTMAS STORY

At that time a proclamation came from Caesar Augustus that ordered everyone in the known world to be registered. So everyone went to be registered, each to his own town. Joseph went up from Galilee from the town of Nazareth to Judea, to the city of David known as Bethlehem. Joseph was from the family of David. Mary traveled with him to Bethlehem. While they were there, the time came for Mary to have her baby, and she gave birth to her firstborn son. She wrapped him in swaddling clothes and laid him in a manger, because there was no room for them in the inn.

Out in the fields near Bethlehem, there were shepherds keeping watch over their flock. An angel from the Lord appeared to them and the brightness of the Lord's glory shone around them. The shepherds were frightened. The angel said, "Do not be afraid; I have come to announce good news that will bring joy to all people. Today, in the city of David, a Savior was born for you. He is Christ, the Lord. I have given you a sign: you will find an infant wrapped in swaddling clothes, lying in a manger."

Suddenly, the sky was filled with angels, all praising God and saying:

'Glory to God in heaven!

Peace to God's people on earth.'

When the angels left, the shepherds said to one another, 'Let us go to Bethlehem to see what has taken place, which God has made known to us.' So they hurried to the stable and found Mary and Joseph, and the infant lying in the manger. After they had seen the child, they told everyone about the message they had been given. Everyone who heard it was amazed. Mary thought about all these things and treasured them in her heart. Then the shepherds returned to the fields, giving glory and praise to God for all that they had seen and heard.

Based on Luke 2:1–20

Activity

Think about the meaning of Jesus' birth in our world today. Then write answers to the questions below.

1. If Jesus had been born today, who do you think would be the first group of people to hear about his birth? Why?

_____

_____

_____

2. Where do you think Jesus would be born in today's world? Why?

_____

_____

3. How is the birth of Jesus good news for you?

_____

_____

_____

CHRISTMAS SYMBOLS

Do you take your Christmas tree for granted? Do you put up your tree in December, decorate it with colorful ornaments, string the lights, and place a star on top? Did you ever wonder where the custom of the Christmas tree came from and why we decorate it the way we do? Although some people are not aware of it, the Christmas trees we place in our homes have a spiritual meaning.

The custom of the Christmas tree began in Germany in the Middle Ages, the time of knights and castles. At that time, the Feast of Adam and Eve was celebrated on December 24. Often the citizens of a town would present a play in church that told how Adam and Eve disobeyed God's command by eating the fruit of the forbidden tree. This tree, which was known as the Paradise Tree, was represented by an evergreen with apples hanging on it. Evergreen trees were symbols of life because they stayed green all winter.

When the custom of the play died out, people began to put these trees in their homes. One reason the trees became known as Christmas trees was that the play had been presented on Christmas Eve. But a more important reason had to do with the meaning of the trees. They came to represent Christ, who was born to overcome the sin of Adam and Eve.

The people of the Middle Ages decorated the trees by hanging apples from the branches and placing lighted candles on the limbs. The apples represented sin, and the candles represented Jesus, the Light of the World.

Soon more symbols were added. A star of Bethlehem was placed on top, and round bread wafers, symbols of the Eucharist, were hung on the branches. Eventually, people added more decorations—candy, cookies, fruits, tinsel, and glass balls—to express the blessings and the beauty of the season.

The Christmas Crib

The custom of setting up a crib with people and animals surrounding the baby Jesus was started by Saint Francis of Assisi on Christmas Eve in 1223. Francis asked his friend John to set up a scene with real people, in the town of Greccio, Italy.

"I want to see with my own eyes how the infant Jesus was deprived of all the comforts that babies enjoy," Francis said.

And so John set up a manger scene by making a crib, filling it with straw, and bringing in a donkey and an ox. Francis came to see the scene and was touched by its beauty. A joyful midnight Mass was celebrated there.

Soon the custom of the Christmas crib spread. Live manger scenes were created in many places. Where this was not possible, people made statues of the figures and placed them in churches or homes. First, statues of Jesus, Mary, and Joseph were placed in the manger scene. Then the shepherds, the Wise Men, and the animals were added to the scene.

The custom of the Christmas crib can still remind us, as it did Saint Francis, that Jesus was born into poverty.

Activity

Draw a line from Column I to Column II to match the Christmas custom with its meaning.

Column I	Column II
Christmas candle	Gave warmth to Jesus
Yule Log	Jesus is the Vine.
Ox and donkey	Jesus is the Light.
Ivy	Poverty of Jesus
Mistletoe	Warmth and hospitality
Poinsettia flower	Love and peace
Christmas crib	Resembles star of Bethlehem

Adoration of the Magi (oil), Botticelli, 15th century, National Gallery of Art, Andrew Mellon Collection, Washington, D.C.

JESUS COMES FOR ALL PEOPLE

After the birth of Jesus, magi or astrologers from the East arrived in Jerusalem. They had been on a special journey, following a star. When they came to Jerusalem, they asked everyone, "Where is the newborn king of the Jews? We have seen his star rising and have come to honor him."

This question caused a great uproar, especially with Herod, whom the Romans had made king over the Jews. Herod was afraid of losing his power. He gathered the leaders of the people for questioning and asked them where Christ would be born. They answered, "In the town of Bethlehem in Judea." Herod told this to the magi, hoping to find out from them exactly where this newborn king was. Secretly, Herod hoped to kill Jesus.

The magi set out for Bethlehem, following the star that went ahead of them. Finally, the star stopped over the place where the child was. When they found the child Jesus, they were overjoyed. They bowed down before him and then presented gifts to him. They gave him gold, frankincense (a type of incense), and myrrh (a special spice).

In a dream, the magi received a message not to go back to Herod. They returned home by another route.

Based on Matthew 2:1–12

The Epiphany

Epiphany is a word that means "manifestation" or a shining out. It is used to describe the story of the magi, who have sometimes been called the Wise Men. The light of Jesus was manifested, or shown, to them. When Christ came among us, he came for people of every nation. During his life he often cared for people who were not Jews. Even at Jesus' birth, people of other nations came to honor him.

Activity

See how well you can complete this puzzle.

Across

1. *Epiphany* is a word that means _____.

6. Jesus is the _____ of all nations.

9. One of the gifts that the magi gave the newborn king was _____.

10. The newborn king, Jesus, was born in the town of _____.

11. The travelers found the newborn king by following a _____.

12. The travelers were so happy to find Jesus that they presented him with _____.

Down

2. Jesus came for people of every _____.

3. The magi came from the _____.

4. The people who study the stars are called _____.

5. King _____ was angry and afraid of losing his power.

7. The travelers were warned in a _____.

8. There are still many people in the world who do not know _____.

CHRISTMAS CRIB ORNAMENT

This Christmas, give a special gift to someone you love. Make an ornament of the Christmas crib below by following these instructions.

1. Cut out along the dotted line of the crib.

2. Paste the cutout onto a sheet of cardboard.

3. After the paste dries, cut around the crib to remove the excess cardboard.

4. Use a hole puncher to punch a hole through the top of the crib ornament.

5. Place a ribbon through the hole and tie the ends together. This will be used to hang the ornament from the tree.

6. On the back of the ornament, write a Christmas greeting to the person or persons who will be receiving your special gift. Don't forget to sign your name.

PRAYER OF THE CRIB

Leader: Today we remember how Jesus was born. As we place each figure around his crib, let us ask Jesus to help us imitate the qualities that each figure shows us. As each figure is presented, we will say, "Jesus is born to give us his love."

Ox: The ox breathed on Jesus to help keep him warm. Let us welcome Jesus by doing good deeds.

All: Jesus is born to give us his love.

Donkey: The donkey carried Mary on the road to Bethlehem. Let us carry Jesus to all those in need.

All: Jesus is born to give us his love.

Joseph: Joseph sought a place for Jesus to be born. Let us make a place for Jesus in our hearts.

All: Jesus is born to give us his love.

Mary: Mary said yes so that Jesus could be born. Let us say yes and bring him to our world.

All: Jesus is born to give us his love.

Jesus: Jesus was born as a poor and helpless child. Let us accept hardship with faith and trust.

All: Jesus is born to give us his love.

Angels: The angels sang of peace and goodwill to all. Let us bring peace by forgiving those who hurt us.

All: Jesus is born to give us his love.

Shepherds: The shepherds heard the angels and went to look for Jesus. Let us look for Jesus in one another.

All: Jesus is born to give us his love.

Sheep: The sheep followed the shepherds and saw the child Jesus. Let us follow Jesus, who is the Good Shepherd.

All: Jesus is born to give us his love.

Wise Men: The Wise Men followed the star and found Jesus. Let us follow Jesus as he leads us to the Father.

All: Jesus is born to give us his love.

Closing Song: "O Come, All Ye Faithful"

Our Church Celebrates Lent

A TIME OF ENLIGHTENMENT

Enlightenment is a word that describes what happens to a person who begins to see, or understand. For example, if you were working for a long time on a difficult math problem and suddenly solved it, you might say you became enlightened.

Lent is a time of enlightenment for those who are preparing for the sacrament of Baptism. It is also a time of enlightenment for all of us. During Lent, the Holy Spirit helps us to see and understand Jesus. The Gospel of John tells us the story of a man born blind who was enlightened by Jesus. This story is a good example of what should happen to us during Lent.

One Sabbath day as Jesus was walking along the road, he saw a blind man. Jesus stopped, spat on the ground, and made a paste of mud. Then he put the paste over the man's eyes and said to him, "Go and wash."

The blind man went off and washed himself. Suddenly, he could see.

When people realized that this man who had been blind since birth could now see, they could not believe it. Some even said he was not the same man. They took him to the Pharisees, who began to ask him questions. Some of the Pharisees did not like Jesus because he did not keep the rule that said no one should work on the Sabbath. These Pharisees considered healing to be a kind of work. "This man is a sinner," they said.

But the man who had been blind stood up to them and professed his faith in Jesus. "If he were not from God, he could not have healed me," he said. With that, the Pharisees grew angrier and ordered the man to leave.

Later, Jesus found the man. Jesus asked the man, "Do you believe in me?"

"Yes, Lord, I believe," the man said.

Based on John 9:1–38

The man who had been blind is a good example of enlightenment because he not only saw Jesus, but also understood who Jesus was. Lent is a time when we try to deepen our faith in Jesus. We join with those who are preparing for Baptism and trying to recognize Jesus' presence among us. We try to understand more clearly his call to love.

By the time Lent is finished, we hope to be able to say a little more strongly "Yes, Lord, I believe." We hope to grow in our understanding of what Jesus really means for us.

Activity

To help you reflect upon the important parts of your faith, think carefully about the questions below and answer them in your own words on the lines provided. Then think about these questions during the season of Lent and pray that you may be enlightened with a deeper understanding.

1. Who is God? _____

_____

2. Who is Jesus? _____

_____

3. Who is the Holy Spirit? _____

_____

4. What is the Church? _____

_____

A Time for Looking at Ourselves

Lent is a time for taking stock. It is a time for us to look at ourselves and ask ourselves if we are the best Christians we can be. Lent is the springtime of the liturgical year. It is a time for preparing for Easter by trying to be better. It is the time for new beginnings.

Lent began in the Church because everyone was concerned about helping people who were preparing to join the Church at Easter. At Easter the new members were baptized and confirmed, and they then shared in the Eucharist for the first time. They became part of the Christian community, and everyone welcomed them with great joy.

The new Christians were not strangers. Everyone in the Church already knew them. During Lent the Church prayed for them, taught them about Jesus, and listened to God's word with them. Those who were already members of the Church became friends with the new members, making them feel welcomed and accepted.

When Christians saw the new members, they would say to themselves, "Look how hard these people are working to become Christians. I am already a baptized Christian, but I could be a better one. I should care more about others."

A Time to Live Our Baptism

Today we still welcome new members to our Church at Easter. We still try to be the best Catholics we can so that we can be good examples to them. We do this by caring for one another. That is what it means to live by the call we received at Baptism. The activity below shows some ways we can do this.

Activity

Try to find out if your parish has people who will be baptized at Easter. Write their names here.

_____

_____

_____

What are some ways you could help these people prepare for Baptism?

_____

_____

_____

One of the ways we care for people is by accepting them as they are. Do you know anyone who is not accepted by others because of the way he or she looks or acts? How can you show that person you care?

_____

_____

During Lent, Christians make sacrifices. They also remember that this is a special time for prayer. We pray for those who are preparing for Baptism, for those who are not easily accepted by others, and for those who are suffering. We pray for ourselves so that we may learn how to care for others. Write a Lenten prayer asking Jesus to help you become a more caring person.

_____

_____

_____

A Time for Changing

For almost 1,600 years, Lent has been the Church's official period of preparation for Easter. Although some Lenten practices have been changed somewhat over time, the purpose of Lent—to change our hearts, our attitudes, and our lives—is still the same.

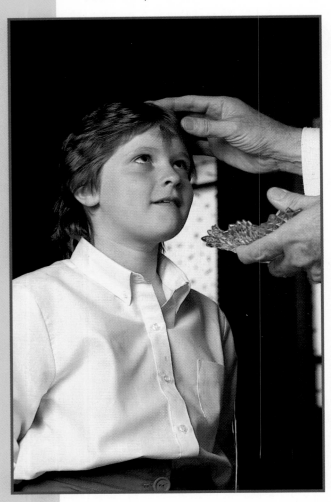

The forty days of Lent begin with Ash Wednesday. On Ash Wednesday the priest or other minister traces the sign of the cross on our foreheads with blessed ashes. The ashes are a sign to us of our need for God and for his help in order to become more like Jesus. As the priest or other minister marks our foreheads, he or she says the following.

"Turn away from sin and be faithful to the gospel" (Based on Mark 1:15).

During the six weeks of Lent, we think about what it means to live as baptized members of the Church and as we try to change the things that keep us from following Jesus. The common traditional Lenten pratices— praying, fasting, and giving to those who are poor and in need (known as almsgiving), have been practiced since the earliest days of the Church.

As baptized Catholics we have the responsibility and privilege to pray. Praying helps us to grow closer to God. It is important to take time to pray alone and with our Church families. Lent is a time when we have many opportunities to pray with our Church communities. Some parishes invite the Church community to participate in special devotions, such as the Stations of the Cross, and special celebrations of the sacrament of Reconciliation. The Stations of the Cross help us to spend time thinking about Jesus' passion, death, and resurrection. The celebration of the sacrament of Reconciliation offers us the opportunity to examine our conscience and to look for ways to live God's law of love more faithfully. It is a way to express sorrow for our sins.

Catholics are obliged to express sorrow by doing penance. This includes fasting and abstaining. **Fasting** involves eating one full meal a day and two smaller meals. **Abstaining** involves not eating meat.

The chart below explains what the Church asks us to do.

Regulation	Who?	When?
Fasting	Adults from the age of 18 to 59	Ash Wednesday and Good Friday
Abstaining	Catholics who have reached the age of 14	Ash Wednesday and the Fridays of Lent

Fasting is a reminder of our longing to be united with God. Although children are not required to fast, they are encouraged to give up a favorite food, a television program, or an action or habit that keeps them from showing their love for Jesus and others. The sacrifice of abstaining reminds us of Jesus' great sacrifice on the cross.

Another traditional Lenten practice is almsgiving—taking special care of those who are poor and in need. During Lent, we are invited to give food, time, or money to help those in need. We can choose to donate to a food pantry, collect toys or clothes for a shelter, or help a friend, relative, or neighbor with chores. By doing these things we remember all that Jesus has done for us.

Activity

Each Scripture verse below describes one of the traditional Lenten customs of prayer, fasting, or almsgiving. Read each verse and then tell how you will put the custom described into practice in your life during Lent.

"Lord, to you I call. Listen to my voice. Let my prayer rise like incense before you" (based on Psalm 141:1–2). _____

"O God, you are the one I seek. My body hungers for you. My soul thirsts for you" (based on Psalm 63:2). _____

"Feed the hungry. Shelter the homeless. Clothe those who have no clothes. Don't turn your back on others" (based on Isaiah 58:7). _____

OPPORTUNITIES TO CHANGE

Jesus said to his disciples, "When you do good deeds, don't try to show off. When you give to the poor, don't blow a loud horn. That's what the showoffs do on the street corners, because they are always looking for praise. Give your gift in secret. Your Father knows what is done in secret, and will reward you.

"When you pray, don't act like the showoffs who love to stand up and pray in the synagogues or on the street corners. They do this just to look good. I promise you that they already have their reward.

"When you fast, do not look gloomy as the showoffs do when they go without eating. Instead, comb your hair and wash your face. Then others won't know that you are fasting. But your Father sees what is done in private and will reward you."

Based on Matthew 6:1–6, 16–18

We have learned that baptized Christians have certain responsibilities and obligations during Lent. We are called to pray, fast, and give alms. These traditional Lenten practices can be used either as opportunities or obligations.

An opportunity is a chance to do something that is good, while an obligation can be thought of as something we must do because the law demands it. The showoffs that Jesus describes are acting out of obligation because they are fasting, praying, and giving to the poor only to impress others. Their sacrifices are phony. Jesus tells us that his true followers will not make sacrifices to impress others or because they are required to. True followers will make sacrifices because they want to grow closer to Jesus.

Jesus wants us to recognize that praying, fasting, and caring for those who are poor and in need are opportunities to show that we are sorry for our sins. These opportunities also help prepare our minds and hearts for Easter.

Activity

Think about the different ways you can get ready for Easter. Then read the list below. Put an **O** next to the things you think are opportunities. Put an **X** next to those things that you would do only out of obligation.

_____ Go to Mass on a weekday.

_____ Give up eating between meals.

_____ Celebrate the sacrament of Reconciliation.

_____ Collect food for the hungry.

_____ Stand up for someone who is being treated unfairly.

_____ Spend time each day reading the Bible.

_____ Visit residents in a nursing home.

_____ Contribute money to the missions.

_____ Read stories to or play games with a younger brother or sister.

_____ Avoid watching television.

Choose one of the activities above or something else you plan to do during Lent. Use your own words to describe how the activity can be used as an opportunity to grow closer to God.

_____

_____

_____

_____

The Lenten Times

Et harumd dereud	Ut enim ad minim	Itaque earud rerum

JESUS HEALS BLIND MAN

Lorem ipsum dolor sit tempor incidunt ut labor veniam, quis nostrund ex commodo consequat. esse molestiae consequat et iusto odio dignissim qu excepteur sint occaecat c deserunt mollit anim id e distinct. Nam liber temp quod maxim placeat fac Temporibud autem quin err epudiand sint et mole delectus au aut prefer ex quid est cur verear ne ad memorite tum etia ergat cum conscient to factor pecun modut est neque nulla praid om undant. I dodecendesse videanteur fidem. Neque hominy ir conetud notiner si effece but tuntung benevolent cum omning null sit caus explent sine julla inura a

Concupis plusque in l Itaque ne iustitial dem re Nam dilig et carum ese non ob ea solu incomm mult etiam mag quod c

nulla praid om undant. I dodecendesse videanteur fidem. Neque hominy ir conetud notiner si effece but tuntung benevolent cum omning null sit caur explent sine julla inura a

Concupis plusque in ij Itaque ne iustitial dem re Nam dilig et carum esse non ob ea solu incomm mult etiam mag quod c expetend quam nostras utent tamet eum locum s dictum est, sic amicitian amicis insidar et metus p confirmatur animuset a v despication adversantur

Lorem ipsum dolor sit metpor incidunt ut labor veniam, quis nostrund ex commodo consequat. D esse molestiae consequat et iusto odio dignissim q excepteur sint occaecat c deserunt mollit anim id e distinct. Nam liber temp quod maxim placeat fac Temporibud autem quin

veniam, quis nostrund ex commodo consequat. De esse molestiae consequat et iusto odio dignissim qu excepteur sint occaecat c deserunt mollit anim id e distinct. Nam liber temp quod maxim placeat fac Temporibud autem quin er repudiand sint et mole delectus au aut prefer e quid est cur verear ne ad memorite tum etia ergat cum conscient to factor pecun modut est neque

fidem. Neque hominy ir conetud notiner si effece but tuntung benevolent cum omning null sit caur explent sine julla inura a

Concupis plusque in i Itaque ne iustitial dem re Nam dilig et carum esse non ob ea solu incomm mult etiam mag quod c Ectamen nedue enim hae cronylar at ifle pellis x expeting ea in motwon x doler, non solut in indu Ectamen nedue enim hae

JESUS ENTERS JERUSALEM

Lorem ipsum dolor sit tempor incidunt ut labor veniam, quis nostrund ex commodo consequat. D esse molestiae consequat et iusto odio dignissim qu excepteur sint occaecat c deserunt mollit anim id e distinct. Nam liber temp quod maxim placeat fac Temporibud autem quin err epudiand sint et mole delectus au aut prefer ex quid est cur verear ne ad cum conscient to factor pecun modut est neque nulla praid om undant. I dodecendesse videanteur fidem. Neque hominy ir conetud notiner si effece but tuntung benevolent cum omning null sit caus explent sine julla inura a

Concupis plusque in i Itaque ne iustitial dem re Nam dilig et carum esse non ob ea solu incomm mult etiam mag quod c expetend quam nostras tuent tamet eum locum s dictum est, sic amicitian amicis insidar et metus p confirmatur animuset a s despication adversantur

Lorem ipsum dolor sit tempor incidunt ut labor veniam, quis nostrund ex commodo consequat. D esse molestiae consequat et iusto odio dignissim qu excepteur sint occaecat c deserunt mollit anim id e distinct. Nam liber temp quod maxim placeat fac Temporibud autem quin er repudiand sint et mole delectus au aut prefer ex quid est cur verear ne ad

nulla praid om undant. I dodecendesse videanteur fidem. Neque hominy ir conetud notiner si effece but tuntung benevolent cum omning null sit caur explent sine julla inura a

Concupis plusque in ij Itaque ne iustitial dem re Nam dilig et carum esse non ob ea solu incomm mult etiam mag quod c exceptur sint occaecat c deserunt mollit anim id e distinct. Nam liber temp quod maxim placeat fac Temporibud autem quin er repudiand sint et mole delectus au aut prefer e quid est cur verear ne ad memorite tum etia erga cum conscient to factor pecun modut est neque nulla praid om undant. I dodecendesse videanteur fidem. Neque hominy ir conetud notiner si effece but tuntung benevolent cum omning null sit caur explent sine julla inura a

Concupis plusque in ij Itaque ne iustitial dem re Nam dilig et carum esse non ob ea solu incomh mult etiam mag quod c Ectamen nedue enim hae cronylar at ifle pellis x

CLASS NEWSPAPER

To study the activities of Jesus and to understand him better, put together a class newspaper. Give the newspaper a name, such as *The Lenten Times*. Work in small groups to collect stories and facts about Jesus.

Decide whether to report on a particular event or miracle. Pretend you are reporters in Jesus' time and have been assigned to cover a newsworthy event.

You may want to draw an illustration of one of Jesus' actions. You may write a poem about enlightenment or faith. Or, you may draw a map of Israel (or one of Jerusalem) and highlight some places of importance.

To get you started, here are some Scripture references that may help you land a front-page scoop. Just consider them as "hot tips" from an anonymous source!

Matthew 5:1–7:29	Luke 18:18–25
Matthew 14:22–33	Luke 21:1–4
Mark 8:1–10	John 11:1–44
Mark 8:27–30	John 14:1–7

Renewal of Lenten Promises

Opening Prayer

All: In the name of the Father, and of the Son, and of the Holy Spirit. Amen.

Leader: Lent is a time for taking stock. It is a time to reflect upon our lives and ask ourselves if we are the best Christians we can be. Let us pause to remember our Lenten promises and ask God for forgiveness for the times we have failed. *(pause)*

For the times we have been selfish, Lord, have mercy.

All: Lord, have mercy.

Leader: For the times we have been lazy, Christ, have mercy.

All: Christ, have mercy.

Leader: For the times we have been unkind, Lord, have mercy.

All: Lord, have mercy.

Reading

Reader: A reading based on the second letter of Paul to the Corinthians 6:1–2.

As your fellow workers we beg you not to receive the grace of God in vain. For he says, "In an acceptable time I have heard you; on a day of salvation I have helped you." Now is the acceptable time! Now is the day of salvation! The Word of the Lord.

All: Thanks be to God.
(Students place their papers at the foot of the cross. The leader traces a cross on each student's forehead.)

Renewal of Lenten Promises

Leader: Through his cross, may Jesus give you strength.
(After all students have been signed, say the following prayer.)

All: God, our Father, you have called us at Baptism to be followers of your Son, Jesus. Through the gift of your Holy Spirit, give us the strength to follow him more closely during this season of Lent. Help us to be faithful to the promises we have made so that we can celebrate Easter with joy and enlightenment. Amen.

Our Church Celebrates Holy Week

THE TRIDUUM

A triduum is a three-day period of prayer in preparation for a major feast or special occasion. The Easter Triduum celebrates the final three days of Jesus' life on the earth. It begins with the evening Mass on Holy Thursday and ends on Easter Sunday evening. This is the holiest time of the Church year. During the Easter Triduum, we experience again Jesus' journey through death to new life.

Holy Thursday

On Holy Thursday, we remember Jesus' Last Supper, when the Eucharist was given to us. Paul in a letter to the Corinthians tells us:

"On the night he was betrayed, Jesus took bread, gave thanks, broke it and said, 'This is my body, for you.' In the same way, he took the cup, saying, 'This is my blood. Whenever you do this, remember me'" (based on 1 Corinthians 11:23–26).

In the gospels, we are reminded that everyone who receives the Eucharist is called to serve. After washing his disciples' feet, Jesus said:

"If I, your Lord and teacher, have washed your feet, you must wash one another's feet. I have given you an example. What I have done, you must also do for one another" (based on John 13:13–15).

Good Friday

Although Mass is not celebrated on Good Friday, we come together as a community at a special service to remember Jesus' suffering and death. The Good Friday service has three parts: the Liturgy of the Word, the Veneration of the Cross, and Holy Communion. The story of Jesus' Passion, according to the Gospel of John, is read. Then we pray for the Church, for world leaders, and for all God's people.

During the Veneration of the Cross, the priest raises a large cross and says, "This is the wood of the cross, on which hung the Savior of the world." We respond, "Come, let us worship." Then we are invited to show reverence or respect for the cross. We can do this in many ways. We can kiss the cross or genuflect before it. We can also touch the cross prayerfully with our hand.

Finally, the Blessed Sacrament is removed from the tabernacle and brought to the altar. We pray together The Lord's Prayer and we receive Communion.

Holy Saturday

During the day on Holy Saturday, we keep watch at Jesus' tomb by praying and fasting. One way the Church keeps watch is by not celebrating the Eucharist on this day. In the evening we gather for the Easter Vigil. We listen to the story of God's love for us. New members of the Church are baptized and confirmed at this liturgy. Then they are invited to join us at the table of the Lord to receive Eucharist for the first time.

At last, after the long weeks of Lent and three intense days of prayer and ritual, we declare as one: "He is risen! Alleluia!"

Activity

Complete the sentences below by placing the number of the phrase in Column A with its ending phrase in Column B.

Column A

1. The Easter Triduum begins

2. On Holy Thursday

3. Jesus gave us an example of service when

4. At the Last Supper

5. On Good Friday we come together to

6. We show reverence for the cross by

7. On Holy Saturday evening we celebrate

Column B

_____ he washed his disciples' feet.

_____ the Easter Vigil.

_____ remember Jesus' suffering and death.

_____ kissing it or genuflecting before it.

_____ on Holy Thursday evening and ends on Easter Sunday evening.

_____ we remember the Last Supper.

_____ the Eucharist was given to us.

THE EASTER VIGIL

Easter is the celebration of the resurrection of Jesus. In ancient times the people of the Church would celebrate this event with an all-night vigil. With the rising of the sun, they would give thanks for the rising of Jesus from the grave. At the celebration the Church would also welcome new Christians through the sacraments of initiation—Baptism, Confirmation, and Eucharist. Today we continue this celebration of the resurrection of Jesus in the Easter Vigil. Let us look at each of its four parts.

The Service of Light

The people gather quietly in the darkened church. When all is ready and the church is completely dark, the priest lights a small fire near the entrance. He blesses the fire and then lights the large Easter candle and prays that the light of Christ will enlighten the darkness of our hearts. The deacon then carries the candle to the front of the church. He stops three times to sing "Christ our light." Each time, the people respond "Thanks be to God," and the candles they have been given are also lighted. When the deacon reaches the front of the church, he places the candle in a stand and sings a hymn of thanks for the light of Christ.

The Liturgy of the Word

Next, all are seated and listen to the readings. The readings recall how God has always actively loved people. The readings tell the stories of the Creation, of the liberation of the Jews from Egypt, and of God's promise to be close to God's people. After each reading, the people pause to reflect. These are stories not only of God's action in the past, but also of God's action in our lives now. The last reading is the gospel—the story of the resurrection, which is not just a past event but one that continues.

The Liturgy of Baptism

We now come to a very important moment. Those who have been preparing for a very long time are now baptized and confirmed. First we pray for them, using a very ancient prayer called a litany. In it we call on the saints to help those who are to be baptized and confirmed. The water is blessed. We give thanks for the water—a symbol of both life and death. We then renew our baptismal promises.

The Liturgy of the Eucharist

The climax of the celebration comes in the consecration and sharing of the Eucharist. Just as we gave thanks over the light and water, we now give thanks over the bread and wine. Offering thanks and praise to the Father reminds us of the life, death, and resurrection of Jesus. Sharing in the Eucharist makes us one in the risen Jesus. We celebrate our union with the newly baptized, who now receive the Eucharist.

The Easter Vigil is a celebration that reminds us that Jesus rose from the dead and is with us now.

Activity

Fire, water, bread, and light are some symbols we read about in the Easter Vigil. Write a brief paragraph about any one of them and explain how we use it in our lives.

_____

_____

_____

Our Church Celebrates Easter

THE RESURRECTION

On the first day of the week at early dawn, Mary Magdalene, Joanna, Mary the mother of James, and some other women came to the tomb bringing with them the spices they had prepared. They found the stone rolled away from the tomb, but when they went in, they did not find Jesus' body. While they were trying to figure out what happened, two men in dazzling clothes suddenly stood beside them. The women were terrified and turned their faces away. The men said, "Why do you look for the living among the dead? He is not here; he has risen. Remember that he told you the Son of Man would be crucified and would rise again on the third day?" Then the women remembered Jesus' words. They returned from the tomb and announced all this to the disciples.

Based on Luke 24:1–9

We have heard many times the story of Jesus' resurrection. Jesus calls us to think about his resurrection as if we ourselves were there, outside the tomb, witnessing this great mystery. Like the disciples, we are asked by Jesus to trust in his promises to us.

Easter is the greatest celebration of the church year. We celebrate that Jesus passed from death to life and that we, too, will have new life. Through Baptism we share in Jesus' death and resurrection, which save us from sin and death. If we try to follow Jesus in all that we do, God's love will make it possible for us to live forever. The risen Jesus is always with us to help us grow in our faith and to live it out in our lives.

Easter is a time for rejoicing and a time to remember that we want to live as Jesus lived. Like Jesus, we can be loving and forgiving. We can bring peace and comfort to others. Most of all, we can be a sign to others of the good news that Jesus came to bring all people through his life, death, and resurrection.

Activity

Imagine that you were an eyewitness to Jesus' resurrection.
What questions would you ask? What feelings might you feel?
Write about your questions and feelings on the lines below.

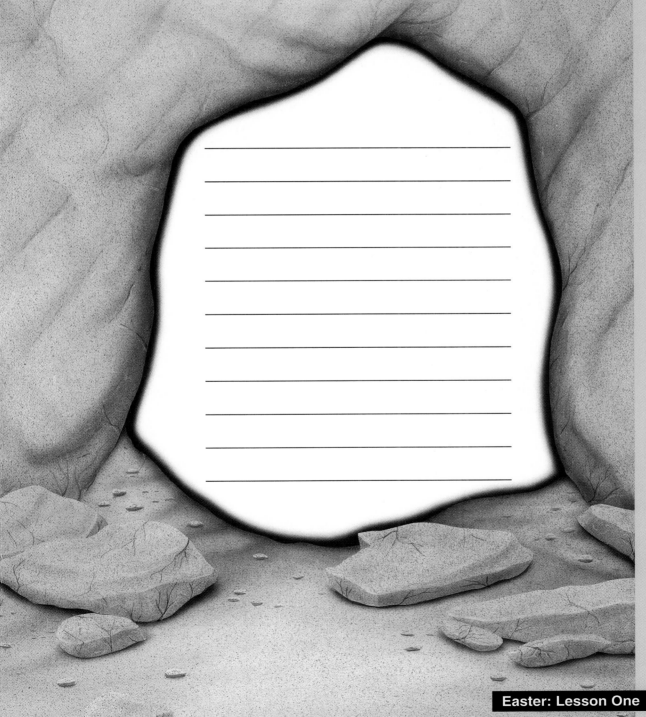

Mary Magdalene at Tomb of Jesus (oil), Duccio, 13th century, Opera del Duomo, Florence, Italy

THE RISEN JESUS SENDS HIS DISCIPLES FORTH

The most important feast of the liturgical year is Easter. During the Easter season we celebrate the fact that Jesus rose from the dead. In doing so, he overcame sin and death. His rising is a sign and a promise of new life for us.

Early on Sunday morning, Mary Magdalene went weeping to the tomb where Jesus was buried. She saw Jesus standing there but she did not recognize him until he spoke her name. He sent her to tell his friends that he had risen from the dead. Mary went to the disciples and said, "I have seen the Lord."

Based on John 20:11–18

Later on Sunday two disciples were walking to Emmaus. They were talking about everything that had taken place. Jesus walked with them, but they did not recognize him. As they walked, Jesus explained the Scriptures to them. They asked the stranger to eat with them. When he was at the table, he took bread, blessed and broke it, and gave it to them. Then their eyes were opened and they recognized him. They returned to Jerusalem and told the disciples what had happened on the road and how they had come to know him in the breaking of the bread.

Based on Luke 24:13–35

We Carry On the Work of Jesus

During Mass, we remember the work of Jesus. We recall his work by praying these words.

To the poor he proclaimed the good news of salvation,
to prisoners, freedom,
and to those in sorrow, joy . . . .
And that we might live no longer for ourselves but for him,
he sent the Holy Spirit from you, Father,
as his first gift to those who believe. . . .

From Eucharistic Prayer IV

We have been given the Holy Spirit to complete the work of Jesus on the earth. The risen Jesus has asked us to carry on his work.

Activity

Show how you understand and can carry on the work of Jesus by completing the following.

Being poor is _____
_____.

Some good news for a poor person might be _____
_____.

I could bring good news to a person if _____
_____.

Sorrow is _____
_____.

I could turn someone's sorrow into joy by _____
_____.

EASTER CUSTOMS

Easter is a joyful time of celebration. The sacrifices of Lent are finished, and everyone rejoices at the new life that spring brings. The word *Easter* was first used to describe the season of spring, when the sun grew stronger. It comes from the word *east*, meaning "the direction of the sunrise." Through the centuries, Christians have created many customs for celebrating the season of Easter.

One custom is the wearing of new or special clothes on Easter Sunday. At the Easter Vigil, the newly baptized Christians are given white garments to express the new life of Christ that they have received. In imitation of this, Christians wear new or special clothes at Easter to celebrate the new life that they, too, have received.

Another custom is the decorating of Easter eggs. Eggs are decorated to show the joy of the season. An egg is also a symbol of new life. The birth of a baby chick reminds people of the new birth that the resurrection brings. The birth of a chick is a symbol of Jesus' rising from the dead. Some even think of the egg's shell as a reminder of the stone tomb in which Jesus was buried.

The most popular Easter flower is the lily. Its great beauty and white color express the glory of the resurrection. Jesus once pointed to the lilies in a field and told his followers, "Not even Solomon in all his glory was as beautiful as one of these" (based on Matthew 6:29). The lily is a sign of God's love and care for us.

People in many cultures bake sweet bread at Easter. Each culture has special ingredients that are put into the dough to make it sweet. Since many people give up sweets for Lent, these breads are a joyful sign that the long period of sacrifice is over. The bread, which is also a reminder of the Eucharist, is sometimes baked in the shape of a cross.

Activity

Each of the words below has something to do with an Easter custom. Unscramble the words and write them on the correct lines. The circled letters will form a special message.

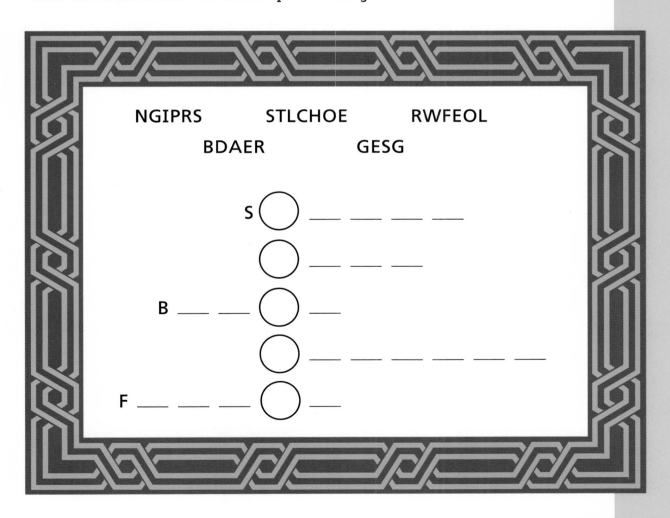

NGIPRS   STLCHOE   RWFEOL

BDAER   GESG

S ◯ __ __ __ __

◯ __ __ __

B __ __ ◯ __

◯ __ __ __ __ __

F __ __ __ ◯ __

EASTER CANDLES

As you have learned, Easter is the season when we celebrate Baptism. At the Easter Vigil, we welcome new members into our Church. During the Sundays of Easter, we often celebrate the Baptism of children. A very important moment in the celebration is when the priest or deacon lights a candle from the Easter candle and gives it to the newly baptized or to a godparent. At that moment, the priest or deacon says, "Receive the light of Christ." The candle you received at your Baptism serves as a reminder of your initiation into the Church.

To remind us that we are one body baptized in Christ, we will make an Easter candle for our class. Cut out a long rectangle from a sheet of posterboard or newsprint. Tape the rectangle to a wall. The rectangle will stand for the candle.

Decorate the candle with symbols of new life. Draw your symbol on a sheet of construction paper; color and cut it out. Now tape or glue your symbol to the candle to make it into an Easter candle.

Some ideas for symbols are pictured on this page. See if you can think of others.

THE RISEN JESUS SENDS US FORTH

Leader: This candle and water remind us of Jesus, the Light and the Life. At the Easter Vigil, we celebrate his resurrection. The light of the Easter candle fills the darkness of the night as we sing "Christ, Our Light!" Then we use this water to baptize the new members of our community, sharing with them the light of Christ. We remember that Jesus sends us forth to share his light and life with those around us. Let us listen to his word.

Gospel Reading

Reader: The Lord be with you.

    All: And also be with you.

Reader: A reading based on the Gospel according to John 20:19–22.

    All: Glory to you, Lord.

Reader: On the evening of the day that Jesus rose, the disciples closed the doors in the room where they were staying because they were afraid. Jesus came and stood among them. "Peace be with you," he said to them. The disciples were overjoyed when they saw him. "Peace be with you," he said again. "As the Father has sent me, so I send you." Then he breathed on them and said, "Receive the Holy Spirit."
The gospel of the Lord.

    All: Praise to you, Lord Jesus Christ.

Sending Forth

Leader: Jesus sends us forth to share his light and his life. Let us come forward to renew our promise to follow him. As we make the Sign of the Cross with the Easter water, let us remember that his Holy Spirit is with us.

Prayer

Leader: Let us pray together that we will obey Jesus' call.
Help us to bring good news to the poor.

    All: Lord, hear our prayer.

Leader: Help us to bring joy to the sorrowful.

    All: Lord, hear our prayer.

Leader: Help us to bring light to those in darkness.

    All: Lord, hear our prayer.

(pause)

Glory be to the Father, and to the Son, and to the Holy Spirit. As it was in the beginning, is now, and ever shall be, world without end. Amen.

Our Church Honors Saints

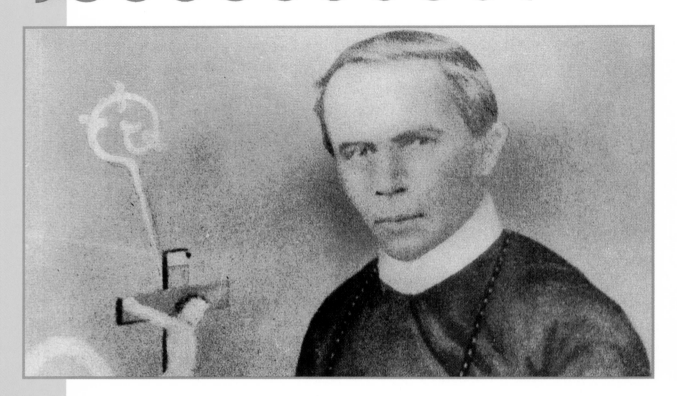

Saint John Neumann

John Neumann was born in 1811 in the European country called Bohemia. Today this country is part of the Czech Republic. As a young man, John entered the seminary to study for the priesthood. He hoped to be ordained and then to go to America as a missionary. John understood the command of Jesus to his disciples, "Go and teach all nations." He wished to follow this call, but when it came time for his ordination, he faced a great disappointment. Because there were already enough priests in his diocese, he could not then be ordained.

John decided he would not wait any longer. In 1836 he decided to set out for America. He traveled across Europe and then by ship to New York. At the age of twenty-five, he arrived with just a suit of clothes and one dollar. In a short time he was ordained a priest. After four years he decided to join the Redemptorists, a society of missionary priests. They are an order that is dedicated to the renewal of the Church through teaching and preaching. John worked as a Redemptorist in parishes in Buffalo, Pittsburgh, and throughout Maryland. Eventually he became the leader of the order in the United States.

One of John's special concerns was education. He wrote books to be used for the study of the Bible and the Catholic faith. He helped Catholic schools to grow stronger. When he was made the bishop of Philadelphia in 1852, he continued the work. As bishop, he built schools and helped to better organize existing schools. He brought sisters to teach in them. Soon there were twenty times more Catholic school students than there had ever been in that city.

What enabled John to be a good teacher of the Catholic faith was the way he lived it himself. As a young man he showed courage and determination in responding to God's call. As a priest he worked hard and was willing to go anywhere to serve. He used his gifts of intelligence and writing to teach others about Jesus.

John Neumann was only forty-eight years old when he died. Although he did not live very long, he accomplished much because he allowed the love of Jesus to work through him.

Activity

One of the books John wrote to teach others about Catholicism was called *The Little Catechism*. A catechism is a handbook that contains all the important Church teachings, sometimes arranged in questions and answers. If you were going to write a catechism, what questions and answers would you include in teaching about Jesus? Write three on the lines provided.

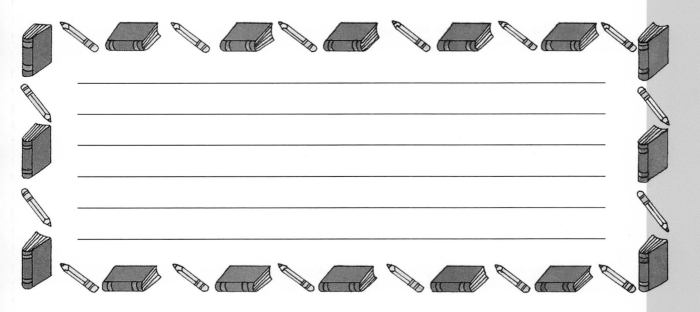

JOHN THE APOSTLE

When John was a young man, he worked as a fisherman with his brother, James, and his father, Zebedee. One day they were mending their torn fishing nets as Jesus was walking along the shore. When Jesus saw John and James, he stopped and called to them. "Follow me," he said. John and James left their father and their boat and followed Jesus.

Based on Mark 1:19–20

John, who was the youngest of the Apostles according to tradition, became Jesus' good friend. Whenever Jesus had something very important to do, he would take Peter, James, and John with him. They were present when Jesus raised a little girl to life. And they were present when Jesus prayed in the garden of Gethsemane before Jesus was arrested.

When Jesus was praying in the garden before his arrest, the three apostles fell asleep. Even though John failed in his faithfulness to Jesus, Jesus still loved him.

According to the gospel that bears his name, John was the only apostle who did not run away when Jesus was crucified. As Jesus was dying, he asked John to take care of his mother, Mary. "This is your mother," he said to John. And from that day, John took care of Mary.

After Jesus rose from the dead, John preached about him to many people. Because John was Jesus' friend, he was able to tell everybody about Jesus' love and forgiveness. We celebrate John's feast day on December 27, two days after the celebration of the birth of Jesus.

Activity

Look at the books of the New Testament found in the Bible. Find three books other than the Gospel of John that bear John's name.

_____

_____

_____

Now imagine that you are going to write a gospel. Fill in your first name and write your responses to the questions.

_____ the Evangelist

What would be the first line of your gospel?

_____

_____

Which one of Jesus' actions would you say is most important?

_____

Which of Jesus' sayings would you put first?

_____

SAINT ELIZABETH OF HUNGARY

Elizabeth of Hungary's childhood sounds like a fairy tale. She was a princess, the daughter of the king of Hungary. After her birth, in 1207, she was promised in marriage to Louis of Thuringia. Thuringia was a country that later became part of Germany. Arranged marriages were common in Elizabeth's time. They helped to keep peace between countries.

At the age of four, Elizabeth was sent to Louis's castle in Thuringia for her education. She was raised with Louis and trained for the royal court. Elizabeth and Louis grew to love one another, and they married when she was fourteen. They had four children.

Elizabeth, who was very religious, spent a great deal of time in prayer and helped the poor who lived outside the castle. She brought people who were sick into her home and nursed them. She stood at the castle gate every day, distributing food. The Wartburg castle was built on a steep hill. Many who came to the castle for help were unable to climb the hill; so Elizabeth ordered a hospital to be built at the base of the hill. She went there daily to feed the patients, to change the sheets on their beds, and to pray with them.

Louis became sick and died of the plague. Elizabeth was heartbroken, but she vowed to continue helping her people. Louis's relatives mocked Elizabeth's good deeds and strong faith. They saw Louis's death as a chance to regain power. They falsely accused Elizabeth of spending all the money in the treasury. Louis's brother ordered Elizabeth and her children to leave the castle. The people of Thuringia were forbidden to help their beloved queen.

Elizabeth and her children left Wartburg and found a simple cottage outside the city of Marburg. Soon she was able to add on a few rooms as a hospital for the sick and elderly. Finally, a reconciliation between Elizabeth and Louis's family was arranged, but she never returned to the castle. Elizabeth joined the Third Order of Saint Francis and spent the remainder of her life in prayer and service to others.

We honor Saint Elizabeth of Hungary on November 17. We pray "Father, you helped Elizabeth of Hungary to recognize and honor Christ in the poor of the world. Let her prayers help us to serve our brothers and sisters in time of trouble and need."

From *The Sacramentary*, The Proper of Saints, Opening Prayer

Write the answers to the following questions on the lines provided.

1. How did Saint Elizabeth recognize and honor Jesus in helping the poor and sick?

_____

_____

_____

2. In today's world, whom can we recognize as Jesus?

_____

3. How can you best follow the example of Saint Elizabeth of Hungary?

_____

_____

_____

_____

_____

SAINT BERNADETTE

Bernadette was the oldest child in a large, poor family. She lived in a mountain village in France more than one hundred years ago.

One day when Bernadette was fourteen years old, she was gathering firewood with her sister Marie and another friend. They came to a stream. Marie and the other girl waded through the water of the stream and reached the other side. As Bernadette was taking off her shoes to cross the stream, she heard the sound of a strong wind. She looked up and saw a young woman standing on the rocks above her. The woman was surrounded by bright light. Bernadette was frightened. She fell to her knees and tried to pray. Then the woman smiled at her. Together, they prayed the Rosary.

After the woman disappeared, Bernadette realized that the other girls had not seen the woman. She tried to tell others about what she had seen, but no one would believe her. Finally, she persuaded her mother to let her return to the place. The lady appeared to her many more times and finally gave her this message: "I am the Immaculate Conception."

Soon everyone believed that Bernadette had truly seen Mary. Sick people went to the stream where Mary had appeared, and some of them were healed of their diseases. The place is called Lourdes. Many still go there today and many are healed. Every year we remember Our Lady of Lourdes and Saint Bernadette on February 11, the day of the first appearance.

Opening

Leader: We are gathered here today to thank God for the many things we have learned this year. Like the saints we have studied, we are called by God to believe in God and love God with all our hearts. We show our belief and love by doing our best in school and by caring for our teachers and classmates. Let us listen to God's call to us.

Gospel Reading

Reader: The Lord be with you.

All: And also be with you.

Reader: A reading based on the Gospel according to John 15:12, 16–17.

All: Glory to you, Lord.

Reader: This is my commandment:
love one another
as I have loved you . . .
You did not choose me,
it was I who chose you
to go forth and bear fruit.
Your fruit must endure,
so that all you ask the Father in my name
he will give you.
The command I give you is this,
that you love one another.
The gospel of the Lord.

All: Praise to you, Lord Jesus Christ.

Prayer of Thanksgiving

Leader: Now let us give thanks to God for all we have received this year. *(Students may offer aloud prayers of thanksgiving for their school, teachers, and classmates.)*

Closing Prayer

Leader: God, our Father, you called Saint John Neumann to be a founder of many schools. We thank you for the work he did and for our school today. Help us to work hard and to respond to the call you have given us to serve you through our schoolwork. We ask this through Christ, our Lord.

All: Amen.

Closing Song: *(Sing the school hymn or another familiar song.)*

Our Church Honors Mary

The Immaculate Conception (oil), Murillo, 17th century, Prado, Madrid, Spain

FEAST OF THE IMMACULATE CONCEPTION

When we think about gifts at this time of year, we usually think of something made or purchased. But there are other kinds of gifts. When we give away these gifts, we receive them from others in abundance. Friendship, love, and compassion are some of these gifts.

The Church teaches that Mary received a special gift or blessing from God because she was going to be the mother of God's Son. This blessing is called the Immaculate Conception. We celebrate the Feast of the Immaculate Conception on December 8. On the Feast of the Immaculate Conception, we celebrate the special gift Mary received when she was conceived without original sin. From the very beginning of life, even before she was born, she was without sin.

Like us, Mary was free to make good choices or selfish choices. Unlike us, she never turned away from God or made a selfish choice. Her entire life was spent caring for Jesus. She even followed him to the cross.

We can always ask Mary to help us be more like her, spending our lives in the service of Jesus. The Feast of the Immaculate Conception occurs in the holy season of Advent. As we recall Mary's gifts, we should think about our own gifts. We, too, have been given special blessings, or gifts, by God. Advent is a good time to think about our God-given gifts and decide how we are going to use them.

God's Special Gift

What are some of the gifts and talents you have received from God? Remember, your gifts and talents are what make you special. A talent is not just the ability to draw, or sing, or play a musical instrument. It might also be the ability to make people laugh, the willingness to put yourself out for other people, or the knack of making other people feel good about themselves.

Activity

Think about the gifts and talents that God has given you. Think, too, about how you can put those gifts to better use. Write a paragraph about your thoughts and title it "My Gifts and Talents."

_____

_____

_____

_____

_____

_____

_____

MARY, A MODEL OF PEACE

Jesus taught his disciples to be peacemakers. In the Sermon on the Mount, he spoke these words.

Blessed are the peacemakers;
they shall be called sons and daughters of God.

Based on Matthew 5:9

Mary was Jesus' mother, and she was also one of his disciples. She was his most faithful follower because she loved him most and never failed to put his words into practice. Mary was a peacemaker because she always responded to violence and hatred with love.

When Jesus was born, King Herod wanted to have him killed. Mary and Joseph quietly took Jesus to live in another country. Even though Herod was trying to kill her child, Mary was still loving. She did not seek revenge.

When Jesus was a man and the people of his own village threw him out of their town, Mary remained peaceful and trusted in God. Even when Jesus was crucified, Mary forgave those who killed him. Mary was a peacemaker, and she is a model for each of us.

The Church has often looked to Mary for help and inspiration in times of war. In 1944, during World War II, Pope Pius XII asked the Church throughout the world to pray to Mary for peace among nations.

Because she was also peaceful in her heart and in her actions, Mary is sometimes called the Queen of Peace. On the Feast of the Immaculate Heart of Mary, we celebrate Mary's peaceful heart. We ask her to pray for us so that we will imitate her example and live in peace.

We can pray to Mary every day to make our world more peaceful. We need to follow her example by being peacemakers.

Activity

Imagine that the following situations happened to you. Before you react to a situation, look up the teaching of Jesus that is listed below the situation. Then write how you would react to the situation if you followed Jesus' teaching.

Situation 1

Robert, the class bully, walks up to you on the playground, shoves you from the back, and walks away, laughing.

Jesus' Teaching: Matthew 5:43–44

I would _____

_____.

Situation 2

Margaret is a new student in your class. She is very quiet and has no one to play with. At recess, you see Margaret standing in the corner of the schoolyard, all alone. You are playing a game with your three favorite friends and only four can play this game.

Jesus' Teaching: Matthew 7:12

I would _____

_____.

Situation 3

Your little brother is sick in bed and cannot go out to play. He asks you to play a board game with him. Your friends come to your house and ask you if you want to play soccer. You love soccer, and you hate that board game.

Jesus' Teaching: Matthew 25:31–40

I would _____

_____.

OUR LADY OF THE ROSARY

Since the earliest days of the Church, Catholics have recognized the special relationship shared by Jesus and Mary. As a way of honoring the major events in Mary's and Jesus' lives, people began to pray the Rosary. In 1571 Pope Gregory XIII set aside a special day for the Church to honor Mary as Our Lady of the Rosary. Today we celebrate the Feast of Our Lady of the Rosary on October 7.

The events of Mary's and Jesus' lives are called **mysteries**. The fifteen mysteries of the Rosary are divided into three major groups: the Joyful Mysteries, the Sorrowful Mysteries, and the Glorious Mysteries.

The Joyful Mysteries

The Annunciation (Luke 1:26–38)
The Visitation (Luke 1:39–45)
The Birth of Jesus (Luke 2:1–10)
The Presentation (Luke 2:22–35)
The Finding of Jesus in the Temple (Luke 2:41–51)

The Sorrowful Mysteries

The Agony in the Garden (Matthew 26:36–46)
The Scourging at the Pillar (Matthew 27:15–26)
The Crowning with Thorns (Matthew 27:27–31)
The Carrying of the Cross (Luke 23:20–32)
The Crucifixion (Luke 23:33–46)

The Glorious Mysteries

The Resurrection (Matthew 28:1–10)
The Ascension (Luke 24:44–53)
The Descent of the Holy Spirit (Acts 2:1–11)
The Assumption of Mary into Heaven (Luke 1:46–55)
The Coronation of Mary as Queen of Heaven (Psalm 24:10)

There are no Scripture texts that describe Mary's assumption or coronation. Instead, we meditate on the Scriptures used on Mary's feast days.

When we pray the Rosary, we meditate, or reflect, on Mary's faithfulness, as we recite the Hail Mary again and again.

Activity

Working with a partner, create a pictorial biography of five scenes from Mary's life. Then find a quotation from Scripture that you feel describes Mary. Write it at the bottom of the page.

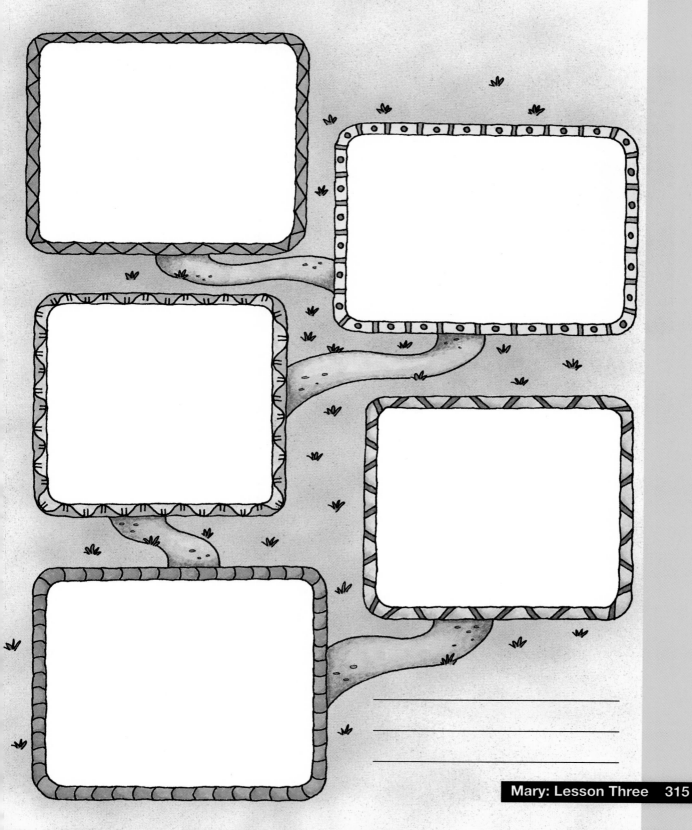

Our Church Celebrates Holy Days

ALL SOULS' DAY

Blest too are the sorrowing;
Happy are those who mourn;
they shall be consoled.

Based on Matthew 5:4

Jesus spoke these words to his disciples in the Sermon on the
Mount; these words speak to us today, too. Death brings us great
sadness. Whenever we lose someone we love, we grieve. Some of us
may have had pets that died. We may have known a person who
died. The person may even have been someone in our family.
Because we have loved someone who has died, we are sad. Being
sad is part of being human and part of being Christian. Even
though we are sad, as Christians we also have hope.

When Jesus rose from the dead, he overcame death for all of us.
Jesus told us that anyone who believes in him would not die
forever but would rise with him.

"In my Father's house there are many dwelling places . . .
I am going to prepare a place for you, and then I shall come to
take you with me, that where I am, you also may be" (based on
John 14:2–4).

We Pray for the Dead

As Christians, we trust in the promises of Jesus. When someone dies, we gather to pray at the wake, at the funeral Mass, and at the grave. After the funeral, we remember the deceased on special occasions such as birthdays, anniversaries, and holidays. We think about the times we have shared together, we give thanks for those times and we pray for the deceased.

Each year, the Church celebrates a special memorial for all those who have died. It is called All Souls' Day. The celebration takes place on November 2. In the special Mass of that day, we listen to readings from the Bible that remind us of the resurrection of Jesus. We pray that those who have died will share his resurrection.

When we participate in the Eucharist, we share in Jesus, who is the Bread of Life. We remember his words.

I am the bread that gives life;
Whoever comes to me will never be hungry.

Based on John 6:35

Those whom we love who have died also share in the Eucharist. The promise of Jesus is true for them, too.

Praying a prayer that we know from memory is another way of praying for the dead. This is one of the prayers we use.

May the souls of the faithful departed,
through the mercy of God, rest in peace. Amen.

Activity

Write a prayer for someone you know who has died.

PENTECOST SUNDAY

The risen Jesus remained with his followers after the resurrection. During that time, Jesus continued to teach them and to prepare them for the time when he would return to his Father.

"I will ask my Father and he will give you another Helper, to be with you forever. I will not leave you orphaned. The Helper, the Holy Spirit, whom the Father will send in my name, will teach you everything, and remind you of all that I have said to you."

Based on John 14:16, 18, 26

Fifty days after Easter we celebrate Pentecost Sunday, the day the early Church received the Holy Spirit. John's Gospel describes the coming of the Holy Spirit on the first Pentecost.

The Acts of the Apostles tell about what happened on Pentecost when the Holy Spirit appeared to the disciples.

On the day of Pentecost, the disciples were all gathered together in one place. Suddenly, a noise like a driving wind came from heaven and filled the whole house. They saw what looked liked fiery tongues, which stood over each person there. They were filled with the Holy Spirit and began to speak different languages as the Spirit directed them.

Many devout Jews from every nation were staying in Jerusalem at that time. When they heard the noise, a crowd gathered. They were surprised because each one heard the disciples speaking to him in his own language. The crowd was amazed and puzzled and they said to one another, "What does this mean?" But others made fun of them and said the disciples had been drinking the new wine.

Peter began to preach to the crowd. He said to them, "Turn away from your sins and be baptized in Jesus' name. Your sins will be forgiven and you will receive the gift of the Holy Spirit."

Based on Acts of the Apostles 2:1–13, 38

The Church was born on Pentecost. Through the signs of wind and fire, the Holy Spirit filled the disciples with courage to continue the work of Jesus. We first receive the Holy Spirit at Baptism. When we are confirmed, the gifts of the Spirit are strengthened within us. On the Feast of Pentecost, we thank Jesus for sending his Holy Spirit to help and guide us. We pray that we will use the gifts we have been given to be a sign of Jesus to others.

Activity

Name a gift, talent, or ability that you have been given by God. Use the lines below to tell how you could use this gift to be a sign of Jesus for others.

_____

_____

_____

_____

_____

_____

THE FEAST OF SAINT PATRICK

Saint Patrick, who is often called the "Apostle to Ireland," was born in the late fourth century. His father was a Roman official who had been sent to work in Britain. At sixteen, Patrick was kidnapped by pirates and taken to Ireland, where he was sold as a slave. He was put to work as a shepherd. Out in the fields, Patrick faced the bitter weather and lived off the land. In his loneliness, he turned to God for comfort and support. He decided that if he ever returned home, he would become a priest.

After six years, Patrick escaped and returned to his family. Although he was happy to be free, he never forgot his experience in Ireland. It is said that in his dreams, he heard the voices of the Irish peasants calling him to return. The dream did not become a reality for more than twenty years. During this time, Patrick studied for the priesthood, was ordained, became a parish priest, and was eventually made a bishop. He was sent as a missionary to Ireland in the year 432 to bring Christ to the Irish.

Patrick was opposed by a group of people who did not want to lose their power over the Irish. But Patrick did not give up. He preached about God by telling stories and using examples the peasants understood. He used a shamrock to help the Irish understand the mystery of the Blessed Trinity. Patrick taught that the three leaves of the shamrock were like the three distinct persons in one God: God the Father, God the Son, and God the Holy Spirit.

Through Patrick's deep faith and hard work, almost everyone in Ireland became a follower of Christ. Yet, Patrick did not want praise. He told people again and again, "I am only an instrument of God."

The Church celebrates the Feast of Saint Patrick on March 17. On that day, many people dress in green and wear shamrocks in memory of this humble saint whose love of God inspired him to bring the good news to an entire nation.

Activity

On each of the shamrock leaves, write something you have learned about Saint Patrick.

_____
_____
_____
_____

_____
_____
_____

_____
_____
_____

Patrick called himself "God's instrument." What do you think he meant?

_____

_____

_____

How are you an instrument of God? On the lines below, write one way that God works through you.

_____

_____

_____

In The Spirit of Jesus

DOROTHY DAY

Dorothy Day was born in Brooklyn, New York, in 1897. When she was a child, her family moved often so that her father could look for work with a newspaper. The family was living in California at the time of the great San Francisco earthquake. When Dorothy wrote her life story, she recalled that event from her childhood. "Another thing I remember about California was the joy of doing good, of sharing whatever we had with others after the earthquake . . . All my neighbors joined my mother in caring for the homeless. Every stitch of available clothes was given away" (*Long Loneliness: An Autobiography*, pages 21–22). This attitude of caring for the needy remained with Dorothy all her life.

As a child, Dorothy was religious. On her own she joined the Episcopal Church. But as a college student, she became more interested in politics than in religion. For a long time she drifted through life, searching for something to give her a purpose. Finally, after the birth of her daughter, Dorothy returned to religion. It was Jesus' concern for the poor that helped her believe in him again and join the Catholic Church.

Dorothy met a man named Peter Maurin. Together they began the Catholic Worker movement in 1933. Dorothy Day and Peter Maurin opened what they called houses of hospitality, where they fed the hungry and sheltered the homeless. This is what Jesus asks us to do. Many people joined them. They were all dedicated to putting Christ's love for the poor into practice. They studied the gospels and the Church's teaching about loving the poor. They recognized Christ in the least of his brothers and sisters—the poor.

Once, Dorothy Day was asked to write for young Catholics about the poor. She told stories about many people, including this one: "An old man who tends a pushcart came in to us one day with a big bag of meat bones 'to enrich the soup.' He had collected them from neighborhood butchers for our New York soup kitchen, where three hundred or so meals are served each day."

Generosity was a very important part of her care for the poor. But Dorothy also emphasized something other than generosity, an even more difficult thing. She called it "detachment." It means doing without things, having only what is necessary to do what God calls us to do. We care for our needy sisters and brothers more than we care about our own comfort.

Dorothy concluded her advice in this way. "It begins with little sacrifices—doing without something in order to help others, whether it is clothes or food and drink."

Dorothy Day died in 1980. She was eighty-three years old.

Activity

Make a list of your five most valuable possessions. Then write a paragraph telling how it would feel to give your possessions away to a needy person.

_____

_____

_____

_____

_____

_____

Habitat for Humanity

Habitat for Humanity International is an organization. It believes that everyone has the right to decent housing. Since 1976, Habitat for Humanity has built more than 30,000 homes worldwide.

Habitat for Humanity began in Georgia. At first, donated money was used to purchase building materials and to help poor families buy houses. It was a good idea, but families still had trouble paying for their houses.

Soon volunteers themselves started building the houses with donated materials. The finished homes are reasonably priced and the loans for the houses are interest free. On moving day, the new owners are given the keys to the house and a Bible. One of Habitat for Humanity's aims is "to witness to the Gospel of Jesus Christ through living acts and the spoken and written word." Their ultimate goal is to eliminate homelessness completely throughout the world.

Habitat for Humanity is an ecumenical housing ministry. The word *ecumenical* means "promoting Christian unity throughout the world." People of all traditions work side by side tiling roofs and installing walls. Many workers had never before used a hammer or a saw. These workers learn how to use tools with the help of skilled volunteers. The new owners help, too. They promise to contribute five hundred hours of work to another Habitat for Humanity project. Everyone involved in a Habitat for Humanity project benefits.

Activity

Habitat for Humanity's spirit of cooperation among people reminds us of the words of Saint Paul. "We are all one body in Christ, we were all baptized into one body, whether Jews or Greeks, slaves or free persons" (based on 1 Corinthians 12:12–13). Find Saint Paul's words to the Corinthians in the puzzle below by drawing arrows from box to box. Not all the letters will be used, and none of the letters is used more than once. The first two words have been done for you.

W	Q	Z	A	Z	T	Z	X	Z	N	X	N	Q
Z	E	B	Q	P	X	I	Q	I	T	O	Z	E
F	A	F	L	X	Z	Z	D	Q	E	O	B	X
K	V	R	Q	L	X	E	Q	T	Z	H	Q	O
X	N	X	E	Z	A	Q	H	R	W	X	D	Z
E	L	O	A	E	Q	E	O	Q	G	Y	E	S
Y	B	L	R	X	Z	R	X	S	R	E	S	K
O	Y	Z	X	E	J	Z	W	Q	X	R	S	L
D	Z	I	Q	Z	W	E	Q	S	E	F	A	Z
Q	N	Q	I	X	Z	E	N	Q	X	E	R	V
C	X	R	Q	S	W	O	Z	R	P	O	E	O
Z	H	K	X	Z	T	Q	S	Q	E	Z	S	X

OUR CATHOLIC HERITAGE

WHAT CATHOLICS BELIEVE

We can come to know and understand our faith in many ways.

 The Bible

The **Bible** is the story of God and God's people. It is the word of God. The Bible has two main parts: the Old Testament and the New Testament. The Old Testament has forty-six books and the New Testament has twenty-seven books. The books of the Bible are called sacred Scripture.

The Old Testament

The book of the Old Testament tells about God and God's people before the coming of the Messiah—Jesus. It contains the sacred writings of the Jewish people and Christians. The Old Testament tells the story of our salvation up to the coming of Jesus. Christians believe that the Old Testament foretells the coming of Jesus.

The New Testament

After Jesus ascended into heaven, people who knew Jesus told and retold stories about him and his teachings to pass on to other generations. Eventually, some of these stories became sacred Scripture.

The New Testament begins with the anticipation of Jesus about to come into the world. In the books of the New Testament, we hear witness accounts of Jesus' life and teachings. In other books, we hear letters of encouragement and guidance written to the early Church. In one book of the New Testament, we hear about the life struggles of the first Christian communities.

The Letters of Paul were written to the early Christian communities that Paul helped to set up. Since traveling in those days was not always possible, Paul relied on sending encouragement and guidance to the Christian communities in the form of letters. Paul wrote about his faith experiences of Jesus.

The Gospel of Mark was written about thirty years after Paul wrote his letters. Mark believed that the only way to follow Jesus is to take up our daily crosses and carry them as Jesus carried his cross to Calvary.

The Gospel of Matthew tells us that we must be people of action. We must do what God commands, not just talk about it.

The Gospel of Luke tells us that Jesus came to bring the good news of his Father's unending love. It contains many stories of healing and forgiveness.

The Gospel of John tells mainly about Jesus' work, which was to do God's will.

The Holy Land

Damascus

● **Caesarea Philippi**

GALILEE

Mediterranean Sea

Cana ●

Nazareth ●

Sea of Galilee

▲ *Mount Tabor*

SAMARIA

River Jordan

PEREA

North

West *East*

South

Plain of Sharon

● **Lydda**

Mount of Olives

● **Bethany**

Jerusalem ●

Bethlehem ●

Garden of Gethsemani

Dead Sea

JUDEA

# The Trinity

We Believe in God

There is only one God, who is revealed to us as three Persons in the Blessed Trinity: God the Father, God the Son, and God the Holy Spirit.

God is all-good, all-holy, and all-knowing. God is always merciful and just.

We believe that God speaks to us. We come to know God in many ways, especially through Jesus, the Scriptures, and the life of the Catholic Church.

God created all things. Human beings are made in the image and likeness of God. We are invited to share the gift of God's life and loving presence as well as the responsibility of caring for our world.

We Believe in Jesus

Jesus is the Second Person of the Blessed Trinity and God's own Son. Jesus has a divine nature and a human nature. When we say that Jesus has a divine nature, we mean that he is God. We believe God's eternal Son became man like us in all things but sin. God's Son becoming man is called the **Incarnation**.

We believe that Jesus is the **Messiah**, or Christ, the anointed one sent by God. Jesus' mission was to announce the good news of God's kingdom; to form a new and everlasting covenant; to free us from sin; and to bring us everlasting life. Jesus carried out his mission by teaching, healing, forgiving, and working miracles as signs of God's love and compassion.

Jesus is the **Savior** of the world. Jesus saves us by his life, death, and resurrection.

Jesus rose to new life and invites us to share this new life with him. The **resurrection** is God's victory over sin and death and the source of our hope. Jesus' resurrection teaches us that death is not an ending but leads us to new and everlasting life.

After the resurrection, Jesus shared his mission with the Apostles. He promised to send the Holy Spirit to be with them. Then Jesus returned in glory to his Father. Catholics call Jesus' return to his Father the **ascension**.

We Believe in the Holy Spirit

The **Holy Spirit** is the Third Person of the Blessed Trinity, one with the Father and the Son, yet distinct. The Holy Spirit is the bond of love and unity between the Father and the Son. The Spirit leads and guides us in living as followers of Jesus.

The Holy Spirit has been at work in the world since creation. Under the guidance of the Holy Spirit, the authors of the Bible wrote God's word. At **Pentecost**, the Holy Spirit descended upon the disciples, giving them the courage to be Jesus' witnesses in the world.

The Holy Spirit is at work in the Church today, helping us to carry on Jesus' mission. At Baptism we receive God's grace and become temples of the Holy Spirit.

ABOUT The Catholic Church

Catholics are followers of Jesus and, under the leadership of the pope and bishops, receive and share God's word, worship God, celebrate the sacraments, and serve others.

The Church has four marks, or qualities, that show its truth and its origin in God. The Church is **one**, in our faith, sacraments, and leadership. The Church is **holy**, because we draw our life from God and offer people the way to God. The Church is **catholic**, or universal, open to all people. The Church is **apostolic**, founded on and faithful to the Apostles' teachings.

The chief teacher of the Church is the pope. The pope is the successor to Saint Peter, the first bishop of Rome. We believe that the pope is the leader of those called to serve God's people on earth.

We describe the Church as the People of God, the Body of Christ, and a Pilgrim People. These images help us understand the mystery of God's love that is revealed in the Church.

Mary

Catholics believe that Mary, the mother of Jesus, was conceived without original sin. This special gift from God is called the **Immaculate Conception**. From the first moment of life, Mary was filled with grace and lived a sinless life.

We honor Mary as the mother of God and mother of the Church. By calling Mary the mother of God, we declare that Jesus is God. As mother of the Church, Mary shows us how to live with faith and love. She cares for us, her children.

We believe that through the Holy Spirit's power, Jesus was conceived without a human father. We honor Mary's purity as a sign of her loving response to God's plan for the world.

Catholics believe that Mary was taken up to heaven, body and soul, and fully shares in Jesus' resurrection. This belief is called the **assumption**.

Life Everlasting

We believe that God's kingdom will be fulfilled, or completed at the end of time. The Church teaches that, at the end of time, Jesus will come again in glory to reveal God's peace, love, and justice. Catholics await Jesus' second coming with hope and faith in all of God's promises.

Our eternal life depends on God's mercy and how we have shown love for God, ourselves, and others. If we have tried to live as faithful followers of Jesus, we will be forever united with God in **heaven**. Heaven is unending happiness with God and all who love God. After death, any remaining faults or selfishness will be cleansed in **purgatory**. This time of purification will prepare us for the complete love and happiness promised by God.

Those who deliberately have refused, in serious ways, to love God and their neighbor separate themselves forever from God and those who love God. We call this everlasting separation **hell**.

The Communion of Saints

When Jesus returns in glory, the **Communion of Saints** will be united. The Communion of Saints is the entire community of God's people, living and dead. It includes those in heaven, those living as God's people on the earth, and those in purgatory waiting to be united with God.

How Catholics Worship

Catholics have a sacred history of **worship**. Worship is giving honor and praise to God. Through the sacraments and prayer, we praise, thank, and adore God, and ask God's help.

ABOUT The Liturgical Year

The liturgical year is the Church's official calendar of feasts and seasons. It celebrates all the important events of Jesus' life and Jesus' presence with us today.

The Church year begins with four weeks of **Advent**—a season of joyful waiting.

During the **Christmas season**, we celebrate Jesus' birth. We also celebrate the Epiphany and the Baptism of Jesus.

Another major season of the Church year is **Lent**. During the forty days of Lent, a time of prayer and sacrifice, we prepare to celebrate Easter.

The last week of Lent is called Holy Week. On the first day of Holy Week we celebrate Passion Sunday (Palm Sunday), when we recall Jesus' triumphant entry into Jerusalem. The last three days of Holy Week are known as the **Easter Triduum**—the holiest days of the liturgical year. On Holy Thursday, we remember the Last Supper. On Good Friday, we remember Jesus' crucifixion. At the Easter Vigil on Holy Saturday, we celebrate Jesus' resurrection. We continue this celebration on the following day, Easter Sunday—the Church's greatest feast.

The **Easter season** lasts for fifty days. During this time we celebrate the ascension of Jesus and the coming of the Holy Spirit on Pentecost.

During the Church year we also have a season called **Ordinary Time**. During this season, we celebrate all that Jesus has taught us, proclaimed in the gospel readings at Mass.

Turn to page 37 to study the Liturgical Year chart.

ABOUT The Sacraments

The **sacraments** are sacred signs that celebrate God's love for us and Jesus' presence in our lives and in the Church. There are seven sacraments. Through the sacraments, we are united with Jesus and share in God's life. Sharing in God's life is called grace.

The Sacraments of Initiation   We become full members of the Church through the three sacraments of initiation. The sacraments of initiation are Baptism, Confirmation, and Eucharist.

Baptism welcomes us into the Christian community, frees us from original sin, and unites us with Jesus.

During the celebration the priest or deacon pours water over the head of the person being baptized as he prays, "I baptize you in the name of the Father, and of the Son, and of the Holy Spirit."

Rite of Baptism

Each of us is born into a sinful condition that separates us from God. This condition is called **original sin**. Baptism frees us from original sin and reunites us with God.

Through the waters of Baptism, which represent death and new life, we share in Jesus' death and resurrection. We are called away from a life of sin to a new life in Christ.

Confirmation strengthens the new life we received at Baptism and makes us living witnesses of Jesus in the world.

During the celebration the bishop or priest lays his hand on the head of the one to be confirmed and anoints the forehead with chrism as he prays, "Be sealed with the Gift of the Holy Spirit."

Rite of Confirmation

Confirmation is usually celebrated with the bishop. The Holy Spirit gives us gifts to help us to carry on the mission of the Church.

Eucharist celebrates the real presence of Jesus' Body and Blood under the appearances of bread and wine.

During the celebration the priest says the words of consecration over the bread and wine, which become the Body and Blood of Christ.

The **Eucharist** is the central celebration of the Church and our greatest act of worship. Jesus taught that he is the Bread of Life. He promised to give his followers his Body and Blood so that they could live forever. Jesus fulfilled this promise at the Last Supper on the night before he died.

The Eucharist makes present Jesus' sacrificial death on the cross and his resurrection from the dead. The word *Eucharist* means "thanksgiving." During the Mass we praise and thank God for all our gifts, especially the gift of God's Son, Jesus.

Jesus is truly present in the Eucharist. The Eucharist still has the appearance of ordinary bread and wine, but, through the power of the Holy Spirit, they become Jesus' Body and Blood.

The Eucharist unites us with Jesus and the Church community. Jesus is also present in the people gathered to celebrate the Eucharist, in the word proclaimed, and in the priest who presides.

The Sacraments of Healing The sacraments of healing—Reconciliation and Anointing of the Sick—celebrate Jesus' forgiveness and healing.

Reconciliation celebrates God's healing and forgiveness of our sins.

During the celebration the priest prays the prayer of absolution, ending with these words: "I absolve you from your sins in the name of the Father, and of the Son, and of the Holy Spirit."

Rite of Penance

When we sin, we choose to turn away from God and one another. In Reconciliation, we are reunited with God and the Church community.

Reconciliation is always celebrated with a priest. We may celebrate individually or communally. We may celebrate the sacrament of Reconciliation any time we feel the need of God's mercy and forgiveness.

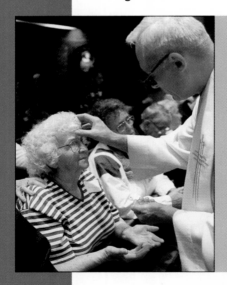

The **Anointing of the Sick** brings Jesus' healing, comfort, and strength to those who are seriously ill, elderly, or in danger of death.

During the celebration the priest anoints the person with the oil of the sick as he prays, "Through this holy anointing may the Lord in his love and mercy help you with the grace of the Holy Spirit. May the Lord who frees you from sin save you and raise you up."

Rite of Anointing

Before the anointing, the sick may celebrate Reconciliation. Following the anointing they may receive the Eucharist. The Eucharist we receive as we approach death is called **Viaticum**. *Viaticum* means "food for the journey," our journey to everlasting life with God.

Like Reconciliation, Anointing of the Sick may be celebrated privately or communally.

The Sacraments of Commitment   In the sacraments of commitment, the Church celebrates two special ways that people serve others by sharing their gifts. The sacraments of commitment are Matrimony and Holy Orders.

The sacrament of **Matrimony** celebrates the permanent and lifelong love of a man and woman for each other.

During the celebration the bride and groom exchange marriage vows, promising always to be faithful to each other.

In the sacrament of Matrimony, the couple's love for one another is a sign of God's love and faithfulness for all people and Christ's love for the Church.

God gives married couples a special grace to help their love grow. Through their love, they share in God's life-giving power and become one.

Catholic parents accept the responsibility and joy of raising their children as members of the Body of Christ. Through their unselfish love and care for their children, parents are a living sign of God's love and forgiveness.

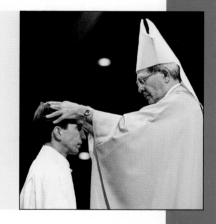

In the sacrament of **Holy Orders**, bishops, priests, and deacons are ordained to serve the Church in a special way.

During the celebration the bishop lays his hands on the head of the person to be ordained. Afterward, he prays a prayer of consecration, or blessing.

The word *ordain* means "to set aside." Bishops are "set aside" or empowered to carry on the work of the Apostles and serve the Church by leading a diocese. Bishops have the special responsibility of teaching, leading, and sanctifying the Catholic Church.

Priests are ordained by a bishop to help him in ministering to the community. Priests, like bishops, celebrate the sacraments, proclaim God's word, and guide the community.

The word *deacon* means "server." Deacons serve by caring for the poor. They also baptize, proclaim the gospel, witness marriages, and preside at funerals.

ABOUT The Mass

Introductory Rites

At Mass we come together to pray and worship as the family of Jesus.

Entrance Procession and Gathering Song ▶

As the priest and other ministers enter in procession, we stand and sing a gathering song.

◀ **Greeting**

We make the sign of the cross. The priest welcomes us by saying, "The Lord be with you." We answer, "And also with you."

Penitential Rite ▶

As a community, we admit that we have sinned and we thank God for his gift of forgiveness. We pray the opening prayer.

Gloria

We sing or say this hymn of praise to God.

Liturgy of the Word

First Reading ▶

The lector usually reads a story from the Old Testament about God's love for us.

◀ Responsorial Psalm

The song leader sings a psalm from the Bible. We join in singing a response.

Second Reading

The lector reads from the New Testament, usually from one of the letters.

Gospel Acclamation

Before the gospel is proclaimed by the priest or deacon, we sing, "Alleluia" or another acclamation.

Gospel ▶

We stand in honor of Jesus as the gospel is proclaimed.

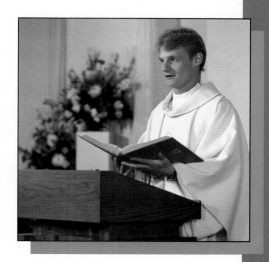

◀ Homily

The priest or deacon explains the readings, especially the gospel, in a special talk called the homily.

Profession of Faith

We stand to declare our beliefs by reciting the Nicene Creed.

General Intercessions

We pray for the pope and the bishops, for our country, and for all God's people.

Liturgy of the Eucharist

Preparation of the Altar and the Gifts ▶

We bring gifts of bread and wine to the altar, as the table is prepared. The priest offers our gifts to God.

◀ **Eucharistic Prayer**

In this prayer of praise and thanksgiving, the priest addresses God the Creator in our name. Together we sing a song of praise to God for his many blessings, especially for the gift of Jesus.

We sing or say, "Holy, holy, holy Lord, God of power and might. Heaven and earth are full of your glory. Hosanna in the highest. Blessed is he who comes in the name of the Lord. Hosanna in the highest."

Together with the priest, we call upon the Holy Spirit and ask that the bread and wine become Jesus' Body and Blood. The priest consecrates the bread and wine.

We proclaim the mystery of faith. We sing or say these or other words of joy and praise,

> "Christ has died,
> Christ is risen,
> Christ will come again."

As the Eucharistic Prayer
ends, we proclaim, "Amen."

Communion Rite

◀ **The Lord's Prayer**
We pray together the prayer that Jesus
taught us—The Lord's Prayer.

Sign of Peace ▶
We offer each other a sign of peace to show
that we are all brothers and sisters in Jesus.

Breaking of the Bread
While the priest breaks the bread, we sing
or say, "Lamb of God, you take away the sins of
the world: have mercy on us.
Lamb of God, you take away the sins of the
world: have mercy on us.
Lamb of God, you take away the sins of the
world: grant us peace."

◀ **Communion**
Jesus invites us to share the Bread of Life.

Concluding Rite

Blessing
The priest blesses us in the name of God the Father, God
the Son, and God the Holy Spirit. We answer, "Amen."

Dismissal
The priest tells us to go in peace to love and serve God
and others. We sing a song of thanks and praise.

ABOUT Reconciliation

The sacrament of Reconciliation, or Penance, celebrates God reaching out to us through the ministry of the Church.

Preparation I prepare for the sacrament of Reconciliation by looking back over my words and actions since my last confession. I ask myself these questions: How do I fulfill God's command to love my neighbor as myself? Have I hurt others by unkind words? How have I shown my love for God? Have I been helpful at home? Have I given good example? Am I sorry for having sinned?

Rite for Reconciliation of Individuals

Priest's Welcome The priest welcomes me in the name of Jesus and the Church.

Reading from Scripture The priest may share with me a reading from the Bible.

Confession I tell my sins to the priest. This is called my confession. The priest then suggests ways that I might serve God better. Then he asks me to say a prayer or do some act of service to help me grow to be a better person. This is called an act of penance.

Prayer of Sorrow The priest then asks me to tell God that I am sorry for my sins. I say a prayer of sorrow, called an act of contrition.

Absolution Acting in the name of the Christian community, the priest extends his hands over me and asks God to forgive me. The priest forgives me in the name of the Father, and of the Son, and of the Holy Spirit. This is called absolution.

Prayer of Praise and Dismissal After receiving absolution, I praise God with the priest. Then he says, "The Lord has freed you from your sins. Go in peace." I answer, "Amen."

Celebrating Reconciliation in Community

Sometimes we gather together as a community to celebrate the sacrament of Reconciliation.

Introductory Rites   We sing an opening hymn. The priest greets us and invites us to pray for God's forgiveness.

Celebration of the Word of God   We listen to readings from the Bible. The priest reads the gospel and preaches a homily.

Examination of Conscience   We examine our conscience and tell God we are sorry for our sins.

Rite of Reconciliation   We pray together an act of contrition and sing or pray The Lord's Prayer. Then, one by one, we go to confession and receive absolution.

Proclamation of Praise for God's Mercy   When individual confessions are over, the priest invites us to praise and thank God for his mercy.

Concluding Rite   The priest blesses us and dismisses us. We sing a song of praise and thanksgiving.

How Catholics Live

The teachings of Jesus and the Church show us how Catholics live happy and loving lives.

ABOUT The Beatitudes

They teach us to love God and others, and promise us a place in the kingdom of heaven. Christians believe that they will be happy forever if they live the Beatitudes. The Beatitudes are Jesus' teachings on how to find everlasting happiness.

The Beatitudes	How We Live the Beatitudes
Happy are the poor in spirit. The reign of God is theirs.	We are poor in spirit when we know that we need God more than anything else in life. We obey God and trust in God's goodness.
Happy are the sorrowing. They will be comforted.	The sin and suffering in the world make us sad. We try to help those who are hurting. We know that God is with them.
Happy are the gentle. They will receive all that God has promised.	We are kind and loving. We use the gifts that God has given us to help others.
Happy are those who hunger and thirst for justice. They will be satisfied.	We long for God's peace, love, and justice to rule the world. We work to help God's kingdom grow. We share the things we have with those in need.
Happy are those who show mercy to others. They will receive mercy.	We forgive anyone who has hurt us. We accept others and are patient with them.
Happy are the single-hearted. They will see God.	We want only to do what God wants us to do. We show our love for God by loving our neighbor.
Happy are the peacemakers. They will be called children of God.	We try to bring God's peace to the world. We help people make up after a fight. We work for unity.
Happy are those who are treated unfairly for doing what is right. The reign of God is theirs.	We carry on Jesus' work in the world. We speak out against injustice. We stand up for what is right, even when it is not always easy.

ABOUT The Commandments

Jesus taught that it is important to obey the Ten Commandments. The Commandments guide us in living as children of God.

The Ten Commandments	The Commandments Help Us to Live
1. I, the Lord, am your God. You shall not have other gods besides me.	We believe in God and love him more than anyone or anything else in life. We remember God's gifts to us. We talk and listen to God in prayer.
2. You shall not take the name of the Lord, your God, in vain.	We use the names of God, Jesus, and all holy persons, places, and things with respect and love. We never say God or Jesus' name in anger.
3. Remember to keep holy the Sabbath day.	We worship God by celebrating the Eucharist together on Sunday. We relax and do special things on Sunday in honor of God.
4. Honor your father and mother.	We love, respect, and obey our parents and all adults who care for us.
5. You shall not kill.	We show respect for God's gift of life by caring for all human life. We never fight or hurt others.
6. You shall not commit adultery.	We respect our bodies and the bodies of others. We use our sexuality according to God's plan.
7. You shall not steal.	We never take things that belong to someone else. We are careful with other people's things. We do not cheat.
8. You shall not bear false witness against your neighbor.	We are truthful and honest. We never tell lies or hurt others by what we say.
9. You shall not covet your neighbor's wife.	We respect the promises that married people have made to each other.
10. You shall not covet anything that belongs to your neighbor.	We are satisfied with what we have. We are not jealous or greedy.

The Great Commandment

"You shall love the Lord, your God, with all your heart, with all your being, with all your strength, and with all your mind, and your neighbor as yourself" (Luke 10:27).

Jesus summed up the Ten Commandments in the **Great Commandment**. The Great Commandment teaches us that God's laws are based on love of God and love of neighbor.

The New Commandment

"This is my commandment: love one another as I love you" (John 15:12).

Jesus' love is the perfect example of how we are to live. We must love as Jesus loved. We live the New Commandment by acting with mercy, peace, kindness, justice, and forgiveness.

ABOUT The Works of Mercy and the Precepts of the Church

The Works of Mercy

Jesus teaches that when we serve others, we serve him. The loving acts described in Matthew 25:31–46 are called the **Corporal and Spiritual Works of Mercy**. The Works of Mercy tell us how to respond to the basic needs of all people.

The Corporal Works of Mercy
1. Feed the hungry.
2. Give drink to the thirsty.
3. Clothe the naked.
4. Visit those in prison.
5. Shelter the homeless.
6. Visit the sick.
7. Bury the dead.

The Spiritual Works of Mercy
1. Help others do what is right.
2. Teach the ignorant.
3. Give advice to the doubtful.
4. Comfort those who suffer.
5. Be patient with others.
6. Forgive injuries.
7. Pray for the living and the dead.

The Precepts of the Church

The Precepts, or laws, of the Church list the responsibilities of all Catholics.

The Precepts of the Church

1. Assist at Mass on Sundays and holy days of obligation. Do no unnecessary physical work on those days.
2. Confess serious sins at least once a year.
3. Receive Holy Communion during the Easter season.
4. Fast and abstain on the days appointed.
5. Contribute to the support of the Church.
6. Observe the laws of the Church concerning marriage.
7. Join in the missionary spirit of the Church.

ABOUT Moral Living

Obstacles to Living a Moral Life

Sin prevents us from living as followers of Jesus. Sin is a free decision to do what we know is wrong and to omit doing what we know is right. When we sin, we make a conscious choice to turn away from God and the Church's teachings. However, even when we sin, God's mercy and love never leave us.

Very serious sins that turn us away from God and the Church community are called **mortal sins**. There are three conditions that make a sin mortal.
- The act must be seriously wrong.
- We must know that the act is seriously wrong.
- We must make a free choice to commit the sin.

Mortal sins must be confessed in the sacrament of Reconciliation. Through Jesus, we receive God's mercy and forgiveness.

Less serious sins are called **venial sins**. Venial sins weaken our relationship with God and the Church community.

Helps in Living a Moral Life

The Holy Spirit helps us overcome sin and live according to the teachings of Jesus and the Church. The Spirit guides our **conscience**, the ability to judge whether something is right or wrong. The Spirit helps us to resist **temptation**, the attraction or pressures that may lead us to sin. However, the Spirit does not force us to make the right decisions. One of our greatest blessings is the gift of **free will**. Free will is freedom to choose to do what is right or wrong.

Catholics call God's loving presence in our lives **grace**. Grace gives us the strength to say no to selfishness and to act as the good people God created us to be. God's loving presence, his grace, helps us choose what is good.

Through the sacraments, especially Eucharist and Reconciliation, we receive **sacramental grace**, or help from God, to live as Jesus taught us.

ABOUT Virtues

Through the Holy Spirit, we receive **virtues**, or spiritual powers, which help us to do good and avoid sin.

The most important virtues are **faith, hope,** and **love**. They help us to believe in God, trust in his promises, and show our love for him by living as Jesus taught.

ABOUT The Gifts of the Holy Spirit

The seven gifts of the Holy Spirit describe the ways the Holy Spirit helps and guides us.

The Gifts of the Holy Spirit

1. **Wisdom** helps us to know how God wants us to live.
2. **Understanding** helps us to be aware of all that God has taught us through Jesus, the Bible, and the Church.
3. **Knowledge** helps us to know that God is more important than anything else in life.
4. **Right Judgment** helps us make good decisions.
5. **Courage** helps us to be strong when faced with problems.
6. **Reverence** helps us to love God as our Father and to show our love in prayer.
7. **Wonder and Awe** help us to be filled with wonder and thanks for all that God creates.

ABOUT Vocations

For most of us, our baptism was celebrated when we were infants. Our parents and godparents wanted to share with us their Catholic faith. They knew that we would need strong values and guidelines in order to live full and happy lives.

As we have grown in the Church community, we have learned about Jesus, and he has become an important part of our lives. Our relationship with God has become stronger, and our identity as Catholics is more clear.

Now, as we are getting older, we are beginning to think about what we would like to be when we are grown up. Some of us might want to be pilots, teachers, computer experts, or engineers. Because of our life in the Church, we know that these choices will include devoting time to service in the Christian community.

Every Christian has a **vocation**—a calling from God to live in a way that allows each of us to serve others in the Christian community and in the world. Although people live different lifestyles—some single, others married; some raising a family, others living in a community—all of us are invited to hear and respond to the message of Jesus in the gospels.

Many Ways of Serving

Lay Persons   Most Catholics live out their baptismal vocation as lay persons. Lay persons usually hold jobs in society and are either single or married. As part of their Christian vocation, lay persons often volunteer their time and skills in serving the local parish community, or even the local diocese. They may care for the poor, teach religious education classes, plan and lead the liturgy, help with parish organizations, or invite others to join the Church. In these and other ways, lay persons help the parish community fulfill its mission to reach out to all in the spirit of Jesus.

Some lay men and lay women choose to work full time in Church ministries. These lay persons serve in various positions, such as teachers in Catholic schools, directors of religious education, leaders of diocesan offices or organizations, or as pastoral associates.

Vowed Religious   Some men and women choose to devote their entire lives to the ministry of the Catholic Church. These people join religious communities of sisters or brothers. Vows or promises of poverty, chastity, and obedience are taken so that the sisters or brothers can be completely devoted to their ministries and to becoming closer to God. Each religious community chooses particular ministries, such as teaching, working with the poor, preaching, prayer and contemplation, nursing work, or parish work.

Ordained Ministers   In the Catholic Church, there are also ordained ministers — bishops, priests, and deacons. Persons called to ordained ministry have the special vocation of leading the community in worship, as well as serving in a wide variety of ministries within the Church.

Bishops are the chief teachers of the faith. They administer dioceses and celebrate the sacraments. Priests are ordained to lead the community in worship and to teach and guide the faithful. Diocesan priests serve in positions such as pastors of parishes, educators, and counselors. Priests who belong to religious communities may be assigned as pastors or teachers, or they may be assigned to the particular ministry of their communities.

Deacons   Most deacons are called permanent deacons. These men usually assist the pastor of a parish by leading the celebrations of Baptism and Marriage, preaching at Sunday Mass, and helping with parish management. Unlike priests, permanent deacons can be married and live with their families.

Discernment

As we get to know more men and women who are answering God's call to serve in these ways, we begin to wonder about God's invitation to us. In what ways are we being called? Answering this question is called **discernment**. To find the answer, we can pray for understanding of what the gospel is calling us to do. A teacher, parish minister, religious sister, or priest can also tell you more about discerning God's call.

ABOUT Religious Brothers

Religious brothers are men who have decided to devote their lives to working in various Church ministries. Each order or community of religious brothers has a particular mission or purpose in the work of the Church. Some orders are dedicated to teaching in Catholic schools, others to missionary work around the world. Some communities of brothers work among the poor, others take care of the sick in hospitals, and still others work in parishes.

Each religious order of brothers has houses throughout the world where the brothers live in community. Living in community means that the brothers share the responsibilities of running the house, support each other in their work, pray together often, and help each other in any way they can.

Religious brothers take the vows of poverty, chastity, and obedience. The vow of poverty means that they

A Maryknoll brother working with Bolivian students

do not own anything in their own names. The brothers depend on their community for everything they have. In this way the brothers are freer to become closer to God and serve the needs of the people. The vow of chastity is a promise not to marry. The brothers feel that God's people are their family, and they want to give them all their time. By taking the vow of obedience, the brothers pledge that they will do the work assigned to them by their religious order and carry out the wishes of the bishop of their diocese. Religious brothers have chosen a life that they believe will help them be better ministers in the Church and bring them closer to God.

HOW CATHOLICS PRAY

Through prayer, Catholics show their love for God. The Church is united through the celebration of the sacraments and the prayers of all its members.

ABOUT Kinds of Prayer

Prayer can best be described as conversation, listening and talking, with God. When we pray, we call out to God. We can express our happiness at the wonderful world God has given us. We can ask God to help us live more in the way Jesus taught us to live. In prayer, we can express our need to be closer to God.

Sometimes we may find it hard to pray because we are distracted by what is going on around us. Sometimes it is difficult to trust that God is always listening to our prayer, since we don't always get what we ask for. We need to continue to trust in God's love, to listen for God's guidance, and to let God know that we are listening and are ready to respond.

When we are in the habit of praying each day, we will find it easier to pray even when we are not asking God for something special. Just as we can enjoy spending time with a good friend, we can get to know and better appreciate God through everyday prayer. Then we can begin to think of God first in everything we do. We can realize that, like a loving father, God cares for us, watches over us, and knows what is best for us, even before we ask.

Blessing   We give a sign that God cares for us and for others.

Adoration   We show our love for God who is great and wonderful.

Sorrow   We ask forgiveness for the times we did not live in the way God has taught us.

Thanksgiving   We offer thanks for all that we are and all that God gives to us.

Intercession   We say that we trust that God cares for others and their needs as much as he cares for us.

Praise   We recognize that God is our creator, and that he cares for us, forgives us, and watches over us.

Petition   We ask God's help to do what is right.

Liturgy of the Hours

The **Liturgy of the Hours** is the official morning, daytime, and evening prayer of the Church. It is made up of prayers, psalms, readings from the Bible, and the writings of some of the saints. By praying the Liturgy of the Hours, we are united with the whole Church throughout the world, since Catholics everywhere pray in the same way every day.

As we pray the Liturgy of the Hours, we are reminded of how Jesus taught us to live, and that we should put God first in our lives. Jesus encourages us to pray always. By joining the whole Church in morning, midday, and evening prayer, we continue a Catholic tradition that has lasted for hundreds of years.

Devotions

Sometimes we pray directly to God. Other times we express our love for God in special forms of prayer called devotions, which remind us of the life of Jesus, Mary, or the saints.

The Way of the Cross

The Way of the Cross, or Stations of the Cross, is a traditional Catholic devotion most often prayed during the season of Lent. The Way of the Cross helps us remember the passion, death, and resurrection of Jesus Christ.

The Way of the Cross

1. Jesus is condemned to death.
2. Jesus accepts the cross.
3. Jesus falls the first time.
4. Jesus meets his mother.
5. Simon helps Jesus carry the cross.
6. Veronica wipes the face of Jesus.
7. Jesus falls the second time.
8. Jesus meets the women of Jerusalem.
9. Jesus falls the third time.
10. Jesus is stripped of his garments.
11. Jesus is nailed to the cross.
12. Jesus dies on the cross.
13. Jesus is taken down from the cross.
14. Jesus is buried in the tomb.
15. Jesus is raised from the dead.

The Rosary

The **Rosary** is a devotion honoring Mary. When we pray the Rosary, we repeat the Hail Mary and other prayers over and over to show our love and respect for Mary, the Mother of God. As we pray, we reflect on the joyful, sorrowful, and glorious events in the lives of Mary and Jesus.

The Mysteries of the Rosary

The Joyful Mysteries
The Annunciation
The Visit of Mary to
    Elizabeth
The Birth of Jesus
The Presentation of Jesus
    in the Temple
The Finding of Jesus in
    the Temple

The Sorrowful Mysteries
The Agony of Jesus in
    the Garden
The Scourging at the
    Pillar
The Crowning with Thorns
The Carrying of the Cross
The Crucifixion and Death
    of Jesus

The Glorious Mysteries
The Resurrection of Jesus
The Ascension of Jesus
    into Heaven
The Descent of the Holy
    Spirit upon the Apostles
    (Pentecost)
The Assumption of Mary
    into Heaven
The Crowning of Mary as
    Queen of Heaven

 Meditation

Meditation is a way of praying in which we concentrate on listening to God. We may begin by reading a passage from the Bible, by thinking about a holy person, or by focusing on a sacred object or the beauty of creation. During meditation we can call upon the Holy Spirit to help us think about our relationship with God and how to respond to his love for us. Meditation involves our thoughts, imagination, and emotions.

There are many different ways to meditate. Christian meditation always focuses on trying to understand what God wants us to do as followers of Jesus. It helps us better understand the mission of Jesus and what Jesus means in our lives.

Meditating on the Bible

1. Find a quiet place.

2. Choose a familiar passage from the Bible.

3. Read the passage slowly and carefully.

4. Imagine yourself as part of the Bible story.

5. Think about what the Bible passage might mean for your life.

ABOUT The Lord's Prayer

Jesus taught his followers to pray. We call the prayer of Jesus **The Lord's Prayer.** The Lord's Prayer is in the form of seven petitions. The first three petitions honor God and his plan for the coming of the kingdom. In the next four petitions, we present our needs to God, who is our loving Father.

Our Father, who art in heaven, hallowed be thy name.	God, who made us and continues to love and care for us, is our Father. We acknowledge God's greatness and holiness.
Thy kingdom come,	We recognize that through Jesus Christ, the kingdom of God has been established. We look forward to the realization of the kingdom in the final coming of Christ.
thy will be done on earth as it is in heaven.	We ask that God's plan for the salvation of the world be fulfilled.
Give us this day our daily bread;	Daily bread refers not only to the nourishment of our bodies, but to the Eucharist: Jesus, the Bread of Life.
and forgive us our trespasses as we forgive those who trespass against us;	We ask God to forgive us for the harm we have done to others. We realize that we can only be truly reconciled with God if we are willing to be forgiving toward those who have harmed us.
and lead us not into temptation,	We ask God to help us avoid sin. We ask God to give us the strength and understanding always to choose what is right.
but deliver us from evil.	We pray that God will help us overcome the evil in the world that can distract us from following the way Jesus taught us to live.
Amen.	The word at the end of a prayer expresses our agreement. It can mean "so be it."

Glossary

absolution

the prayer and declaration of forgiveness for sins prayed by the priest in the sacrament of Reconciliation *(page 219)*

abstaining

not eating meat *(page 284)*

Advent

four weeks of preparation before Christmas *(page 37)*

anoint

to apply sacred oil to a person's body to signify that a person is set apart from others or given a special mission *(page 175)*

apostolic

one of the four marks, or qualities, of the Church that show its truth and its origin in God. The Church is apostolic, founded on and faithful to the Apostles' teachings. *(page 331)*

ascension

the returning of Jesus in glory to his Father *(page 330)*

assumption

the taking up of Mary, body and soul, to heaven *(page 332)*

Baptism

the first sacrament of initiation, through which we are freed of original sin and welcomed into the Church *(page 175)*

baptized

welcomed into the Christian community *(page 115)*

basilica

a Catholic Church that the pope honors for a special reason *(page 27)*

blasphemy

an insult to God or to his holy leaders *(page 75)*

Blessed Sacrament

the Eucharist bread kept in the tabernacle as a continuing sacrament of Christ's presence with us *(page 199)*

blessing

a prayer praising or thanking God for someone or something and asking God to be present *(page 19)*

breaking of bread

the New Testament name for the Eucharist *(page 135)*

canonize

to name a saint of the Church *(page 47)*

catechumenate

a process of formation during which candidates pray, study, and learn about the Catholic faith. It is the Church's way of initiating adults and older children into the Christian community. *(page 173)*

cathedral

the official church of the bishop or head of a diocese *(page 29)*

catholic

one of the four marks, or qualities, of the Church that show its truth and its origin in God. The Church is catholic, or universal, open to all people. *(page 331)*

chasuble

a garment worn by bishops and priests during the Mass *(page 237)*

chrism

a perfumed oil, blessed by the bishop *(page 175)*

Communion of Saints
the entire community of Jesus' followers, both living and dead *(page 47)*

compassionate
caring for and about other people *(page 73)*

Confirmation
a sacrament of initiation in which we become fuller members of the Church and in which the Holy Spirit makes us stronger to live and share our faith in Jesus *(page 183)*

conscience
our ability to judge whether something is good or bad *(page 347)*

consecration
prayer and action by which bread and wine become the Body and Blood of Jesus *(page 197)*

conversion
to turn away from our selfish ways and turn back to God *(page 215)*

Corporal Works of Mercy
the loving acts described in Matthew 25:31-46 that tell us how to respond to the basic physical needs of all people *(page 346)*

covenant
an agreement or a contract between two people or groups *(page 245)*

deacon
a person ordained to assist in the ministry by preaching, baptizing, distributing the Eucharist, visiting the sick, and witnessing marriages *(page 235)*

diocese
a Catholic community made up of many parishes *(page 29)*

discernment
asking God to help us know in what ways we are being called to serve *(page 350)*

Easter Triduum
the three holiest days of the year. On Holy Thursday, we remember the Last Supper; on Good Friday, we remember Jesus' crucifixion; on Holy Saturday, at the Easter Vigil, we celebrate Jesus' resurrection. *(page 333)*

Easter Vigil
the most important of all the Church's celebrations. On Holy Saturday night we celebrate Jesus' victory over death. *(page 173)*

Emmanuel
a title for Jesus that means "God is with us" *(page 93)*

Eucharist
a sacrament of initiation and of unity and love in which we receive the Body and Blood of Christ *(page 195)*

fasting
eating one full meal a day and two smaller meals *(page 284)*

free will
the freedom to choose what is right or wrong *(page 348)*

grace
God's loving presence in our lives *(page 175)*

Great Commandment, the
the commandment in which Jesus summed up the Ten Commandments by teaching us that God's laws are based on love of God and love of neighbor *(page 346)*

Glossary

heaven
unending happiness with God and with all who love God and one another *(page 332)*

hell
eternal separation from God and others *(page 332)*

holy
one of the four marks, or qualities, of the Church that show its truth and its origin in God. The Church is holy because we draw our life from God and offer people the way to God. *(page 331)*

holy days of obligation
six special days of the liturgical year celebrated in the Church of the United States *(page 37)*

Holy Land
Israel, the land where Jesus lived *(page 25)*

Holy Spirit
the Third Person of the Trinity who leads and guides us in living as followers of Jesus *(page 331)*

Immaculate Conception
the belief that Mary, the mother of Jesus, was conceived without original sin *(page 332)*

Incarnation
God's Son becoming human while remaining God. Jesus Christ is both God and man. *(page 93)*

Last Supper
when Jesus gave us the gift of himself in the Eucharist *(page 290)*

Lent
forty days of preparation before Easter *(page 37)*

liturgical year
the cycle of seasons and feasts celebrating Christ with us always *(page 37)*

Liturgy of the Hours
the Church's official prayer prayed at certain hours of the day and night *(page 137)*

Matrimony
another name for the sacrament of Marriage, in which a man and a woman promise to love one another for the rest of their lives as husband and wife *(page 245)*

meditation
a way of praying in which we concentrate on listening to God *(page 354)*

messiah
the one God had promised to send to free God's people *(page 330)*

mission
a sending or being sent out with authority to perform a special service *(page 179)*

mortal sin
a very serious refusal to follow the teachings of Jesus, one which turns us away from God *(page 219)*

mysteries
the events of Mary's and Jesus' lives *(page 314)*

nuptial blessing
the prayer prayed by the priest during the sacrament of Matrimony that asks God's blessing on the couple and the Holy Spirit's help for them in living as one in mind and heart *(page 247)*

one
one of the four marks, or qualities, of the Church that show its truth and its origin in God. The Church is one in our faith, sacraments, and leadership. *(page 331)*

ordain
to give someone the special role and dignity of bishop, priest, or deacon *(page 235)*

original sin
the first selfish act of the first human beings, and the sinful condition into which we are born *(page 175)*

parish
a local church where the Catholic community gathers *(page 29)*

Pentecost
the day the Church began with the coming of the Holy Spirit upon the first disciples *(page 331)*

persecute
to cause another to suffer because of his or her belief *(page 143)*

personal sins
mortal and venial sins. Personal sins have social consequences and often hurt others or tempt them to turn away from God and the Church. *(page 347)*

pilgrimage
a religious journey to a sacred place *(page 25)*

prayer
conversation with God *(page 83)*

presider
priest who leads the eucharistic celebration *(page 195)*

prophet
someone called by God to speak in his name *(page 63)*

psalms
prayer songs from the Old Testament *(page 89)*

purgatory
after death, the process of purification from all traces of sin *(page 332)*

rabbi
Hebrew word that means "teacher" *(page 63)*

reconciliation
making up with someone through sorrow and forgiveness *(page 213)*

resurrection
Jesus' rising from death to new life *(page 330)*

ritual
a ceremonial act or action *(page 165)*

Rosary
a devotion honoring Mary *(page 354)*

sacrament
a special sign within the life of the Catholic Church through which Christ truly becomes present with us and acts in our lives *(page 137)*

sacramental
a blessing, an action, or an object that reminds us of Jesus' presence with us and God's care for us *(page 15)*

sacramental grace
help from God to live as Jesus taught us *(page 348)*

sacraments of commitment
Matrimony and Holy Orders—the Catholic Church's two sacraments of commitment *(page 169)*

Glossary

sacraments of healing
Reconciliation and Anointing of the Sick—the Catholic Church's two sacraments of healing *(page 169)*

sacraments of initiation
Baptism, Confirmation, and Eucharist—the Church's three sacraments of welcome and belonging *(page 167)*

saint
someone the Church singles out as an outstanding model of what it means to be like Jesus *(page 47)*

Savior
Jesus Christ, who brought us God's mercy and forgiveness and freed us from sin *(page 93)*

seven sacraments
seven powerful signs and rituals given by Christ to the Church to give grace *(page 165)*

shrine
a sacred place where God is worshiped *(page 27)*

sin
a free decision to do what we know is wrong or not to do something we know is right *(page 219)*

social services
organized activities that help people who are sick, poor, and in need *(page 123)*

Spiritual Works of Mercy
the loving acts described in Matthew 25:31–46 that tell us how to respond to the basic spiritual needs of all people *(page 346)*

stole
a narrow strip of cloth worn by bishops, priests, and deacons as a sign of their service to the community *(page 237)*

synagogue
house of worship and a community center of the Jewish people *(page 63)*

tabernacle
the special container in church where the Blessed Sacrament is kept *(page 199)*

temptation
a pressure to think, say, or do something we know is sinful *(page 348)*

Trinity
the one God who is Father, Son, and Holy Spirit *(page 183)*

venial sin
a less serious act of selfishness, one which weakens our relationship with God *(page 219)*

vestments
the special clothes that symbolize the various ministries of those who are ordained *(page 237)*

Viaticum
the Eucharist given to a person in danger of dying *(page 227)*

virtues
spiritual powers which help us to do what is good and avoid sin *(page 348)*

vocation
God's call to use our gifts for our own good and the good of others *(page 349)*

vow
a solemn promise *(page 247)*

witness
a person who informs others about what he or she has seen or heard *(page 115)*

Index

Index